BABY BOOMERS GUIDE TO CARING FOR AGING PARENTS

By Bart Astor

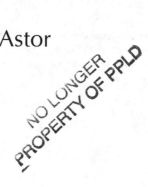

MACMILLAN SPECTRUM

An imprint of Macmillan • USA

A Simon & Schuster Macmillan Company

119488062

To my father, who taught me to value independence.

A Spectrum Book

MACMILLAN and SPECTRUM are registered trademarks of Macmillan, Inc.

Manufactured in the United States of America

10   9   8   7   6   5   4   3   2   1

Library of Congress Number: 96-078163

ISBN: 0-02-861617-0

Disclaimer: Material contained in this book should not be considered legal advice. Neither the author nor the publisher assumes liability for loss or damage as a result of reliance upon information, suggestions, or data printed in this publication.

CONTENTS

Foreword v

Opening Remarks xii

Introduction: In the Good Old Days xiv

 1 How It Is Now 1

 2 Tough Talk 10

 3 With a Gentle Hand 24

 4 Blind Justice 53

 5 I Got You Covered 68

 6 Show Me the Money 95

 7 Visiting Hours 118

 8 I've Fallen and I Can't Get Up 135

 9 For the Long Haul 158

 10 Ugh, I Hate Going There 173

 11 You Don't Have to Go Broke 195

 12 Facing the Inevitable 207

Appendix A   State Agencies on Aging 230

Appendix B   American Health Care Association
              State Affiliates 235

Appendix C   State Home Care Association
              Phone Numbers 240

Appendix D   Sample Power of Attorney 244

Appendix E   Sample Living Will 247

Appendix F   Health Care Aide Job Application 249

Appendix G   National Association for Home Care:
              Patient Bill of Rights 254

Appendix H   Questions to Ask About
Long-Term-Care Facilities 256

Appendix I   Funeral Directors Code of Ethics 263

Appendix J   General Release—Background Checks 264

Appendix K   Medicare Supplement Coverage Plans 265

Appendix L   Resources and Referrals 266

Appendix M   Emergency Response Systems 273

Appendix N   Sample Employment Contract 275

FOREWORD

by Thomas J. Humphrey
Executive Director,
Children of Aging Parents

Never before have the times so clearly pointed to a need for a good "how-to" book for family caregivers watching their parents age. For never before have so many people lived so long; never before have so many children seen their parents become so dependent on them for care. And never before have so many American workers faced such conflicting responsibilities for caregiving and careers.

Why are these times so different? And why do caregivers today require so much more help than caregivers of our youthful memories?

Many caregivers living today can recollect memories of Grandma coming to live with Mom and Dad. Perhaps she was "acting funny" or getting confused. Or, it was whispered, she was getting "senile." Perhaps, also, she was reaching the ripe old age of seventy. Those who can't recall their parents as caregivers are more apt to say, "I can't remember my grandmother. She died when I was very little" or "She didn't live to see any grandchildren." This was not uncommon in the 1930s and 1940s. In those early decades of the twentieth century, the elderly were those who had escaped death from heart attack, strokes, TB, and cancer, and lived to an old age of sixty-five or seventy. How times have changed!

Today's elderly are protected, medicated, regulated, and monitored sufficiently to reach their eighties, nineties, and beyond. In these later years, many fall victim to other disabilities like Alzheimer's, Parkinson's, strokes, osteoporosis, and frailty. Their dependency on others occurs at later ages, but it surely occurs and in far greater numbers.

Although many exceptions can be singled out, most caregivers today are between the ages of fifty and sixty-four. These are the children of the elderly. Few Americans will escape this call to be a caregiver. The group just now facing this responsibility are the "baby boomers," the largest segment of people in the country. This group is seventy-eight million strong. They started life in 1946 after World War II and continued to break all birth records until 1964. The first baby boomers are just beyond fifty years of age; the youngest of them are about thirty-three years old. In another twenty years, some of the youngest boomers may be caregivers for some of the first baby boomers—fifty-three-year-olds caring for seventy-year-olds.

The baby boomers have always changed their world as they passed through life's stages. As newborns, they triggered a response to a real shortage of pediatricians. As newly marrieds, they triggered a housing boom. Today, their members are triggering a call to reform the Social Security system and to encourage more geriatric specialties in medical schools. They will also redefine caregiving. They will exemplify the true "sandwich generation."

Those of the sandwich generation are so named because they are still caring for their own children (or just experiencing their maturing and leaving the nest) while at the same time beginning to care for the parents who raised them. They're sandwiched between two forces like between two pieces of bread. The top slice represents their parents' needs and the bottom slice represents their children's needs. Sometimes an added pulling force is a retired spouse with dreams of travel and free time.

Looking ahead to the twenty-first century we see a new challenge looming. This new challenge is for a system to deal with chronic care. By definition, this means care for conditions that are not curable and will be long-lasting, usually with specific health consequences. More familiar to us are the traditional health care systems that concentrate on acute care—like hospital care to cure or repair our illnesses and maladies. A look at some statistics will help us understand why the baby boomers of the sandwich generation will probably redefine the caregiver's role as we deal with this new challenge for chronic care.

Longer life expectancy means that the number of elderly persons is increasing. In 1900 only 4 percent of all Americans were over age sixty-five. By the year 2000 they will account for 13 percent, and in 2040 they'll be 21 percent of the population, or one out of every five Americans. Among elderly Americans, chronic conditions are and will be commonplace. These chronic conditions may be heart disease, Alzheimer's, paralysis from strokes, crippling arthritis, emphysema and pulmonary disease, or mental confusion or dementia.

Often these chronic conditions do not require hospitals or medical care. In fact, most people with chronic conditions live and work among us and are struggling to remain independent and continue in the work force. But not all can do so, and many require some assistance to lead normal lives.

In 1995 an estimated 99 million of us were living with chronic conditions with recurring health consequences. By 2030 nearly 150 million are projected to have chronic conditions, and 42 million of them will be limited in their daily activities or dependent on assistance. Among them, about 12 million will be unable to live without involving caregivers in their lives.

The services these 12 million chronically ill and dependent persons will need will not all be medical, but assistance with daily living and activities. Some of the providers of these services will be paid medical personnel in the home. But many services will be provided by volunteers, family, community, and government agencies. Today's caregivers must learn how to access various services and orchestrate the care each can provide. They will be involved with:

- social services for transportation and homemaking assistance
- custodial services for safety and day care
- rehabilitation services for speech or mobility
- psychological services for depression or feelings of isolation, and
- family services for shopping, housekeeping, cooking, banking, driving, and bathing

According to the U.S. House of Representatives, the average woman will spend seventeen years caring for her children and eighteen or more years caring for her aging parents. Her tasks will increase in time and intensity over those years. They may begin as grocery shopping, driving, cooking, housekeeping, and banking chores, and develop into providing housing and personal care with bathing, feeding, and assistance with walking.

The sandwich generation will experience many strong forces pulling them from opposite ends. A report from the American Association of Retired Persons (AARP) indicates that 14 percent of all caregivers have switched from full-time jobs to part-time work to care for a loved one, and another 12 percent have left the work force to be a full-time caregiver. Imagine the dilemma when a parent's need conflicts with the demands of a career. Even without leaving a job, the demands may affect your productivity at work. In 1995, *The Met-Life Study of Employer Costs for Working Caregivers,* prepared by the Washington Business Group on Health and Gibson-Hunt Associates, revealed that a large U.S. employer in the manufacturing sector had 1,739 caregiver employees, representing about 2 percent of its 86,952 employees. The cost of caregiving to that employer was over $5.5 million per year, or $3,163 per caregiver per year. The study suggests that many other companies face similar costs and recognizes that employers must be aware of what caregiving means to their individual employees and to their own business bottom lines.

Furthermore, a Robert Wood Johnson Foundation study, *Chronic Care in America—A 21st Century Challenge,* prepared in August 1996 by the Institute for Health and Aging at the University of California in San Francisco, reveals that 60 percent of employed caregivers report that their caregiving interferes with their work. Either they work fewer hours, rearrange their schedules, take time off without pay, or leave the work force entirely. Today few companies offer family illness days or flexible hours to assist caregivers, although there are indications that more and more companies are beginning to show a concern for caregiver employees and for their impact on business profits. They have determined that the cost of employee wellness is a worthwhile expenditure if an employee is worth keeping.

Businesses have learned that productivity depends on workplace stability and dependability. Workers who are sole caregivers for elderly parents are grateful for family-friendly workplace policies. These include such new options as flex-time, shared jobs, day care and respite options, and family long-term-care insurance plans extended to cover aging parents. Some employers will take more aggressive steps to keep valuable employees, like opening on-site adult day care programs for parents of workers. We were not surprised when we saw child day care options at the workplace. And in twenty years the existence of adult day care options will be no less surprising. We can expect to see employers continue to adopt new policies as America ages.

Adding to the demanding schedules and stresses of caregiving is the reality of few potential caregivers. In 1970 there were twenty-one potential caregivers for every person over age eighty-five. By 2030 there will be only six potential caregivers for each very elderly person. This results not only from the number of baby boomers who are aging, but also from later marriages that produce fewer children. The impact on the housing options for the elderly will be great.

The housing options we now have reflect the changing demographics. Despite the "graceful, leisurely, carefree" life in retirement communities, as depicted in the media, and despite the rapid growth of the nursing home industry, the fact is that elderly people, even those with chronic illnesses and disabilities, prefer an "at-home" setting. And, in fact, only about 5 or 6 percent of the population over age sixty-five live in nursing homes. The rest are either living alone, living with a spouse, living with adult children, or living in a life care/retirement community. To maintain that degree of independence, they have come to rely on the support and care provided by family members. Their living arrangements account for the rapid growth rate of home health service agencies, geriatric care managers, and adult day care centers, and the building of new living centers geared toward the elderly. New concepts of respite care and long-distance caregiving are producing a new vocabulary unknown to families fifty years ago.

Caregiving roles vary significantly from one caregiver to another. Stereotyping is risky. And no time frames can be applied universally. What starts out as an occasional need for a driver, companion, or cook often progresses to a need for one to bathe, dress, medicate, or toilet an aging parent. What starts out as a caregiving role as a visitor two or three times a week may ultimately become, for many, a live-in caregiver's role shared by husband and wife, children, and parents. By 2020, it's estimated, one-third of all American workers will be responsible for the at-home care of an elderly parent. Again, this is the reality of a sandwich generation.

New questions that deal with issues of caring for our aging parents continue to pop up. But the answers don't keep pace. Our hope is that answers will grow out of innovation, creative and collective grass roots endeavors, and out of the American genius for capitalism and competition. We can hope that compassion and concern form the foundation for these yet-to-be-discovered solutions. We should not live by hope alone, and that's why self-help, "how-to" books remain helpful to those who make their own way.

"How-to" books can be lifelines for the determined do-it-yourselfer. Good ones can save time, money, marriages, sanity, and more. They can help readers analyze a problem, organize themselves to tackle it, avoid unexpected pitfalls in seeking answers, and reach workable solutions. Getting the right books into the hands of the right people is the key to a publisher's success, while the author's chief duty is to present clear information and to destroy the myths that often inhibit success. Books that deal with serious and rapidly increasing problems of caring for aging parents demand both the correct information and the destruction of these myths.

But the magnitude of this problem, the aging of America, means that social services and charitable, nonprofit organizations must continue to flourish and present viable options to families seeking answers.

Children of Aging Parents (CAPS) is one of many such organizations. It was formed in 1977 and now enjoys a twenty-year reputation for reliable service to caregivers of the elderly. Services include national information and referrals to service providers for the elderly and for caregivers, educational outreach to inform the public of the needs of caregivers to ensure better care of the elderly, and a network of support groups to help caregivers cope with stress and problems and to learn to affirm their self-worth and dignity.

CAPS welcomes the publication of this practical, simplified guide for caregivers. For the healthier caregivers are, the better will be the care they provide for the elderly.

Author's Note: We are extraordinarily grateful to Tom Humphrey and the staff of CAPS for their guidance and assistance. The organization provides an invaluable service, and we encourage everyone to join as a member. Membership is an incredible bargain, costing only $20 per year. For this small amount, you stay current on all the latest trends in caregiving, regularly receive tips and assistance for your own situation, *and have access to a national network of caregiver support groups that can give you unparalleled assistance as you face the joys, commitments, and burdens of caring for your aging parent. For more information, you can call Children of Aging Parents at 800-227-7294. Or you can write to them at:*

Children of Aging Parents
1609 Woodbourne Road, Suite 302A
Levittown, PA 19057

The test of a people is how it behaves toward the old.

—Abraham J. Heschel

OPENING REMARKS

What we owe the old is reverence, but all they ask for is consideration, attention, and not to be discarded or forgotten.

—Abraham J. Heschel,
address at the 1961 White House Conference on Aging

I confess: I'm a baby boomer. One of almost eighty million Americans born between 1946 and 1964. We boomers have been branded with numerous labels: self-indulgent, self-centered, self-important, self-satisfying. We're preoccupied with instant gratification; we're cocky, brazen, and individualistic. We changed the world by the mere fact that we were born in such numbers. We have the most money and have achieved the highest level of education of any generation in the history of the world. What we want, we get. We're like the elephant swallowed by the snake, a massive entity moving steadily along the continuum. The snake's entire body must focus all of its flexibility and strength in that one spot to keep the elephant moving through; society has had to do the same to deal with us. New schools were built to accommodate us, yet there still weren't enough, and we had to attend double or triple sessions in high school. New housing developments were constructed, and still there weren't enough. So we extended the suburbs.

With so many of us around, competition was fierce: to excel in school, to get accepted to college, to get a job. There were so many of us that those who rose to the top to serve as our leaders had to have incredible leadership skills. We disrupted society; we pushed its very limit whenever we could. We rebelled, and in so doing, nudged society in the direction we wanted. Then we left school, got jobs, got married, and started having families of our own. We needed new products; we got them. We needed more houses; we built them. We improved our cars and transportation to take us to our jobs in the city. When we got tired of the long commutes into the city center where the jobs were, we started moving the jobs to the suburbs. When we started to become more conscious of our health and fitness, we built sophisticated, high-tech treadmills and stair-steppers, baked low-fat cookies, and now have started a new concept: nutriceuticals and cosmeceuticals—hybrids of food and drugs and cosmetics and drugs that make us look and feel young.

Through it all, we were idealistic. We had visited Camelot and knew that all we had to do was set our sights on something and it was ours. Nothing stood in our way. We could do anything. Perhaps that's what being spoiled means: feeling you can have anything you want.

We're a confident bunch. We have faith that there will be a future because we've always had so much control of everything. Despite all the talk of Social Security going bankrupt when we reach retirement age, we're not really worried. We jokingly say that we weren't counting on it anyway. Or as I've heard it said, "There are so many of us that if we need more money for our retirement, we'll sell the Louisiana Purchase."

Yet we continue to confound all prognosticators: the many that said we would not marry, would not have children, and would not move to the suburbs. For the most part we have. Many said, too, that our self-indulgence will conflict with our ideals and responsibilities. We've confounded the prognosticators again. What the prognosticators didn't count on was that the basic values we grew up with are still with us. Like our parents, we know that it's up to us to take care of our children and family.

But there's one big difference between boomers and the older adults, our parents. Our parents grew up in the Depression era and had no expectations for what government could do for people. For the most part we've accepted government intervention (our political differences are in how much intervention, not whether to intervene). Not only that, we believe that government *must* help, that it's the responsibility of government. And because we believe good health care, adequate housing, and having enough food are rights, not privileges, we're concerned about our seniors, our parents—more concerned than the prognosticators thought we would be. Perhaps because we see ourselves there very soon. Perhaps because the numbers of us who have breast cancer or AIDS remind us of our vulnerability. We insist that when we are old, we won't be useless to society. We won't let society reject us because we're old.

And so we take care of our mothers and fathers and aunts and uncles, just as our parents did. Maybe not out of duty, like our parents. I like to think it's because we believe what we owe the old is reverence.

Introduction: In the Good Old Days

by Dr. Joyce Brothers

Many of us cherish a sentimental picture of a family "in the good old days," when three or more generations lived happily together under one roof. In this family, traditions were automatically passed on from one generation to another, the older members teaching the young children about life and about the family's unique history.

But the fact is that though widely shared, this picture is largely a fantasy. Few American families ever lived this way. And in the past, few grandparents lived long enough to know their grandchildren well. Aging is a gift of time. Most of us who have parents who live to a ripe old age consider ourselves quite lucky.

My mother and father were both attorneys. When my father died in his seventies, my mother retired from her law practice and busied herself with her family. She lived to the age of ninety-one as she wished—near her children and in her own apartment. As she grew into her late eighties, she needed a cane but was too proud to use one. My sister and I bought sturdy shopping carts, later, fancy umbrellas, and finally, pretty walking sticks. We just left them around the apartment, knowing that eventually my mother would come to use them. She did. Later, when my mother was wheelchair bound, she ultimately needed round-the-clock care. Fortunately, we were in a position to pay for that care. But even though we had the funds available, there were shoals and eddies and raging torrents we had to navigate, just as most people who belong to the "sandwich generation" do. By the sandwich generation, we mean those adults who are caring for their parents at the same time as they are bringing up their own children.

My sister and I gloried in our mother's older years and would try to have birthday celebrations, each one better than the previous one. The greatest blessing my mother's old age bestowed on our family was the stories she told her grandchildren: about her family and about her life. Certainly the richest moments of my own life include the holidays when my extended family gathers at the farm my late husband and I bought years ago. These events are often hectic and crowded—when we run out of beds, we ask people to bring their own sleeping bags. But these inconveniences are more than balanced by the joy we find in being together and in rediscovering, or establishing for the first time, our own family traditions.

Knowing where our roots are helps to ground us. Knowing that within the family circle we are unconditionally loved and valued provides a vital refuge from a world that's sometimes cruel. So it has been for my family. So it is for many families.

Grandparents and other older adults who are part of a child's life can contribute a great deal to the child's development. Given the opportunity, children can learn from their elders that life is likely to turn out okay (or, sadly, they can learn the opposite too). Children may find that grandparents are more willing and able than their parents to listen to their minor concerns. A wise mother I know understands this. "When my son is upset," she says, "he has permission to call Grandma long-distance." That family is lucky to have a grandparent so accessible and so much a part of the family structure, despite the distance.

Grandparents and older relatives can sometimes talk to children in ways parents cannot. Says the same mother, "When my son says he hates his sister, I feel I have to defend the sister—after all, she's my child too. But Grandma tells him that she, too, felt the same way as a child."

Older family members want very much to play these important roles. They often feel intense disappointment if they're consigned to the sidelines whenever the family gets together. Older people may look or be physically frail. But many feel strong and vital and know that they have much to offer children. When they talk about the past and about their own lives, they're providing a great service to the family. They're providing the continuity and family oral history. At the same time, reminiscing is good for them too; studies show that older people who are encouraged to talk about their experiences are physically and mentally healthiest.

If you've heard Grandpa's stories too often for comfort, try asking him to entertain your four-year-old for a while. Children are often enchanted by tales of "the olden days." They also may enjoy the responsibility of "keeping Grandpa company." One three-year-old I know takes being his great-aunt's "eyes" very seriously. "She doesn't see very well," he explains, "so I help her go where she wants to go. When we eat, she cuts things up for me because I'm not allowed to use a knife."

Today many families are so geographically scattered that they simply can't get together very often. Luckily, there are other ways families can keep in touch with one another and keep their special traditions alive.

My grandchildren prepare long tape recordings about their activities to send to their Arbisser grandparents in Israel, and they receive wonderful tapes in return. One grandmother I know publishes *Grandma's Gazette* for her family: a monthly newsletter featuring grandchildren's drawings and stories, interviews with family members, and general family news. "The kids love seeing their work in print," one of Grandma's daughters says. "And I love reading about what's happening in my brother's and sister's families. It helps make up for the fact that we can't see each other often."

Compiling family scrapbooks and making family trees are good ways of teaching children about the people in their past. Maintaining unique family activities and treasures is another. One four-year-old I know loves a lap-bouncing game not simply because it's fun, though certainly it is to him. But he talks about the game "that my daddy plays with me and his granddaddy played with him." The lap-bouncing is more than a game for him—it's his legacy. I cherish a simple, covered earthenware dish that belonged to my grandmother, whom I never knew. The dish reflects my family's history and perhaps one of my grandchildren will continue to keep it close to her heart.

As parents we can tell our children about relatives they cannot often see or can never know. "This is my grandmother's recipe" or "Let me tell you about the Halloween costume my mom made for your Aunt Sally one year." Comments like these help make those people real in your children's minds.

Families everywhere are looking for new ways of relating to each other long-distance. Fortunately, love knows no geographical boundaries. You can help your children feel a part of family traditions and memories—no matter how many years or miles stand in the way.

I mentioned the contribution older people can make toward the development of the children because that's the essence of how we can deal with seeing our parents age. We all want to see our parents live to a ripe old age, at the same time hoping that they remain vital and healthy. Yet most people actually dread old age itself. They picture it as an inevitable but terrible accident that will leave them forever altered. Like Mrs. Jones down the street, they'll suffer rheumatic aches and pains. Or like Mr. Smith up the street, they'll lose their memory, become garrulous, and repeat themselves incessantly.

"That's just not the way it happens," says the University of Chicago's Bernice Neugarten. She says that older people have less in common with each other than they have with who they've always been. "In other words," she says, "if I know the life history and personality of a person, I can predict the kind of old age he or she will have."

The vigorous tend to remain vigorous; the studious continue to function intellectually. Those with a history of poor health may continue the pattern, but it's not a new one for them. Those with a history of good health can expect to continue their good luck. And it's not true that liberals turn into conservatives with age, or become rigid in their thinking. Old age is just a continuation of an individual's life—and it remains an individual experience for everyone.

When does old age begin? That, too, differs from person to person. But it certainly doesn't begin for most people at sixty-five, the age at which you can begin to collect Social Security benefits. Most sixty-five-year-olds today are more youthful than their parents were and they have a longer life expectancy. Indeed, the number of people in our population aged seventy-five and over is increasing rapidly. [Author's Note: The fastest-growing population today are those eighty-five and over.]

Why do we have such a dismal picture of old age? Why do we see so many malfunctioning oldsters among us? There are two reasons. One is that in our over-seventy population today there are a disproportionate number who have achieved old age despite the handicaps of poverty, malnutrition, and lack of education and medical care. Tomorrow, far fewer oldsters will suffer from these early disadvantages.

The second reason we see old age as catastrophic is that we've bought the myth that it must be. We label as "old" those people who are suffering, forgetting that many young people suffer too. We don't call the respected old judge old, or the white-haired opponent who just beat us on the tennis court. They are merely "mature" or "wise with experience." If we realized that they, too, represent old age, we might dread aging less.

We see Grandma ask, "What was the name of that young man you introduced to me last night?" She then apologizes, "I'm getting old. I don't remember anything anymore."

But Grandma, a musician since she was a little girl, can sit at the piano and play almost any piece of music written—often from memory. The truth is that Grandma always had a memory for music, which, to her, was the most important thing in her life. And she never had a memory for names—not even when she was in her twenties, at the peak of her physical prowess.

The sad fact is that she, and probably her family as well, have bought the fallacy that old age means deterioration in mental abilities.

That can act as a self-fulfilling prophecy, warn psychologists Paul Baltes and K. Warner Schaie of West Virginia University. The person who thinks that because he's forty—or sixty-five or seventy—he should be getting senile, *will* probably become senile. But he's more apt to be the person who knows he will be retired at sixty-five, or was retired at sixty-five, than the octogenarian heading a government, sitting on a Supreme Court bench, or serving as a senator or congressional representative.

As people grow older, age can take a toll. So they may need social or financial support from others. Often that support comes from their children. Research has produced a mixed set of findings about the psychological consequences of being on the receiving end of such support. Some studies show that assistance from children improves the psychological well-being of older people, while other studies find that it actually increases distress, the exact opposite finding. What's the truth of the matter? Is support a good thing? Can there be too much of a good thing?

The researcher Merril Silverstein and her associates surveyed a sample of 539 older participants in the University of Southern California Longitudinal Study of Generations. To measure social support, parents had been asked who they relied on for assistance in terms of household chores, transportation and shopping, advice, emotional support, financial assistance, discussing life decisions, and care when ill. The participants had also been surveyed for positive and negative feelings, the degree of control they thought they had over their lives, and what their expectations were in terms of how much responsibility adult children should have for their parents.

The study produced a finding that should be of great interest to any family faced with the problem of how much help to offer, and may be startling to many: Getting support from one's adult children is psychologically beneficial at moderate levels and psychologically *harmful* at high levels. In short, receiving support makes older people happier up to a point. Beyond that, however, it actually reduces feelings of well-being. Furthermore, being alone has an even more pronounced effect on how older people feel about support. While we may expect people who are alone to be more receptive to support, the finding was just the opposite: our widowed parents respond more negatively to "oversupport" than do our married parents.

Beyond this global finding, there are two specific patterns that merit highlighting, specifically in regard to the interaction between the parents' expectations of support from their children and the amount of support they actually received.

First, we would expect that those parents who expected that their family would provide support, but who did not get it, would be more depressed than those who got what they expected. But they were not any more depressed. Undersupport, despite expectations, did not seem to have the effect one would predict.

Given the result that older people receiving high levels of support were less happy than those receiving lower levels, it may well be that intergenerational oversupport is *more* harmful than intergenerational undersupport.

A second pattern that should be of interest to us all is that parents who had low expectations of support experienced a rise in well-being with increases in the amount of assistance they received. We conclude from this finding that these people were pleasantly surprised by unexpected support, which led to greater emotional good.

Dr. Silverstein's findings clearly demonstrate that there are definite psychological benefits to older people associated with receiving social support from their adult children. But her study also shows that such support is not a panacea for the elderly. Older adults may not well tolerate receiving more than moderate amounts of support from their well-meaning children, because such support means that they are no longer independent and autonomous, two qualities that adult human beings value greatly.

In another study that explored similar terrain, K. D. Pyke and V. L. Bengstson gathered data from twenty families. They observed that when older parents received care that was in excess of the amount they desired, rather than responding with gratitude, they felt resentful and infantilized.

So showing that you care for your parent is important. But so is helping to maintain the parent's sense of autonomy. Adult children need to learn how to walk the line between giving and giving too much.

Bart Astor's excellent book, *Baby Boomers Guide to Caring for Aging Parents* helps the sandwich generation walk that line with caring and concern.

ACKNOWLEDGMENTS

Some special people: to my wife Kathie, my sister-in-law Roberta, my niece Katy, and my nephew Rob (together we lived through the ordeal so I could write about it). To Gary Mazart, Susan Palla, Diane Welsh (from AARP), Bill Gillett, Joyce Brothers, Tom Humphrey, David Levy, and Leah Weiss for their guidance and information. To Nancy Janow and Elaine Clark in the South Orange Library for their direction and referrals. To Kathy Nebenhaus, Christy Wagner, Fred Bidgood, and the professionals at Macmillan for pulling it all together. And to Debby Englander for her support.

How It Is Now

In 1982 my in-laws retired. My father-in-law retired from a company for which he had worked for over fifty years. His colleagues gave him a few going-away presents and the company provided a small pension. My in-laws sold the New Jersey home they had lived in for almost forty years because they decided that the house was too big for just the two of them, and they moved to California to be near my wife and me.

At our suggestion, they rented a town house, even though renting was against their makeup: How could they live at the whim of a landlord—what if they got evicted, where would they go? But they also knew that they needed to live off the income from the sale of their house and that buying another place, particularly in such a high-priced area, wasn't prudent. So they compromised and settled for a long-term lease. Of course, they still worried about being thrown out. And the money they had was all put into safe, but low-yielding, investments. Nevertheless, with the Social Security income they received, the small pension, and the return on investments, they had enough.

We lived nearby and got together almost every weekend. We'd change lightbulbs for them, help fix a meal or two, and we'd go out once in a while. Our visits were social occasions.

Then it started. My father-in-law's adult-onset diabetes started catching up with him. He started having circulatory system problems. He needed to have his carotid artery opened up, which his doctors successfully did. But later, despite many efforts, they were unable to save a leg. Here was this older man who had been an extraordinary athlete in his time (an Olympic sprinter), now facing life on one leg.

He rallied unbelievably. And with the help of numerous professionals, he learned to walk on his artificial limb. He drove his car, he went shopping with my mother-in-law, and he visited with his new friends.

But the scars were deep and time took its toll. Over the next couple of years our visits became less and less social calls and more and more helping them take care of things. Changing lightbulbs became helping him stand up and go to the bathroom. Helping her prepare a meal became cooking for them. Going out was more and more a challenge to get them both into the car, into a restaurant, and managing with the canes or walker he needed. We started having to read the menu for them in the dimly lit restaurant. We waited to order while they counted out the pills they each had to take with dinner and listened while they reminded each other not to eat certain foods because it would keep them up. We tipped the waiter a little more after he had to show them three times that the coffee he served them was, indeed, decaf.

Because of a job change a few years later, we had to move back to the East Coast. We gave my wife's parents the option of staying in California or moving back east near us, at our expense (fortunately the company was helping us out). They moved to a retirement community not too far away from where we had moved to. Whether that was the smartest or dumbest thing to do, we'll never know. We do know that things deteriorated rapidly soon after.

The visits we had with them during that period were more and more work, less and less social. They had bought the retirement house, which meant that when something went wrong, they had to fix it. There was no landlord or super to take care of maintenance. I became Mr. Fix-it while my father-in-law stood watch. My wife took charge of her mother's usual duties as her failing eyesight made her less and less able to clean the house, fix dinner, or shop for food or clothing. They didn't bother making many new friends: it was easy to stay inside.

Then my father-in-law's health took a rapid drop and, a year and a half later, he died. With almost no one to talk to in the retirement community and bad memories of the new house, my mother-in-law had to leave. So she moved into her own apartment, closer to us and in the town where she had lived for forty years. She wanted to be near the friends she had from the old days, perhaps hoping that reliving the past would help her forget the present.

By then our roles had taken on significantly more caregiving and caretaking. My mother-in-law paid the bills, but not always. She cooked for herself, but not always, and, certainly, not healthy meals. She couldn't shop, so we did some ourselves and worked out an arrangement with a local grocery to have things delivered. The prices were higher than supermarket prices, and we fought with her to pay the extra amount for the service. We threw in a little extra tip once in a while knowing that she gave the delivery person the bare minimum. Every time we visited, which was now twice a week, we walked around the apartment, checked that everything was in order, checked to see that there was food in the cupboard, checked whether the food was spoiled and the bathroom clean. We looked over the stack of bills and offered to help her take care of them. We started out just writing the checks for her to sign and gradually signed them ourselves because it was just easier that way. We'd surreptitiously review her financial statements and checkbook to make sure everything was okay. It was, but because we kept it so. She maintained control—before she agreed to buy anything, we had to show her that she had enough money.

Then she fell. No broken bones, no injuries. But she had lain on the floor for an unknown length of time (although she thought it was only minutes). She got checked out, and they didn't find anything. Then she fell again. And again. So we signed her up with the local police service: She had to call in every morning or they would come by.

Then she fell and couldn't get up to go to the phone. She had lain on the floor for hours this time. So we signed her up with one of those companies that provides a pendant for her to wear around her neck. When she fell, she could press the button and yell, "I've fallen and I can't get up." The company notifies the police, a neighbor, and us. After a while, the police had to come by too often. She was falling a lot.

We didn't know what to do. We had no guidance, no role models. We talked about having her move in with us. No, that wouldn't do. We had no bedrooms on the first floor, no room we could convert, and only a tiny powder room on that floor. Besides, we both worked long hours and traveled fairly often with our jobs.

We called every day, often more than once, to make sure she was okay. Our visits were now three or four times a week, as our schedules permitted. There was very little socializing now: the visits were more the business of making sure that everything was taken care of. We had already arranged to have all bills sent to us, and we had joint control of the checking account. It was much easier that way. We paid her bills when we paid ours. It just meant doing two sets of books. We hired a series of aides to come in a few times a week: to make sure everything was okay, to clean, to prepare meals, and to make sure that she was taking all the pills she had to take at the right times. She hated every one of them and told us so.

We took her to doctors; we picked up her prescriptions; and we made sure that all the business of her life was taken care of. We took care of her bills, watched over her investments, and filed all the insurance claims! Since this was back in the days when doctors weren't required to file Medicare claims, we did it. We made copies of all the bills, sent one to Medicare, one to a secondary insurance company (Medigap), and one to a tertiary insurance company (another Medigap). We paid the doctors and kept records of all the benefit statements and checks, and made sure that the checks came to us (not to the doctor, therapist, or laboratory) and that all of the claims were accounted for. Because she was still covered under her late husband's retirement insurance benefit plan, we got to do the same for all the prescriptions she had filled.

It was a full-time job. And we weren't even physically taking care of her.

After a time, it became clear she needed more than part-time supervision. It had become that obvious. Perhaps it had become obvious earlier. But we had no model to look at to make any determination. And my mother-in-law certainly wasn't going to tell us she needed more help.

We began the search for someplace where she could get the care and supervision she needed: a long-term-care facility. Of course, back then we called it a nursing home. We didn't look at day care—it didn't really exist. We went through all the steps that are outlined in this book. We visited perhaps a dozen or more places: some that accepted Medicaid, some that didn't; some that offered different levels of care, some that only offered skilled care; some for which you must buy into, most that you don't; some that had availability, some that had a waiting list. If we liked the place, we put her name on the waiting list. There was no obligation, so why not?

We gathered all the information and sat down with pen, pad, and calculator. We crunched the numbers and figured out that with her Social Security and the income from her investments, her money would last her about ten years. That was based on the assumption that the nursing home charges would increase at a reasonable rate and that her investments would get about the same rate of return she had been getting. Of course, we knew her cash flow would fluctuate wildly as bills came due but dividends didn't. So we tried to account for that by using our most conservative estimates.

The initial visits to scout out the nursing homes were just as we feared. Many of them were depressing. Some had that awful smell we had anticipated but hoped to be spared. We got so we could walk in and, within seconds, know that it wouldn't be the right place. Actually, we found to our dismay that none of them was the right place. Yet we had no choice. She had no choice. She needed full-time care, and we couldn't provide it. We had ruled out hiring a twenty-four-hour, seven-day-a-week private nurse's aide because we knew that she needed both skilled and unskilled care, which would have been much too expensive to arrange. We also knew that we were not in a position to oversee the process or to make sure that someone always showed up. There weren't geriatric care managers or the kinds of assisted-living agencies that exist now.

My mother-in-law knew that she needed full-time care. But she resisted going to a home. We did everything we could to convince her to go. Finally, my wife and I both said to her, in the most determined voice she had ever heard from either of us, "Mom, you have no choice. You're going."

There was one big compromise on our part: We told her that it would be temporary until she was well enough to live in her apartment again. We lied. We knew that it wasn't temporary. In fact, we only waited a month before canceling the lease on her apartment. But we didn't tell her. For months, even years, she would ask, "When am I going home?" We usually said, "When the doctors think you're well enough." I think she eventually figured out that she wasn't going home, but she never said it to us. And we were smart enough to not bring it up. Besides, what was "home"? Back to the house they had sold nine years before? Back to the life with her husband? Home certainly wasn't the apartment she had lived in only for a few months. Home, we suspected, was the past.

We helped her move into the nursing home and visited her a couple of times a week, even more often in the beginning. We brought a couple of pieces of her furniture to make it her room, as we were instructed. We brought pictures of the family and hung them on the walls. But there was little we could do to make it like home. It was an institution. We spoke with the dietician, head nurse, administrator, social worker, activities director, and just about everyone associated with the home. We spoke to someone at almost every visit. We always wanted to know how she was doing, whether she was adapting, and whether the alternating anger and despair we were seeing was typical. We were told that she was doing well, that she was adapting, and that her anger and despair were indeed typical. We were also told something else: that she was much happier than she showed us. She participated in activities more than she told us she did; she talked with the staff more than it seemed she did. She even talked with other residents more often than she told us she did. She had always told us that she couldn't stand any of them—they were all old people and none of them could hear.

In one important way we were lucky: My mother-in-law had a terrific roommate, a woman several years younger who was interesting and talkative, but who also respected my mother-in-law's privacy and desire to not talk at times. My mother-in-law had made a friend of sorts. And how convenient that she was in the next bed.

That didn't last long though, because the roommate had to go to the hospital. By the time she was released, her bed had already been filled by someone else. An empty bed is a valuable commodity. My mother-in-law went through a series of roommates. They were never friends. They rarely talked. They would just live in their own private worlds and watch different TVs—sometimes the same program.

Then the nursing home raised its prices. A huge jump. They told us that they had to, that the costs were escalating, that the rates hadn't changed in years, and that they couldn't make it at the current price. We believed them because we saw how expensive everything was. So we again sat down and crunched the numbers. It wouldn't work now. Her money would run out much too quickly.

We talked with my mother-in-law about Medicaid and buying down assets. She wouldn't hear any of it. She refused to go on "welfare." She'd rather die. We respected her wishes and started looking at alternatives. Her other daughter lived in Texas, and we discovered that the prices there were considerably lower.

So my sister-in-law did all the same running around looking at facilities, talking with administrators, social workers, and nurses. We compared prices and notes, and, after crunching more numbers, told my mother-in-law that she'd be moving to Texas, to be near her other daughter. We told her that she'd be moving to a much nicer place (again, temporarily until she was well enough to go "home"), to a place near her grandchildren, and (perhaps this was the most important reason to her) to a cheaper place.

It was a much nicer place, and my sister-in-law and her kids took on the role of weekly visitors. We kept control of the business stuff. We still paid her bills. We still oversaw her investments. And we still dealt with submitting and keeping track of all the medical claims. Fortunately, by this time doctors were required to submit the forms to Medicare, so we were relieved of that burden. But we still had to deal with the Medigap policies and prescription reimbursement, the complicated nursing home bill, the cash-flow problems, and the fact that she could easily outlive her money.

We had just arrived at the hotel in Texas to see her when we got a call from my sister-in-law telling us that my mother-in-law had died that morning. We hadn't even known that she was sick. In fact, as the doctors thought, she really wasn't. She had died of "an infection," they said. She really died because she had no more reason to live.

The funeral was to be back in New Jersey where she would be buried next to her husband. We emptied the nursing home room of her belongings and flew back to New Jersey to make the arrangements. We used the funeral director closest to the home she and her husband had lived in for forty years. They were terrific. They made sure that we knew all the options and, without pressuring us, made sure that we made decisions. We weren't traumatized by our grief or by having to make all the funeral arrangements. While she hadn't had any life-threatening illnesses, she had been close to death for a long time. It didn't come as much of a surprise when she died.

Caring for her didn't end when she was buried. We still had all the financial obligations to deal with. We had to pay the bills, file the final tax return, divide up the estate according to the terms of her will, uncover and cash in the life insurance policy, make sure all the reimbursement checks for medical claims were received, and dispose of all her personal belongings.

Three years later we still have boxes of her stuff in among all our own stuff.

It is this story and the fact that we didn't have a model on which to draw that led to this book. We needed to know what to do when. We had to figure out what questions to ask and of whom to ask them. We looked for guidance from doctors, nurses, physical therapists, accountants, lawyers, and clergy. We asked our friends and relatives to help us with the decisions.

But mostly we stumbled through it all. We made phone calls to insurance companies and spoke with secretaries, file clerks, account representatives, and administrators. We argued, cajoled, and, eventually, learned what to say when we needed to get the right answer. We learned to ask the right questions and to make it easy for the person on the other end to answer the way we wanted. We learned to keep asking until we got the answer we wanted to hear.

Something inside us told us to try to respect our parents' independence. Never did we think that we were taking over the role of parent to our parents. They were always adults to us, no matter how frail or dependent they were on us for daily living. They were not children to us, just adults who needed us to do things for them, even if one of those things was decision-making. They didn't need to be taught anything by us—there were no lessons of life to learn from us. The only things they needed to learn were how to walk on one leg or how to make an arthritic hand do what they wanted it to do.

It's not easy watching our parents grow older and to deal with the changes that naturally occur as they age. When physical or mental ailments strike them and compound their struggles, it can be heartbreaking. We immediately want to jump in and help. We tried that many times with my mother-in-law and were often rejected. Why? Because we started challenging her feeling of independence.

She never wanted to become a burden on her children. She always wanted to be able to cope by herself. She couldn't, of course. Not fully. And at times, barely at all. But she always wanted to. We tried to let her handle things herself when we could.

We didn't always do the right thing. We made many decisions, some of them wrong, some right. We sometimes made decisions *for* my mother-in-law. But we always tried to bring her into the decision-making process. What we didn't know, we tried to learn. Unfortunately for us, we often had to learn it on our own.

We hope that this book will help you revere the old. We hope that we can answer the questions you have, and we hope that we can prompt you to ask your parents, yourselves, and the professionals who will care for your aging parents the questions you have.

Abraham Heschel said many brilliant things in an address he delivered at a White House Conference on Aging way back in Camelot (in 1961). Among them, he said, "The tragedy is that old age comes upon us as a shock for which we are unprepared."

We cannot let old age come upon our parents as a shock. We cannot let our parents be unprepared. There is too much to lose if we do. Heschel suggests that old age is an age of opportunity for inner growth: "The years of old age may enable us to attain the high values we failed to sense, the insights we have missed, the wisdom we ignored."

It is up to us baby boomers to see to it that our parents are not only cared for in their old age, but that their old age is rich in opportunity. The first responsibility in planning for our parents' old age will rest with us, the family. But, as Hillary Rodham Clinton would suggest, it takes a village not only to raise our children, but to care for our elderly.

Tough Talk 2

Caring for your aging parents begins with a conversation. Actually, it probably begins with several conversations, since it's unlikely that you and your parents will be able to cover everything in one discussion.

The idea of this talk is to learn as much as you can about their financial, insurance, and legal affairs, their health status, and their wishes to be carried out after their deaths. The more you talk about these issues, the more you'll learn. The more you learn, the better you'll be at making sure that they're as well cared for as possible. While few of us want to talk to our parents about aging, it's absolutely essential. In this chapter we will list all the areas you should discuss.

As you begin these conversations, you may find that some topics flow from others, or that you or your parents are more willing to discuss certain topics gradually. And you may find out, to your surprise, that some aging parents are quite willing to talk about sensitive topics, even about their own deaths. The fact is, many older people are more comfortable discussing death than younger people, especially if they're in good health. Perhaps it's because they've faced it more: with their own parents, with their friends, and with other relatives. Or maybe they've come to grips with their own mortality as they've seen their bodies change. As my stepmother says, "To be old is to be faced with death." We young people often don't realize how well our older relatives have coped with the death of their friends and relatives and how well prepared they are for their own deaths.

This is not to say that talking about aging is an easy thing. Nor will many aging parents feel comfortable discussing it with their children. But don't be too shocked if, when you begin to bring up the various subjects, all having to do with their aging, they appear much more comfortable than you are. After all, they face aging every time they look in the mirror or at each other. They saw their own parents and aunts and uncles go through the aging process. Chances are that they want for themselves better later years than what your grandparents had. They know all too well that they need to make sure you and others whom they trust know what their wishes are and as much as possible about their state of affairs. So your parents may be more open than you think they'll be.

At the same time, don't be surprised if you meet quite a bit of resistance. The fact is, many parents don't want to discuss some of these important matters with their children. Later in this chapter we'll talk more about the responses you get when you bring up the subject. The more you talk about their aging, the more they'll experience their own fears. They'll have to think about their own mortality and of the potential pain associated with dying and disease. They'll also have to confront the potential loss of control over their lives, the interruption of the goals they had for themselves, the fear of being a burden on you and other survivors (or, similarly, the fear of living without a spouse), and, for those who believe in an afterlife, the fear of punishment.

Don't Assume

You know the old joke about assuming: When you assume, you make an "ass" of "u" and "me." There's so much to cover about a person's state of affairs. It would be easy to miss some areas or to gloss over some because you assume that it's already been dealt with.

The primary purpose of this chapter is to make sure that you cover the important topics and find out what you have to know to make sure that you are caring for your aging parents as effectively as possible. Some of the following will be relevant to you and your parents while other areas may not apply. Try to address them all, since it's often the case that you know less about your parents' affairs than you think you do. For example, because your father is an attorney, you might reasonably assume that he has set up his papers appropriately, that a proper will has been executed, and even that a durable power of attorney has been set up. This could be an example of the shoemaker's children going without shoes. So, rule number one is: Don't assume, ask!

One word of caution: Keep in mind that when you discuss your aging parents' financial and legal affairs, health concerns, housing, and their wishes after they are gone, you are taking on more

Ten Purposes of Talking with Your Aging Parents

1. to learn as much as possible about your aging parents' current legal and financial affairs

2. to learn as much as possible about your aging parents' wishes, both before and after their deaths

3. to provide information to your aging parents about resources available to them and about their health and legal and financial affairs

4. to help them make decisions about their affairs and their future

5. to learn about their lives

6. to learn about you, your life, and your relationship with them

7. to provide a sense of heritage for you and your children

8. to help them maintain their dignity and as much control over their own lives as possible

9. to help them cope with their aging and adapt to changes

10. to talk about their feelings and reactions

responsibility for them. Be prepared to accept this responsibility. And if, for example, your aging father balks at talking with you or another one of his children about legal issues or his finances, you should encourage him to bring along your mother (or you) the next time he talks with the lawyer, accountant, or advisor.

Who Should Participate in the Discussion

You might think that everyone who will have responsibility for your aging parent should either be involved in these discussions or, at least be privy to the information that is shared. But that's not always desirable, nor is it practical. While the person designated as the primary caregiver should certainly participate, it doesn't necessarily follow that everyone be involved with all aspects, even the primary caregiver. If you and your family have decided to split up the responsibilities, each party should certainly know as much as possible about his or her immediate area of responsibility. So the person(s) who will be making sure that all the legal and financial areas are covered should know as much as possible about your parents' affairs. But that person need not necessarily be involved in handling some of the other day-to-day decisions.

Splitting Up the Work

Although more and more families are working out ways to split up the duties and responsibilities, they are usually *not* equally shared. So the first thing you and your family must work out is who will be the designated primary caregiver. More often than not, other than your aging parent's spouse, the first designated primary caregivers are women, while men more often take on the logistical and financial responsibilities of aging parents. We encourage you to agree on whatever arrangements work out best for you. But, for your information, the primary caregivers, in the order most frequently seen, are:

1. the spouse
2. the oldest daughter
3. a daughter still living at home
4. a daughter-in-law who lives nearby
5. a son

When to Have Your Discussion

A logical question is: "When should I have this discussion?" The quick answer is: "Now, since you can never have this discussion too early, but clearly you can try to have this discussion too late."

Discussing the future can help you and your parents prepare emotionally for the inevitable, and you'll also be better able to help ensure that their wishes are carried out. And there are also some logistical reasons for discussing your parents' future earlier than you might have thought.

Why to Have Your Conversation Now

1. You may be able to help them take advantage of resources available to them that they might not have known about. These include such things as free or low-cost services, discounts at stores, free rides, activities they can participate in, and alternative living arrangements.

2. You may be able to help them make sure that they've done everything they can to preserve their estate, regardless of its size, and that they're properly covered by insurance. This means that they may need to go to see a lawyer, accountant, or other advisor, and will need to take a more active part in ensuring that their legal, financial, and insurance affairs are all in order.

3. If their health and ability to take care of themselves are a growing concern to you and you believe that they may eventually need to move into a long-term-care facility, you may need to get your parent's name on a waiting list at a facility you feel will be best for them.

4. There are a growing number of multilevel communities and long-term-care facilities that require people to move in before they need skilled nursing care. There are also a growing number of so-called "retirement communities" which offer services and activities to older citizens that your parents may want to avail themselves of. It's much better for them to move to one of these places when they're young enough (and healthy enough) to take advantage of what they have to offer.

Finding the Words

If you and your parents have a close relationship, possibly live nearby, and talk often about most topics, you're probably in a fairly good position to talk about the various topics discussed in this chapter regularly and also to deal with the changes your parents will undergo. But even for those who appear to talk freely and openly, starting that first conversation can be tough. Here are a few approaches and suggestions. You'll probably want to use a combination of these.

Approaches

- ◆ The Direct Approach: "I'd like to talk with you about the future. There are lots of things I need to know about. Is this a good time to talk?"

- ◆ The Written Approach: "Here's an article/book/chapter I think might be good for you to read. I think it's really good and helpful. After you've had a chance to digest it, I'd like to talk with you about what it says."

- ◆ The Third-party Approach: "I'm concerned about the future and wondered if you've talked with your lawyer/accountant/advisor. If not, would you do so? If you have, do you think it would be good for me to talk with him/her or to have all three of us talk together?"

Whatever approach or combination of approaches you use, don't overlook your parents' lead. Appreciate how difficult it may be for them to talk and try to set aside any old resentments.

Some Likely Responses and What You Can Say

- ◆ Closing off the conversation or constantly changing the subject. Your response might be: "I'd like to talk about it, but I'll wait until you're ready." Then be sure to bring it up again.

- ◆ Strong emotional outpouring from one or both of you. Your response might be: "Why don't we talk more when we're both ready." Again, be sure to bring it up again and again. The level of emotion will likely subside.

- ◆ Denial. Your response might be: "It's very important that I know some things just in case something happens to you."

Be assertive about your desire to talk, but pay attention to your parents' lead and to your own feelings and reactions. Often, touching helps, as does empathy and active listening. At the same time, keep in mind that you're trying to gather information, not counsel them emotionally. So while this conversation often results in a discussion of feelings, what you're really after are facts, plans, and a status report. Whether that comes as a result of many discussion or a written response to a list of questions

Important: Be sure to listen to your parents and be open-minded about their wishes. They are *their* wishes. You can certainly express your own desires and feelings, and even try to persuade them if necessary. But remember that people want to remain in charge of their own lives as long as possible. Unless they're in danger, your parents have a right to take risks and even to make foolish decisions about their own lives. Your parents may be physically feeble but that doesn't mean they're feeble-minded. Treat them with the respect you would want.

doesn't really matter. The aim is to get answers to your questions.

Organize Right Away

As time progresses and you take on more responsibility for your parents' well-being, you'll need to be well organized. The best time to start organizing is before you begin your conversation. Good organization will not only help you deal with all the issues you must face, it will also help you keep the discussion centered on the facts. That, in turn, will likely make the conversations easier. It will also ensure that you get your questions answered. Take notes, or if that's awkward, write up your observations immediately afterward. In our experience, tape recorders and video recorders make it much more difficult for people to open up. So unless you're actually preparing your parents' will, stay away from recorders. They'll just make it more awkward for everyone, and you then won't get answers to your questions.

We strongly suggest that you get a notebook that you designate specifically for all those issues you and your aging parents will face. If you wind up taking on more responsibility for the business of your parents' life later on, you'll find that you may need several notebooks: for appointments, key addresses, important personal and medical information, financial papers, medical insurance claims, etc. This is as good a time as any to get that started. You can put it all in the first notebook and later transfer the information to your paper filing system, or, if you're comfortable with electronics, to a computer database program.

There will be an incredible amount of detail for you to remember or be able to access, so it's wise to get organized early, before it becomes overwhelming.

You Can Still Do It from a Distance

If you live nearby and see your parents often, you obviously have some advantages over those who live farther away. But long-distance caregiving is quite possible, and quite common. In today's world, people are mobile and families are often spread throughout the country, if not the world. You won't be the only ones dealing with aging parents from afar. There will be lots of support from others available if you need it and take advantage of it. As you read in the Foreword by Thomas J. Humphrey, Executive Director of Children of Aging Parents (CAPS), there are local support groups springing up everywhere. You're not the first one to deal with this problem, and you obviously won't be the last. Take advantage of what others have learned and are willing to share with you. Your situation is unique, certainly. That's still no reason to reinvent the wheel. If you feel isolated and don't know where to turn, call CAPS at 800-227-7294. They can tell you about a local support group, give you some information, or refer you to a local resource.

For those who don't live near their parents, or don't have a close relationship with them, it's even more important to be well organized. Caregiving and caretaking can both be done successfully from a distance. It just takes effort and a clear notion of what must be done and when. When you're visiting, for example, you'll want to take notes about your parents' health and living situation and about the network of support that's available or set up, you'll want to meet their doctors/lawyers/advisors as needed, and you'll want to have an alert system set up. When you're talking on the phone, you'll want to listen for clues about their health and status. You'll also want to be sure that certain questions are answered, and that means keeping track, usually in a notebook, of what outstanding issues have yet to be resolved.

Subjects to Cover in Your Conversation

Traditionally, for your parents' generation, husbands handled most of the financial, legal, and "business" connected with the household while wives dealt with the family and the home. Therefore, major changes occur more often and cause potential problems when your father dies, leaving your mother to fend for herself. Some of these very capable women can handle the new responsibilities quite well, but others not so well. This is not a statement about ability or a political ideology. The fact is that your parents lived at a time when things were different and there were many more gender-specific roles that people had to fit into. So, for example, we see that over 80 percent of older women have no pension. And of those that do, the median amount is just $3,000 per year. As a result, women make up almost three-quarters of the elderly poor. The numbers are far better for older men.

The Top Ten Subjects

Here are the top ten subjects to cover and the questions you must eventually know the answers to. The more you and the other care-givers know about each issue, the better off you'll be when decisions have to be made.

1. Personal Information

- ◆ Social Security numbers—make sure that you know the numbers of *both* your parents
- ◆ Medicare/Medicaid identification cards
- ◆ the name, address, and phone number of your parents' mortgage holder (don't forget second mortgages and home equity loans or lines of credit)
- ◆ the approximate balance of each mortgage
- ◆ if your parents rent, the name, address, and phone number of your parents' landlord
- ◆ bank accounts—be especially careful to find out *all* the accounts and the exact names they're under
- ◆ the location of safe deposit box and where the keys are kept
- ◆ credit cards—bank name, card number, current balance (if any), and the name(s) on the account (given the difficulty many women have in establishing credit after they're widowed, it's a good idea to have your mother establish her own credit now)

2. Health

- your parents' present condition (including normal blood pressure and cholesterol levels, dental health, normal degree and location of pain/discomfort)

- long-term and short-term illnesses and their prognoses

- allergies, especially allergies to any drugs

- current prescriptions—put together a list of the drugs your parents take, what they're for, who prescribed them, the frequency they should be taken, how long they are to be taken, and whether the prescription can be refilled

- degree of hearing and sight loss (if known) and last date both were checked

- usual complaints, including constipation, toothaches, dry eyes, dry mouth, fatigue, insomnia, arthritic pain, sensitivity to cold (chilblains), and ringing in the ears (tinnitus)

- inoculations (including the last flu shot)

- names, addresses, and phone numbers of all the doctors and health professionals who currently care for your parents (include their family doctor and specialists who have treated them, and don't forget podiatrists, chiropractors, physical and occupational therapists, and optometrists)

3. Documents and Other Important Items

You should know the location (and/or have copies) of all the following:

- birth certificates

- marriage certificates

- death certificate of spouse

- divorce decrees

- military discharge

- Immigration and Naturalization Service card (known as the "green card")

- home deed/title or lease

- auto title or lease

- appraisals of valuables
- life, home, and auto insurance policies
- disability and medical insurance policies and identification cards
- burial plot deeds
- wills and codicils
- living wills
- power-of-attorney forms
- durable power-of-attorney forms
- health care proxies
- home security system codes
- duplicate house keys
- duplicate keys to post office boxes
- duplicate car keys

4. Insurance

- Medicare/Medicaid identification card number
- Medicare supplement insurance plans, the so-called "Medigap" insurance (kind of coverage, company name and address, and policy number)
- long-term-care insurance (kind of coverage, company name and address, and policy number)
- life insurance policies (company name and address; the agent's name, address, and phone number; policy number; policy face amount; beneficiary; cash value, if any; and the amount of any loans that have been taken against the policy)
- auto insurance policy (coverage, company name and address, and policy number)
- homeowner's or renter's insurance policy (coverage, company name and address, and policy number)
- disability insurance (coverage, company name and address, and policy number)

5. Religious Concerns

- ◆ place of worship, if any
- ◆ name of personal clergy
- ◆ wishes for a religious or nonreligious funeral service
- ◆ religious rules for handling of funerals
- ◆ religious beliefs as they relate to health care

6. Finances

- ◆ financial advisors (names, addresses, and phone numbers)
- ◆ bank accounts—checking, savings, and investment accounts (names and addresses of banks and account numbers); it may be a good idea either to get your name on the account or to have signature authority through a power of attorney (see chapter 4, "Blind Justice")
- ◆ brokerage accounts
- ◆ complete list of assets
- ◆ complete list of debts and liabilities
- ◆ terms and balance of their home mortgage
- ◆ property tax receipts
- ◆ list of routine household bills (mortgage/rent, utilities, insurance premiums, etc.)
- ◆ list of real estate holdings and rental property
- ◆ copies of tax returns for the last three years
- ◆ personal loan records (including loans made to family members and partners)
- ◆ open lines of credit
- ◆ duplicate key and signature authority to access safe deposit box
- ◆ location and appraisals of valuables (jewelry, art, precious metals, silver, stamp and coin collections, etc.)
- ◆ retirement and pension policies (make sure you know whether benefits are extended to the surviving spouse)

- partnerships and interests in other business ventures
- credit cards and balances
- receivables from business or personal loans
- moneys set aside for funeral and health care

7. Friends, Relatives, and Neighbors

- a complete list of the immediate neighbors, their addresses, and their phone numbers (including daytime phone numbers)
- list of those who have an extra key or access to the house
- list of friends and relatives who live nearby who can visit or stop in
- list of emergency contacts

8. Plans for the Future

- funeral arrangements made or wishes for a service
- whether they want a burial or cremation
- if a cremation, what to do with their ashes
- wishes about housing arrangements
- wishes regarding medical and crisis care
- whether extraordinary or "heroic" measures are to be taken in life-threatening emergencies
- holiday and birthday plans

9. Legal Issues

- name, address, and phone number of attorney(s), if any
- location of last will and testament plus all codicils
- location and a copy of durable power of attorney
- location and copy of health care proxy
- deeds (home, burial plot, rental property, autos)
- birth certificates

- marriage certificates
- death certificate of spouse
- divorce decrees
- military discharge papers

10. Personal Contacts

- associations, clubs, and fraternal organizations (many offer services and benefits)
- pet's veterinarian
- geriatric care manager
- day care provider
- family therapist(s)

In the next chapter you'll learn about how you can help keep your aging parents as fit as possible. We'll talk about good nutrition, proper exercise, and specific health concerns of the aging. We'll also point out what to look for and the key decisions you must make when your parents show signs of deterioration, dementia, Alzheimer's, and other physical or mental distress.

WITH A GENTLE HAND

Age may be relative, but aging is not. So, while everyone is surely different, and the aging process affects people differently, there are definite characteristics of aging that are common to most people. Our goals, of course, are to live as long a possible, to be as healthy as we can, and to minimize the suffering we experience in our older years. Our goals as children of aging parents are to do what we can to help our parents realize their goals.

In this chapter we'll talk about ways we can help our parents stay as healthy as possible in mind and spirit. We'll talk about keeping fit, good nutrition, and some common medical conditions that occur in older people, such as Alzheimer's disease, adult-onset diabetes, dementia, osteoporosis, heart disease, depression, substance abuse, hypochondriasis, and gum and dental disease. We'll also discuss things you can do when your parents' eyesight begins to fail or their hearing becomes impaired.

The focus will be on what you, as caregivers and children of aging parents, should look for to make sure that your parents are not experiencing some physical or mental distress for which some treatment is needed. We'll give hints to help you and your parents choose doctors and other medical personnel. We'll talk about ways that you can make your parents' home more suitable to their needs and more accessible if they have any physical limitations. And we'll discuss medications—their effects and keeping track of them.

Young at Heart: Keeping Fit

First, let's make something very clear: Fit does not mean youthful. In fact, our whole definition of "old age" has, by necessity, changed dramatically in recent years. It's a common sight to see senior citizens running in marathons or triathlons or performing some other physically challenging task (many of us who are much younger can't run a mile or swim 100 laps in a pool). It's become even more common to see senior citizens in health clubs, pumping iron, mastering stairs, and aerobically stepping. The point is, the goal of an older person is *not* to be young again. There's nothing wrong with getting older (like the old joke, "consider the alternative"). Most older people wouldn't trade their age for anything. They love being exactly who they are: a composite of all the experiences they've amassed over a lifetime. You obviously can't stop time and you can't stop aging. But you can delay some or all of the physical deterioration that comes with aging. One of the best ways to do that, for most people, is through exercise: a regular, appropriate routine.

Important: Needless to say, everyone starting to exercise, regardless of age, should be certain to choose an appropriate regime given their age and physical condition. With your aging parents, it's especially recommended that they consult their doctor or physical therapist before starting any exercise regime.

The Goals of Exercise

What do we mean by a regular, appropriate routine of exercise? This is the same for us baby boomers as it is for our parents. Simply put, there are three ingredients:

1. aerobic activity for a healthy heart and lungs

2. flexibility exercises so that muscles and joints don't atrophy from lack of use

3. strengthening exercises to maintain muscle tone and prevent injury

The specific routine your parents adopt should be designed by them and their medical consultants. It should be something they can do often and with little hassle (otherwise it will be much too easy to put off). Furthermore, whatever routine they choose should be one they enjoy doing and look forward to.

Walking is certainly one of the best activities your parents can do regularly. And more and more we're seeing hordes of retirees dressed in their workout clothes and specially designed sneakers "walking the mall" in the morning hours before the stores open. Walking meets all three of the goals of exercise. And walking the mall means that there's always a lot to see and other people with

Note: If your parent has some physical disability, it may be possible to get a doctor to prescribe an exercise regime. In that case, all or part of a club membership or activities fee may be covered by health insurance (classified as physical therapy) or tax deductible (but be sure that your parent checks this out with a tax advisor).

Warning: Remind your parents that if, at any time while exercising, they feel faint, light-headed, or short of breath, or feel any sort of chest pain or "palpitations," they should immediately stop exercising. If the condition persists, they should seek medical attention immediately!

whom your parents can interact, which makes it more enjoyable. As a bonus, weather is almost never a problem.

If there's a mall near your parents' house, there's likely a group of seniors who are there every morning limbering up and then walking briskly from one end of the mall to another. In some malls there's even an organized club or association that sponsors the exercise or, at least, keeps it safe and supervised.

To learn more about mall walking, check with the central administration office of the mall or with a nearby senior community center.

If your parent is in a wheelchair, uses a walker or cane(s), or has some other disability, physical exercise should be an essential part of his or her life, as any physical therapist will say, to maintain muscle strength and flexibility. Be sure that your parent works closely with the therapist and has a recommended exercise routine mapped out.

Where to Go

In addition to mall walking, there's always the great outdoors. While in some places your parent will have to deal with weather, traffic, and other barriers, there are many towns and areas that offer walking trails and park courses. There are also many fitness and aerobics classes available for seniors offered through local community recreation centers, adult schools, senior centers, YMCAs and YWCAs, and churches and synagogues. These are usually low-cost or free, run by professionals, and supervised.

In addition, many health clubs and gyms offer reduced rates for seniors or lower-cost limited memberships to people who will use a club during off-peak hours (usually between 9:00 A.M. and 4:00 P.M.).

For more information about fitness for seniors, the American Association of Retired Persons (AARP) offers a great deal of information to members. You can call the headquarters at 800-424-3410 or your local chapter office (there are nearly 4,000 local chapters). You can also visit the AARP Web site at:

http://www.aarp.org

We Are What We Eat

One of the biggest problems facing older people is maintaining good eating habits and getting well-balanced meals. In fact, it may surprise you to learn that many older people suffer from anorexia. There are several reasons for these nutritional problems.

Ten Reasons for Poor Nutritional Habits in Older Persons

1. Appetite is based largely on our senses: taste, smell, and sight in particular. But the senses are not as keen in older people and these sensory deficits and insufficient internal cues lead to a decrease in appetite.

2. As our bodies age, we need different kinds of foods and in different proportions. Yet most of us, the elderly especially, are fairly rigid in our eating habits and likes/dislikes. What we've always eaten (and like) is what we always *want* to eat, regardless of whether it's "good" for us or whether we're getting the nutritional value we need.

3. Many older people experience worsening economic conditions as they are forced to live on fixed incomes. The amounts they're living on are often considerably less than what they've been accustomed to. As a result, they buy and eat less, trying to save money wherever they can.

4. Many older people are on daily doses of a number of different medications. Many of these medications cause changes in appetite and body chemistry. Some may even cause nausea or some other condition that will decrease appetite. Sometimes the combination of drugs leads to decreased appetite or shortages of certain vitamins or minerals.

5. Many older people suffer from diseases such as adult-onset diabetes that require special nutritional care. Yet they may

not always be able to keep up with what their bodies need as their conditions change.

6. Many older people have various aches and pains of unknown origin and generally just "don't feel well." As a result, they don't want to eat or even go through the trouble of eating.

7. Many older people live alone and just don't bother cooking or shopping for themselves.

8. Many older people are unable to cook or shop for themselves, but don't let others know.

9. Many older people are in the early stages of Alzheimer's disease, dementia, or senility that lead to poor eating habits.

10. Depression, loneliness, confusion, alcoholism, substance abuse, and other conditions affect an increasing number of adult people, leading to decreased appetite and poor eating habits.

Good Nutrition

Maintaining a well-balanced diet is no less important for older people than it is for younger ones. In some ways, actually, many older people need to be even more careful that they're getting all the nutrients they need, for several reasons:

♦ The many medications they're taking affect their chemical balance.

♦ Their life is slower and, as a result, so is their metabolism.

♦ They generally eat smaller quantities than younger people, making what they eat even more important.

♦ Their taste buds and other senses are less keen, which means that they have decreased appetites and eat less.

♦ They are prone to many more illnesses, diseases, and conditions that affect the appetite.

♦ They are frequently on low-fat, low-salt diets, which means that foods tend to have no taste (or so they'll complain), which means that they'll eat less.

♦ Their bodies are less able to cope with deficiencies.

Meals-on-Wheels

Almost every locality offers a "meals-on-wheels" program for seniors in which both hot and cold meals are delivered to seniors. These meal programs are *not* necessarily based on need or geared exclusively toward low-income people. Local agencies administer the programs, and many offer the same meal program for a small fee ($2 or $3 per meal) or donation. Of course, for low-income seniors the service is completely subsidized. But for others, there can be a shared cost. The service is available seven days a week. To find the name of the organization that administers a meal program in your parents' area, you can contact:

National Meals-on-Wheels Foundation
2675 Forty-fourth Street SW, Suite 305
Grand Rapids, MI 49509
800-999-6262

To the extent possible, you should make sure that your parents are getting all the nutrients they need, and you need to pay close attention to any changes you see. Here are a few suggestions to help your parent eat well:

◆ Be sure that your parent's physician is informed of any deficiencies. The doctor may either put your parent on a diet or make a referral to a nutritionist/dietician.

◆ Help your parent shop for groceries.

◆ Arrange to have groceries delivered.

◆ Help your parent plan meals that are nutritious and easy to make.

◆ Make some prepared meals that require only warming or microwaving.

◆ Eat meals with your parent so that mealtime is not depressing.

◆ Encourage your parent to eat one or more meals with others or at a community or senior center.

◆ If your parent is eating alone, encourage him or her to actually sit down and have a meal, on a plate, with food

Dehydration

Important: In addition to various stages of malnutrition, many older people suffer from *dehydration*. This can be caused by the same reasons as other nutritional disorders, or simply by not taking in enough liquid. Make sure that your parent drinks enough water or other non-alcoholic drinks (keeping a water bottle at bedside can help).

that's been prepared, not just eat out of the can or standing over the sink.

♦ Encourage your parent to take vitamin and mineral supplements as recommended by a physician.

♦ Experiment with new spices (in small quantities at first) to compensate for a low-salt, low-fat, and low-sugar diet. Lemon, garlic, and fresh herbs add zest without the negatives.

♦ If your parents can't or won't cook for themselves, consider hiring someone to come in and prepare meals once a day or so (or at least a couple of times per week).

♦ Have your parent take advantage of free or low-cost meal programs at churches and synagogues, community and senior centers, senior day care centers, hospitals, and other groups.

Depression

Depression is the most widespread mental problem among older people: estimates are that *half* the people age 65 and older are depressed. Its causes are numerous and its ramifications endless. As caregiver, you're in the best position to see that your parent is depressed. But because you're so close to the situation, you may not be able to realize that your parent is suffering. You may see sadness or any of the other symptoms of clinical depression (see below). But it's easy to dismiss any one or two symptoms or find logical reasons for them. For example, your parent may have lost a little weight, not be eating well, and feel "empty" or sad. Those are normal feelings in and of themselves. You could easily dismiss them as reactions to some sad event that has happened recently (the loss of a friend or relative, for example—something that occurs all too often), or perhaps from a medication your parent has started to take, or even from a change in the season (yes, winter months with decreased numbers of daylight hours do, in fact, lead to a form of depression known as Seasonal Affective Disorder).

But taken together and in combination with some other symptoms they may indicate that your parent is clinically depressed. Here are the twelve symptoms of depression according to the U.S. Department of Health and Human Services.

The Twelve Symptoms of Clinical Depression

1. persistent sadness, anxiety, or "empty" mood
2. loss of interest or pleasure in ordinary activities, family, or friends
3. decreased energy, listlessness, fatigue, feeling "slowed down," especially in the morning
4. sleep problems and changes in sleep patterns (for example, insomnia, oversleeping, early-morning awakening)
5. eating problems and changes in eating patterns or foods consumed (also indicated by a loss or gain of appetite or weight)
6. difficulty concentrating, remembering, or making decisions
7. feelings of hopelessness or pessimism
8. feelings of guilt, worthlessness, or helplessness
9. thoughts of death or suicide
10. irritability
11. excessive crying
12. recurring aches and pains (headaches, backaches, etc.) that don't respond to treatment

How to Know If Your Parent Is Depressed

It isn't "normal" for people to feel depressed all the time, old or young. In fact, most people, and most older adults, feel quite satisfied with their lives. So as a general rule, if you see more than three or four of these symptoms over two or more weeks, you should take some action.

Causes of Depression

There are numerous causes of depression. Again, we're not talking about just sadness or feeling down. We're talking about more than three or four of the symptoms previously listed.

Medications: A common cause of depression is the side effects of medications. Certain drugs used to treat high blood pressure and arthritis, for example, have been known to cause depression. In addition, older adults are often taking several drugs at once. Some of the interactions among drugs can cause depression. Make sure that your parent's physician knows what drugs your parent is taking regularly. Don't forget to ask about over-the-counter medications your parent is taking. Often those drugs are just weaker versions of prescription drugs. They may have the same chemicals, just in different proportions. (See more about medications below.)

Important: If your parent talks of suicide, *always* take it seriously. Talk to your parent's physician or call the local suicide-prevention hot line listed in the blue pages of your local telephone book. Talk of suicide may be serious or may be just talk. This is not a time to gamble.

Alcohol: Alcoholism or excessive drinking is not usually thought of as a cause of depression but as a symptom. However, even moderate amounts of alcohol *in combination with* other drugs or medicines can cause depression. Furthermore, alcohol can cause or increase forgetfulness, confusion, and an ability to concentrate. This can make depression worse.

Physical Illness: Illnesses can be either a cause or a symptom of depression. For example, diabetes, strokes, hormonal changes and disorders, Parkinson's disease, and cancer can cause many of the symptoms of depression. Similarly, people with life-threatening diseases such as cancer, those who have had a stroke, and those whose physical condition is deteriorating (loss of hearing or vision, for example) react to their condition by becoming depressed.

Internal Chemical Changes: As we age, our body chemistry changes, and some of the chemicals we normally produce are either no longer produced or are produced in smaller amounts. Some of these reductions in what our bodies generate may lead to depression. Correlated with this is stress, since stress has been shown to change our body makeup and chemical balance.

Life Events: Many external events and major changes in lifestyle can lead to depression. The death or illness of a loved one (and, of course, as we age, we see more and more of our peers die) can cause depression. Even the loss of a pet can have the same effect. In addition, so many older adults have financial problems that it's surprising even more aren't depressed. Many older people are forced to move (either because of finances or physical condition), another highly stressful event and a leading cause of depression. And even some positive changes, such as retirement, can lead to depression, in part because of the stress that results.

Genetic Personality: Some causes of depression are directly linked to your genes. For example, it has been shown that people with very low self-esteem for a prolonged period, or those who are very dependent on other people, can trace the disorder to a genetic proclivity.

Treatments for Depression

Depression is often easily treated. In fact, it's estimated that over 90 percent of those treated for depression respond successfully. One of the key factors in successful treatment is early intervention.

Common treatments include medication (antidepressants) and counseling or, more often, a combination of the two. Your parent's physician will be in the best position to make the determination about how to treat your parent's depression. So it's especially important that when you see the signs of depression, you and your parent speak with a physician.

Counseling is offered most places, and often there are geriatric psychiatrists or psychologists who specialize in treating depression in older adults. To find the right professional for your parent, you can ask your parent's physician for a referral. Or you can check with the local senior center, hospital, or social service agency.

What You Can Do When Your Parent Is Depressed

Early intervention is one of the most effective ways to treat depression, so it's extremely important that you pay attention to the symptoms your parent displays. If you notice your parent experiencing several of the symptoms previously listed for an extended period (more than two weeks), you should consider intervention.

1. Seek professional guidance or have your parent seek professional help. You and your parent should talk openly with his or her physician about the symptoms. Remind your parent that one of the symptoms of depression is the feeling that treatment won't help.

2. Make sure that your parent's physician is aware of all medications your parent is taking regularly. Also make sure that the physician knows about any over-the-counter medications your parent is consuming.

3. Make sure that your parent's physician knows your parent's medical history so that physical disorders can be ruled out as causes.

4. Have your parent take advantage of counseling that is recommended. Your parent should seek a professional with whom he or she is comfortable sharing some inner feelings. Most people are resistant to seeing a counselor. You should encourage your parent as much as possible, using whatever influence you can muster. Remind your parent that there is no longer a stigma attached to seeking professional help, that many older adults benefit from the help they get, and that depression can be treated successfully.

5. If medication is prescribed for your parent, make sure that it is being taken and at the prescribed times (see the discussion of medication below). Make sure, if it is so prescribed, that the medication is being taken on a full stomach, or that certain foods and beverages are not consumed (be especially watchful if your parent consumes alcohol).

6. Pay attention to any side effects of the medication and be certain to report them to your parent's physician. Ask your parent about side effects he or she notices.

7. Be a part of the treatment. Encourage activity and participation in your family and his or her community. Also encourage physical exercise, which can increase the benefits of medications and, by itself, lead to feeling better.

Confusion, Delirium, Dementia (and Alzheimer's)

Most people lump these three conditions into one and call it "dementia" or "senility." But these three are different, despite the fact that they refer to a disorder in thinking and rational processing and all three may have physical causes. In brief, not all confused people are demented, but all demented people are confused.

- *Confusion:* Confused people are aware of their state and are often distressed by it. Confusion is typically a temporary condition.

- *Delirium:* People experiencing delirium may or may not be aware of their state as they drift in and out of consciousness. Delirium, too, is often a temporary condition.

- *Dementia:* People with dementia rarely have insight into their condition. Dementia is often progressive and irreversible. Alzheimer's disease is one kind of dementia.

Coping with a parent suffering from dementia is difficult. You experience great sadness as you watch your parent exhibit the behaviors accompanying the disease. You feel totally isolated and helpless as your parent slips farther and farther away from the person you knew and loved.

Here are a few points to keep in mind:

1. Dementia is not a normal part of aging. Not all older people experience dementia.

2. If your parent exhibits an increasing amount of "strange" behavior (confusion, disorientation, etc.) you should have him or her checked by a physician.

3. The more you understand about dementia and Alzheimer's, the easier it will be for you to handle the problems associated with it.

4. Some dementias are treatable with medication. While there is no "cure" per se, recent evidence has shown that sometimes, for some people, with some drugs, the progression can be arrested.

5. There are many conditions that mimic dementia which can, in fact, be reversed with the proper care. For example, poor nutrition and certain side effects or combinations of medicines can lead to increased confusion, which can look like dementia.

6. To be sure that your parent is actually suffering from dementia or Alzheimer's, have him or her diagnosed by a physician. If, indeed, that is the condition, you might consider joining a support group to help you cope. At the very least, you should try to learn as much as you can about your parent's dementia.

For more information about Alzheimer's or to learn about support groups, you can call the local chapter of the Alzheimer's Association (look in the white pages of the phone book). Or you can contact the national headquarters at:

Alzheimer's Association
919 North Michigan Avenue, Suite 1000
Chicago, IL 60611
800-272-3900

Running Hot and Cold

Walk into your parent's house in the winter and you'll most likely get blasted with hot air. Older people get cold easily and for a number of reasons: their blood vessels don't dilate or constrict as well as they used to, they don't have as much fatty tissue or hair for insulation, they're suffering from confusion or dementia, some of the medications they're taking have side effects that cause them to feel cold, etc. As a result, they're more prone to hypothermia, a potentially serious condition characterized in the early stages by listlessness and some confusion and spiraling downward to drowsiness, slurred speech, and unconsciousness. Prolonged overexposure to cold can ultimately be fatal.

If you discover your parents experiencing hypothermia, get them to a warm room, wrap them in sweaters or warm blankets (or have them take a warm bath), and have them drink warm fluids. If the condition persists, make sure that they seek medical attention.

Older adults are also subject to hyperthermia, or heat stress, for similar reasons as hypothermia, and from an inability to feel things because of strokes, diabetes, Parkinson's disease, and other disorders. A person suffering from hyperthermia will usually start out with clammy skin with some sweating (maybe not much sweat since older sweat glands that protect the body from overheating also don't work as well). The progressive symptoms of overheating are heavy sweating, nausea, general weakness, and a rapid heartbeat.

A related condition is dehydration, characterized by confusion, fatigue, and lightheadedness. Older adults are more prone to dehydration because, among other reasons, their kidneys don't work as well as in younger people. As a general rule, older people should drink as much water and non-alcoholic beverages as they can (eight glasses per day is the recommended amount). There is almost no risk of drinking too much water, unless a physician wants your parent on a restricted fluid intake or if incontinence is a problem.

Important: Heat stroke is very dangerous for older people. Heat stroke is characterized by high body temperature, cramps, diarrhea, breathing difficulty, and *dry skin with no sweating,* in addition to confusion. Immediately seek emergency medical attention if you discover your parent (or anyone, for that matter) with these symptoms. As a first aid, have him or her drink plenty of cool water and try to cool the person down with cool (not cold) wet sheets.

Brusha-Brusha-Brusha

Another potential problem many older adults face is dental and gum disease. Dental and gum problems can either be a cause of poor nutrition, leading to even more serious illnesses, or be a symptom of poor nutrition. As a caregiver, you need to be extra careful about monitoring your parent's dental health, especially since most older adults tend to neglect their teeth. They tend to feel that dental problems are an inevitable part of growing older.

Why There's More Tooth Decay as We Age

- ◆ Gums tend to recede, which exposes more root surfaces.

- ◆ Fillings and crowns are old and break off or crack.

- ◆ Medications, especially those used to control incontinence and hypertension (high blood pressure), reduce the production of saliva.

- We naturally produce less saliva as we age, which means that the acids in the foods we eat are not neutralized.

- Reduced saliva production means that food is not washed away as well.

- Reduced saliva production means that our dental tissues get less of the calcium and phosphorus they need.

- The constant changes in the shape and size of dental tissues that we undergo with age means that dentures and artificial teeth no longer fit as well.

- Older hands, particularly on people suffering from arthritis or other similar diseases, cannot grasp toothbrushes and dental floss as easily.

- Visual impairment leads to poorer dental hygiene.

What You Can Do

1. Make sure that your parent visits a dentist at least once a year.

2. Do a visual check of your parent's mouth.

3. Make sure that your parent is eating well-balanced meals and shows no other signs of malnutrition.

4. Check to see if your parent has difficulty chewing.

5. Make sure that your parent is brushing at least once a day.

6. Check that your parent gets a new, soft-bristled toothbrush every six months or more (new toothbrushes make excellent little "gifts").

7. If your parent has arthritis or some other disease that limits hand and arm motion, talk about ways to make brushing easier:

    - enlarging the toothbrush handle with sponges or bicycle grips

    - elongating the handle with a piece of wood

    - using an elastic band to attach the toothbrush to the hand

8. Get your parent an electric toothbrush to make brushing easier.

9. Check that your parent's dentures are not loose.

10. If your parent has drymouth, make sure that he or she is sipping water, sucking on hard candies (stick to sugarless), and using something on the lips to keep them moist.

11. Check your parent's breath. If there is consistent bad breath, have him or her check with a dentist or doctor to see if it could be caused by medication or some disease.

See Me, Feel Me. . .

By now a lot of us baby boomers have grown accustomed to failing vision and wearing reading glasses. We've pretty much accepted that as we age, our arms become too short for us to read the newspaper. Bifocal and trifocal glasses are common, not to mention bifocal contact lenses. Simply put, most of us become more farsighted as we age because the lenses in our eyes are less able to adjust (medical experts keep saying that working on computers all day long doesn't make our vision worse, but we have serious doubts about that).

The correct medical term for farsightedness is presbyopia, as distinguished from myopia, which means nearsightedness. When we go to the supermarket or a large drugstore, we see kiosks that have reading glasses in varying strengths (and now we even see them in some of the larger bookstores—what a terrific idea, we wish we'd thought of that). These reading glasses are little more than magnifying glasses and many of us progress from the low power 1.25 up to the 3.5 strength before we need prescription strength. For many this is fine, although we certainly need to visit the eye doctor periodically to make sure that our failing vision is not complicated by some other problem.

For older adults, failing vision is considerably more complicated because:

1. Effectively, just about every older person suffers from cataracts to some degree (a remarkable statistic for sure), albeit mildly in most cases.

2. They are susceptible to other various diseases that could be causing the failing vision (glaucoma and macular degeneration, to name two common ones).

3. They are more sensitive to glare.

4. They refocus more slowly.

5. They may be subject to some of the other effects of poor vision (driving risks, falling, etc.).

Encourage your parents to see an eye doctor at least every other year, and more often if there are any vision and health concerns. In addition, you can take a few precautionary steps to make your parent's poorer vision less stressful.

- Increase the wattage of the lightbulbs in your parent's house (but be careful not to exceed the manufacturer's suggested wattage for fixtures); 100-watt bulbs should be sufficient for reading lights.

- Make sure that hallways and stairs are well lit and that there are on/off switches at both the top and the bottom of stairs.

- Install nightlights in the bedroom and bathroom (especially the kind that light up even if the power is off).

- Make sure that there's adequate light over the kitchen counter (where knives are used in food preparation) and over the stove.

- Install a large-button telephone.

- Buy or borrow large-print books and newspapers.

- Take advantage of the many products on the market for people with poor vision. You can visit one of the retail outlets or browse through one of a host of catalogs that now offer these products. (Also read *The Do-Able Renewable Home,* available from AARP, which explains how to retrofit a home for older people with physical limitations).

Hear No Evil

Tired of yelling? Tired of being told you mumble (although many of us do)? Well, if so, your parents may be suffering from some hearing loss. In fact, chances are quite likely that your parents are suffering hearing loss, since over twenty million Americans are hearing impaired and a staggering *one-third* of older adults face hearing loss. (Just wait, baby boomers. With all that rock 'n' roll that's been blasting in our ears for so many years, a Walkman plugged in all the time, and city noise pollution assaulting us constantly, it's a wonder we're not *all* hard of hearing!)

Hearing loss has a huge impact on older adults: it basically cuts them off from people. You can literally watch older adults "tune out" of conversations before your very eyes after they get tired of saying "What?" all the time. Imagine the isolation you would feel. Imagine how easy it would be to just withdraw. And despite the fact that there is no rational justification for a stigma, hearing loss seems to affect people emotionally, and they resist admitting that they have a hearing loss. Despite the fact that President Reagan felt comfortable displaying his hearing aid, and none of us would have any problem with a younger person wearing a hearing aid and acknowledging a hearing impairment (we've all easily accepted the fact that President Clinton needs a hearing aid), acceptance of hearing loss by older adults is still limited, albeit significantly improved. The amazing thing is, older adults are not stigmatized by failing vision and have no hesitation about wearing glasses. It's likely that it's just a matter of time before hearing aids are as common as eyeglasses.

How do you know if your parents are losing their hearing? Well, you don't know unless they get checked by a specialist. If your parents' doctor suspects hearing loss, it's likely your parents will be referred to an audiologist, a licensed professional who is not a doctor but who can perform a hearing evaluation. (If their doctor suspects something more serious than just hearing loss, they'll likely be referred to an otolaryngologist, a medical doctor specializing in diseases of the ear.)

Types of Hearing Loss

There are two basic types of hearing loss: conductive and sensorineural.

Conductive hearing loss usually involves the outer and middle ear and can result from a blockage of wax, a punctured eardrum, birth defects, or infections. Many conductive hearing losses are correctable through surgery or medical treatment.

Sensorineural hearing loss is the type of damage to the inner ear most seen in older people, although it can also be caused by infections (both viral and bacterial), head trauma, loud noises, medications, and fluid buildup in the inner ear. Rarely can sensorineural hearing loss be corrected surgically or medically. Instead, it's usually treated with hearing aids and other devices.

The kind of sensorineural hearing loss is unique to each person. Different people lose the ability to hear different pitches or frequencies of sound, not sound in general. In fact, it's quite common for people to lose their ability to hear upper registers as they age, which may explain why your parent has an easier time hearing a man's voice than a woman's. Many women take it personally that they are not heard by their parents, as opposed to their brothers or husbands who seem to be heard better. They sometimes attribute it to not being taken seriously or "not paying as much attention to me," when in reality the cause is a physical difference in the pitch of their voices.

People also commonly lose a degree of sound "clarity" in which certain consonants are not distinguishable from each other ("s" and "f," or "b" and "p," for example). Speaking more clearly and slowly will help your parent understand more, but it won't make up for the loss in clarity.

Tips for You to Use with Parents Who Have Hearing Loss

- ◆ Enunciate your words (consonants can run together and sound muddy).
- ◆ Speak a bit more slowly.
- ◆ Speak a bit more loudly, but *don't shout*!
- ◆ Use greater inflection when you speak.
- ◆ Face the person so that your lips can be seen when you speak and so that the sound can travel directly to the person.
- ◆ Be especially cognizant of background noise, which is quite distracting to people with hearing loss (in particular, turn down the volume on the TV).
- ◆ If there are many people in the room, or if you're outside, pay even more attention to where you face and whether your parent can see your lips.

◆ When talking in a car, try to face your parent, and be aware of wind noise from an open window or sunroof.

◆ Make sure that there's enough light in the room for your lips to be seen.

◆ Use shorter sentences.

◆ If you're asked to repeat what was said, rephrase it.

◆ Use as much nonverbal communication as possible so that hearing is not as necessary.

◆ Get devices that aid those with hearing loss (for instance, telephones with adjustable volume controls or amplifiers, flashing door "bells" and alarm clocks, earplugs for radios and TVs, etc.).

Hearing Aids

Hearing aids are basically microphones and speakers, and therefore they amplify sound. A small microphone in the hearing aid picks up the soundwaves, converts them to sound, and sends them through a tiny speaker directly into the ear.

But hearing aids differ in a number of ways. The most important difference to your parent is in the type of hearing loss they are suffering from. Just as some stereos are better equipped to pick up certain frequencies than others (although equalizers and other high-tech equipment can compensate for this), so, too, do specific hearing aids work better for certain people. Because of this, it's essential that your parents have an audio specialist evaluate the specific type of hearing loss they are experiencing.

Hearing aids also come in different shapes and sizes. Some are self-contained units that fit snugly into the ear while others have ear pieces connected to large transmitters you must carry around in a pocket. The specific model best for your parents is:

◆ the one that best addresses their specific hearing loss.

◆ the one that they can most easily put in their ear.

◆ the one that has controls they can most easily adjust (the really small ones also have really small controls which, for people with limited dexterity, can be difficult to adjust).

♦ the one that addresses their vanity and other similar concerns.

Legal Oversight

The Food and Drug Administration (FDA) is responsible for enforcement of regulations that deal with the manufacture and sale of hearing aids. According to FDA regulations, which have the force of law, all dispensers of hearing aids must meet the following criteria:

♦ Dispensers of hearing aids must advise patients who have a hearing problem to consult with a physician before purchasing a hearing aid.

♦ Dispensers must obtain from the patient a written statement, signed by a licensed physician and dated within the previous six months, which says that the patient's hearing has been medically evaluated and that the patient is cleared for fitting with a hearing aid.

♦ Although anyone over 18 can sign a waiver of the medical examination requirement, all dispensers must advise the patient that waiving the examination is not in the patient's best health interest.

♦ Dispensers must avoid encouraging the patient to waive the medical evaluation requirement.

♦ Dispensers must provide a complete set of instructions for the operation, use, and care of the hearing aid, including a list of sources for repair and maintenance.

♦ Dispensers must provide a statement that "the use of a hearing aid may be only a part of a rehabilitative program."

Ten Rules for Purchasing Hearing Aids

Hearing aids are sold in stores (over the counter), by mail-order (although illegal in some states), and even by door-to-door salesmen who prey upon older people.

1. If the dispenser uses high-pressure sales tactics, it's probably best to find another dispenser.

2. Make sure that there's a *written* warranty.

3. Make sure that the warranty is honored by the manufacturer, not just the dispenser.

4. Choose a dispenser that offers a trial period for use, with
   only a small service fee for returning the hearing aid within the first thirty days (as a rule, dispensers can return
   hearing aids to most manufacturers within sixty or ninety
   days for a *complete* refund).

5. Find out what training and other services the dispenser
   will provide free of charge, and for how long. In particular,
   make sure that the dispenser will explain how to get accustomed to wearing a hearing aid and what to do when there
   is ringing or feedback.

6. Check the reliability of the hearing aid dispenser (Better
   Business Bureau, consumer protection agency, state attorney general's office, etc.).

7. Check the references of the hearing aid dispenser.

8. If you purchase a hearing aid from a door-to-door salesman, you have the right, by law, to cancel the order within
   three business days and get a complete refund, including
   any deposit.

9. Be wary of purchasing a hearing aid through the mail (legal
   in most states). Consider the difficulty of the right fit and
   the correct hearing aid for your needs.

10. Choose a dispenser that will give you a "loaner" hearing
    aid when yours needs to be repaired.

The Medicine Chest

The number of pills your parents are supposed to be taking daily
is probably staggering. Partly, this is a sign of how much our bodies stop working as we age. It's also a sign of the technological
and medical advancements that have given us so much knowledge of how our bodies are supposed to work.

There are several problems that spring from this situation:

♦ Some of the medications prescribed for our parents'
  illnesses and physical shortcomings are addictive. This
  means, essentially, that our parents are hooked on drugs.

Of course, this addiction is lifesaving, rather than life-threatening. Still, it means that they have become physically dependent.

♦ The side effects of some drugs are substantial, so much so that medications are frequently prescribed to treat the side effects of the original prescription. This snowball effect causes problems of its own.

♦ Coordination of the myriad drugs is incredibly complicated. Often, drugs are prescribed by the various specialists that your parents are seeing. This means that unless you or your parents take an active role and report *every* prescribed drug to a coordinating physician, your parents could be taking two drugs that cancel each other out—or even worse, two drugs whose combined effects can cause additional medical problems.

♦ Managing the number of pills prescribed can be a full-time job: some of them must be taken with meals, some on an empty stomach; some cannot be taken with juice while some are better with juice; some should be taken with milk to minimize the stomach upset and some cannot be taken with milk; some must be taken on odd days, some two or more times per day; and it goes on and on.

♦ The cost of these pills is mind-boggling. While some insurance programs reimburse the cost of medications, most do not. And those insurance policies that do cover prescriptions usually don't cover the full price (either there's a co-payment or it just covers a percentage, anywhere from 80 percent to just 50 percent).

Twenty Questions You or Your Parent Should Ask the Doctor About Prescriptions

1. What is this prescription for?

2. What are the potential side effects?

3. Can this new medication be taken with other medications currently being taken?

4. How often should this medication be taken?

5. For how long should this medication be taken?

6. Should your parent avoid taking any over-the-counter medications or eating or drinking certain foods (or alcohol) while taking this medication?

7. Should this medication be taken with meals or on an empty stomach? Does it matter?

8. If with meals, does it matter if it's before, during, or after?

9. Should this medication be taken with water, milk, or juice? Does it matter?

10. Will this medication cause drowsiness?

11. Will this medication cause diarrhea or stomach upset?

12. What should you do if your parent forgets to take a pill? Take two next time or just continue with one?

13. Will your parent feel better after taking this drug?

14. If not, how will you know if it's working?

15. If your parent has trouble swallowing the pill, can it be broken in half or crushed and put into food?

16. If your parent has specific allergies, does the doctor know and will that be a problem?

17. What is the allergic reaction to this drug?

18. Is there any other way to treat this condition rather than through prescription medication (for example, over-the-counter drugs, different foods, etc.)?

19. Is there a generic form of this drug or must your parent take the name brand?

20. Does the doctor have any free samples your parent can have to get started?

Buying Medication

The cost of medication for your parents could be enormous, even if they have some insurance coverage. There are several ways for your parents to save on medication, including the following:

◆ Check to see if your parents' health insurance covers prescriptions, and, if not, investigate whether it would be cost-effective for them to purchase a policy.

- Ask the doctor or pharmacist for the generic equivalent rather than the name brand.

- Ask the doctor for free samples of the medication, which they often have available. In that way, the doctor can prescribe fewer pills, which will lower your cost (doing so also allows your parent to get started on the medication before having to go to the pharmacy).

- Check to see whether one of the mail-order prescription services offers a lower price. But be price-conscious since a mail-order house may be lower on some medications while charging more on others.

- Speak to the local pharmacist and try to negotiate a better price (this probably won't work with one of the large, chain drugstores but often works with small, privately owned "neighborhood" pharmacies).

- If the medication will be an ongoing, long-term prescription, order larger quantities at once. This may allow the pharmacist to negotiate a lower price. It will also mean that people whose insurance requires co-payments will only have to make one co-payment, rather than several.

- If this is a new prescription, check to see whether your parents have used this drug before and have any pills left. *But check the expiration date on the vial and be extremely careful that the drugs are not out of date.*

- If your parent is in a nursing home or other long-term-care facility, compare the price it is charging to the price you would pay at a pharmacy. Sometimes the home will add an administrative or "handling" charge. If nothing else, it will likely charge the full retail price when you could get a lower price.

Choosing a Doctor

Chances are, your parents will have to go about finding and selecting a doctor, whether this is a specialist because of some particular disease or symptom, because they've moved into a new community (or into a nursing home), or because they've joined a new health care insurance program and their previous doctor is not a member of the group. Just as in every profession, doctors differ in how good they are: in their knowledge, in their ability to communicate with patients, in how much they stay abreast of the latest information. Doctors also differ in their points of view: a surgeon may see surgery as the best means to deal with a problem while an internist may look to medication and other nonsurgical treatments to handle the situation before recommending surgery. Both may be right. But the key is, which is more right *for your parent.*

Important: It's up to *you or your parent* to make sure that the doctor knows about all of your parent's other important conditions. When seeing a doctor for the first time, make sure that you or your parent communicate the intangible parts of your parent's condition (worry about the symptom, concern about a family history, etc.). Don't be too passive. It's not good for your parent, and it's not good medicine.

Clearly, it's essential that whichever doctor your parent sees knows as much about your parent as is possible. It's not enough that the cardiologist knows only about your parent's heart or circulatory problems. That doctor should know about all the other parts of your parent, not just the medical history but some of the nonmedical aspects as well: the family history, the lifestyle, the personality, how submissive and passive your parent is with doctors, the feeling they have about medical personnel, what beliefs they have that play into their health, etc. Most doctors would want to take the time to find out these things because they know the importance that nonmedical elements play in a person's health and recovery. But most doctors don't have the time to learn the intangibles. They must treat the patient, and often that means they may treat the symptom or the problem, not the whole person. If, for example, your parent does not respond well to an expert who comes into the exam room, spends a few moments, leaves with barely a few words, and "decides for your parent," you or your parent must let that doctor know that that is not acceptable and you should ask for more information.

Finding the Right Doctor

There's no one doctor that's right: there are many. Sometimes you may have to balance poor bedside manner with brilliance, but the choice should be your parent's. Here are some ways you can go about finding a doctor with whom your parent can be comfortable:

1. Get a recommendation from another doctor. Most know who in their field is good and who should be avoided, although often a referral could be based on social contacts, so ask the referring doctor:

    ◆ Have you ever used the recommended doctor or referred family members?

    ◆ Can you provide three possible names?

    ◆ Is there one of the three you most recommend?

2. Get a recommendation from nurses and other medical personnel. Often, medical people, especially those who work in hospitals, know how good doctors are and how well they deal with patients. They also know about the reputation of doctors since they're privy to some of the comments doctors make about other doctors.

3. Ask family members and friends. When you do, make sure that you ask about doctors to avoid, and always find out why a person recommends or rejects a doctor.

4. Check with a local hospital's doctor referral service.

5. If your parent is in a managed-care program, check the Internet for a list of participating doctors in your area (usually the Internet address will be something like "http://www.insurance-company-name.com"). You can also call the company and ask for the Internet address.

6. Call a local university medical school and obtain a recommendation from the head of the clinical residency program.

7. Call 1-800-DOCTORS, a private, for-profit company that makes referrals. The company refers you to doctors who fit your criteria (ZIP Code, insurance program, and "what you're looking for in a doctor"). The doctors pay to participate in this service so *there is no fee to the caller.*

Researching the Choices

Make sure that you consider:

◆ convenience to your parent's home (including parking concerns or convenience to public transportation)

◆ hours available for appointments (especially if you need to take your parent and the only time you have is in the evening or on Saturdays)

◆ whether the doctor accepts assignment (see the discussion of Medicare in chapter 5, "I Got You Covered")

◆ whether the doctor is a participant in your parent's health plan (if it's a managed-choice program)

◆ whether the doctor accepts payments directly from your parent's health plan or if you must pay and get reimbursed

◆ how much experience the doctor has with older patients

◆ if the doctor is a specialist, whether he or she is "board-certified" (you can check on that by calling the American Board of Medical Specialties at 800-776-CERT)

◆ at which hospital the doctor has staff privileges (partially for convenience, but also to see whether the doctor has staff privilege at a major hospital or not)

◆ whether the doctor has ever been disciplined by the state medical licensing board

Important: When getting recommendations, make sure that you ask about the doctor's knowledge and ability in dealing with older patients (geriatrics). It's not essential that the doctor be a specialist in geriatrics, especially if you're seeking another kind of specialist (cardiologist, orthopedist, etc.), as long as the doctor has experience with older patients.

◆ whether the doctor is a member in good standing of the local medical association

◆ whether the doctor speaks your parent's language (your parent must be able to communicate with the doctor and speaking the same language is critical)

◆ whether the doctor will give a free initial office consultation (if not, the fee for about twenty minutes of the doctor's time should be about $40 or $50); this is a critical step in ensuring that your parent is comfortable with this doctor

◆ whether the doctor will give you an estimate of how much this treatment will cost (and whether your parent's portion can be charged or deferred)

- whether the doctor is available for phone calls or returns them later (and when)

- whether the doctor is available in emergencies

- who covers for the doctor when he or she is away or busy (in which case, you need to ask that physician many of the same questions)

Some people also like to ask whether the doctor likes being a doctor, or something similar, since this may give you insight into the doctor's attitude toward patients. You might also consider asking about the doctor's philosophy toward a specific concern you or your parents have (for example, surgery for older adults, nutrition, second opinions, managed-care health insurance, etc.).

In the next chapter, "Blind Justice," you'll learn about the legal issues that you and your aging parents will have to face in order to protect their rights, their wishes, and their estate. We'll discuss wills, powers of attorney, health care proxies, and other legal documents, and we'll talk about finding a good elder law attorney to handle these matters.

BLIND JUSTICE

When caring for your aging parents, it's essential that you understand the basics of the legal issues involved. A host of legal problems pop up when older persons haven't taken the appropriate steps to plan for their old age. How many times have you heard your parents say, "I don't want to be a burden to my children." In this chapter we'll discuss how you can best protect your aging parents' estate, the steps you must take to ensure that in the event of a catastrophic illness their wishes are carried out, your and your parents' tax consequences, and other important elements of elder law.

Early Planning Can Resolve Problems

Most seniors don't plan for their older years as well as they should, financially or legally. This leads to many problems for them and their children:

- ◆ problems when people are unable to manage their own affairs
- ◆ life-and-death decisions
- ◆ guardianships
- ◆ conservatorships
- ◆ long-term care
- ◆ age discrimination
- ◆ preservation of inheritances

As more and more of our parents age, this will become a greater problem for us as a society, leading to major decisions being made *for* us, not *by* us.

If you've followed the steps suggested in chapter 2, "Tough Talk," you're already well on your way to dealing with potential legal problems. You will have discussed with your aging parent, among other things, wills, living wills, health care proxies, access to assets, and tax issues. Dealing with these legal issues has become a specialized legal practice area referred to as "elder law" and you can now find attorneys who are experts in the field. Later in this chapter we'll discuss how to find an elder law attorney for your aging parents.

Notary Publics

Suggestion: The bank in which you or your parents have your account, or your broker, will probably not charge you to have something notarized. But they are unlikely to notarize anything *unless* you or your parents have an account there.

Before we talk about the legal aspects of caring for aging parents, we should mention that many documents you and your parents will have to sign must be notarized. This means that a third party is testifying that the signer is the person he or she claims to be. So your parent will need proof of identity and must sign the document in front of the notary.

You'll find a notary public at your or your parent's bank, brokerage, real estate office, or attorney's office. Some notaries charge a small fee while others do not. Most attorneys are notaries, so if you're having your attorney draw up a legal document, you can have it notarized at the same time.

Lifetime Planning

An elder law attorney is most concerned with three goals for the client:

1. ensuring that there is an orderly distribution of assets after the client's death with a minimization of taxation

2. ensuring that your aging parents have a personal and financial management system in case they're incapacitated and unable to manage their own affairs

3. ensuring that your aging parents have access to adequate health care without depleting all their resources

Achieving Goal 1: Where There's a Will, There's a Way

The first goal—an orderly distribution of assets after death—can be easily accomplished through a written will. The will is a critical document that transfers assets to heirs. Most seniors already have executed a legal will. But if your parents have not, urge them to do so. Unfortunately, wills are too often neglected or are out of date. Essentially, everyone should have a written will, regardless of age. A will is more than just a document that designates who gets your wealth after you die. Indeed, there's usually little question of who gets the house or the cash. When there are problems, they often result from uncertainty about who gets certain items of personal property. It's the small, less valuable items with high sentimental value that cause problems in families. A written will can ensure the *orderly* distribution of these items. Urge your parents to list individual bequests in detail, including items of low monetary value but high sentimental value (for example, photo albums, a favorite locket or necklace, etc.).

Note: During the talk you have with your parents, which we covered in chapter 2, "Tough Talk," the terms of your parents' will is one of the subjects most likely to encounter resistance. To deal with that, you might say to your parent, "You don't need to talk with me if you don't want to. You can talk with an attorney."

For more valuable items, it may be appropriate to bring in a professional appraiser before actually drawing up the will. To find an appraiser, you can check with the Appraisers Association of America at 212-889-5404, or the American Society of Appraisers at 800-ASA-VALU or 703-478-2228.

If anything has changed since your parents drew up their will, they may need to change it or add a codicil (an amendment). If an attorney drew up the will, it's easiest, and probably cheapest, to have that same attorney make the changes. If your parents choose to have a different attorney execute a new will or make changes, or draw up their own will using a software program or a preprinted form, they should notify the first attorney in writing that they have a new will and that the old one is no longer valid.

In a will, you name one or more beneficiaries who are to receive some of your assets and property, usually just called your "estate." It also names a particular person who will serve as the "executor/executrix," who is responsible for making sure that the property goes to the right person and that all bills are paid. That person is usually a close friend or relative.

To be valid, a will must be written, signed, dated, and witnessed, usually by two people present when the will was signed.

The key here is to make sure that your parents' wishes about their estate are met (and yours too, when your time comes). The more detail that's included in their will, the more likely their wishes about who gets what will be met. You don't want to go through a legal battle with relatives and friends who said they were told "that such-and-such" an item was to be theirs, or who simply feel that because of the closeness, they "deserve" a particular item.

Suggestion: Urge your parents to review their will to make sure that the person whom they designated as executor/executrix is still able and willing to function in the role.

The cost for an attorney to draft a will will likely run from a low of about $50 up to about $1,000 or $1,500, depending on the complexity and the size of the estate. You can certainly have your parents draw up their own will, either on their own, using a software program, or from a preprinted form available in many bookstores and office supply stores. If your parent chooses any of these, however, we caution you to make sure that the will is valid in your state. It would be a shame to have gone through the expense and trouble of drawing up the will only to have it successfully challenged because of the laws in your parents' state. In appendix E we have included a copy of a will that was drawn up in California. Following this template may work in your state. But, again, you'll probably want to double check.

Probate

One other term that should be mentioned here is "probate." It is the process by which:

◆ Property is inventoried and accounted for after the person dies

◆ Any debts are paid off

◆ Taxes owed are paid off

◆ Whatever is left of the estate is given to the rightful heirs

We'll talk more about probate and how to either avoid probate or minimize its effects in chapter 12, "Facing the Inevitable."

Achieving Goal 2: Power to the People

The second goal—ensuring that there's a system in place if your parents become unable to manage their own affairs—is also relatively simple to accomplish. It requires only that your parents complete certain legal documents under the direction of a professional. These documents include:

◆ a power of attorney

◆ a durable power of attorney

◆ a health care instruction directive (usually referred to as a living will)

◆ a health care proxy

Power of Attorney

Simply put, a power of attorney is a legal document that authorizes another person to act as your agent or as your attorney. It's a simple document that many feel can be executed without an attorney (you'll need to have your parent's signature notarized). However, because of the potential ramifications (you're giving over a great deal of responsibility and authority to another person), you should give serious thought to using an attorney, particularly if your parents' estate is significant. In that way you and they will be clear about what powers are authorized.

A power of attorney essentially gives the person designated the power to manage funds, sign contracts, and transact most business on behalf of the signer. It's the kind of paper you might have if your parent travels a great deal or spends the winters in a warm climate but the summers elsewhere. The power can be as limited as the signer wishes (as long as it's spelled out clearly) and can be terminated at any time by revoking the power *in writing*. Powers

Note: If your parent becomes incompetent, through dementia, Alzheimer's, or serious illness or accident, a regular power of attorney is automatically terminated. Under those circumstances you would no longer have the legal authority to conduct your parents' business.

of attorney must be signed, dated, and notarized by a notary public.

A power of attorney does *not* mean that your parent gives up decision-making authority. Rather, it's an extremely useful tool that you can use to handle your aging parents' business affairs.

Signing over the power to act as one's attorney or agent is a serious matter and it is *not* recommended that your parents enter into this lightly. They should be aware that by signing a power of attorney, they are giving the designee full power to conduct their business. If specified in the document, that would include such things as selling and buying stocks, bonds, or property; obtaining insurance; and signing contracts on their behalf.

Appendix D has a sample power of attorney that was executed in New Jersey that may be acceptable in other states.

Durable Power of Attorney

A durable power of attorney is a special kind of document that allows the designee to act on the signer's behalf *even if the signer becomes incapacitated or incompetent.* This fact must be stated in the document itself by including words such as:

> I [your parent] hereby make, constitute, and appoint the Agents, with full power of substitution, as my true and lawful attorneys in my name, and said Power of Attorney shall take effect on the date hereof and remain in effect in the event that I become disabled (as that term is defined in state law), to do each and every act which I could personally do.

A durable power of attorney can be limited to specific areas of responsibility (for example, signing a contract for a house sale) or give broader powers to simply act on your parents' behalf. It's an essential tool in caring for your aging parents, particularly if your parents become incapacitated or incompetent.

But it's also extremely important that the power of attorney be as specific as possible. For example, your parent can set up a *springing power of attorney* that only takes effect if the signer is declared incompetent.

Living Wills (or Health Care Instruction Directive)

A living will is a legal document that informs physicians, lawyers, clergy, and all others of your wishes regarding your health if and when you become incapacitated and unable to make your wishes known. A living will usually specifies that you do *not* wish to have your life artificially prolonged with the use of life-sustaining procedures or high-tech equipment if you have an incurable injury, disease, or illness certified to be a terminal condition. It's a legal, binding document which tells doctors that you give them permission (regardless of what other family members or friends may say) to refuse all medical or surgical treatment and to permit you to die. Usually, the living will allows for merciful administration of medication to eliminate or reduce pain, but demands that physicians and health care personnel remove all machines and halt all resuscitation attempts.

A sample living will is located in appendix E. Note that it must be witnessed and notarized. If you use this sample, be certain to verify with your attorney that it's legal in your state. You can also get a copy either from Choice in Dying by calling 800-989-9455 or from the National Right to Life Committee at 202-626-8800.

Some states will allow physicians to honor a person's wishes if they have made it clear to a number of people but do not have a written living will. However, if the terms specified in a living will are your parents' wishes (or yours, for that matter), clearly it's much simpler to have a written, legal document available.

Living wills generally only cover terminally ill patients. This means that a person who has a serious illness but is not considered to be competent or is in a coma cannot make his or her own decisions about medical care.

Important: If your parents have assets in more than one state, they may need a durable power of attorney for *each* state. So if your parents own a vacation or winter home in a warm climate and their summer home up north, be sure that they get a legal durable power of attorney in both states. They don't have to be identical—it's possible, for example, that they will name a different person to serve as agent or attorney-in-fact for the two different locales.

Furthermore, unless it is specified, it will be unclear whether your parent wishes to be fed intravenously, even if he or she has a terminal illness.

Health Care Proxy

A health care proxy is similar to a living will except that it covers considerably more territory. Essentially it allows the designee to be responsible for the all health care decisions of your parent in the event that he or she is deemed incapable of making a judgment (but not necessarily terminally ill). It's a document that should be *in addition* to a living will. It may, in fact, turn out to be a more important document since health care decisions are more often made when a person is *not* terminally ill.

Note: Many people say that they wish to be allowed to die peacefully and don't want to be hooked up to a lot of machines. It's an easy thing to say, particularly when we're healthy and not facing an imminent threat. Preparing a living will gives someone the chance to reflect on his or her true feelings. Preparing a health care proxy will likely be an even more difficult decision since it doesn't only take effect when you are terminally ill.

A health care proxy is quite similar to a durable power of attorney. However, it does not require that an attorney draw it up (although it will require a notarized signature). You can get a health care proxy form from your local hospital or your state or county Area Agency on Aging.

Do Not Resuscitate (DNR)

A DNR order is an instruction to medical personnel that goes into your parents' medical chart. It's most often found in the chart of a person who is in a hospital, nursing home, or other long-term-care facility. People who have a DNR in their chart have, in essence, instructed the medical personnel that they do not want any heroic measures taken in the event that they go into respiratory or cardiac arrest. A DNR order is something that the patients themselves, or the family that has taken responsibility, can order. Most of the time the instructions are adhered to (most physicians and nurses will think twice before starting CPR on nursing home residents anyway). But since a DNR order is not a legal document, physicians, nurses, or other medical personnel would much prefer to have a living will or health care proxy on file that includes a DNR direction.

Guardianships and Conservatorships

If there is no durable power of attorney on file but your parent is unable to make his or her own decisions, the court will likely step in. If your parent is judged to be incompetent to make his or her own decisions, the court will appoint a legal guardian who will have the authority to make all decisions regarding living arrangements, medical care, and financial considerations. This guardian may be a relative or friend, an attorney, or even an agency. The guardianship may be permanent or temporary, and the court may place limits on the powers of the guardian (for example, the guardian may be limited to financial decisions but not have authority to make health care decisions).

A conservatorship is a type of guardianship that, in most states, limits the powers of the conservator to financial affairs.

The key to caring for your aging parents effectively is to try to avoid having the court decide their fate. By planning ahead, you can make sure that their affairs are taken care of in the manner they would like, not necessarily what an impartial, third party may feel is either expedient or "best for all concerned."

Achieving Goal 3: Getting Care Without Losing It All

Achieving the third goal—ensuring that your aging parents have access to adequate health care and health care coverage without depleting all their resources—is considerably more difficult and complex to accomplish than either of the first two goals. Furthermore, it's highly political, which means that there's a constantly changing playing field. Even just the purchase of long-term-care (LTC) insurance has been affected recently by new legislation that gives tax breaks to people who purchase such insurance. For example, under the new legislation, LTC premiums are now tax deductible (up to certain limits), and LTC insurance benefits received by claimants will be tax-free to recipients (again, subject to limitations).

Important: Joint ownership is rife with problems, two in particular:

1. *Unintended Distributions:* Any one of the owners can remove the assets whenever he or she wants and for any purpose. The other co-owners have no way to prevent this. Upon the death of any one of the co-owners, the money is divided among the other co-owners on a per capita basis, without regard to how much any of the surviving co-owners contributed.

2. *Creditor Liability:* All funds owned in joint ownership are considered available to any of the

continues

The point is, making sure that your parents have health care without spending all their money will not only require a great deal of thought and planning on your behalf, but also constantly staying abreast of the latest developments.

We'll cover this area in great detail in the next two chapters: chapter 5, "I Got You Covered," and chapter 6, "Show Me the Money." We'll also bring this area up again when we discuss specific plans to pay for nursing homes, in chapter 11, "You Don't Have to Go Broke."

Access to Assets: Power of Attorney

Having easy access to your parents' assets will be essential as you take on more of your parents' financial caretaking. As we saw above, one of the ways you can accomplish this is through a power of attorney. Although it is perfectly legal, many clerks, tellers, and others with whom you'll interact are not familiar with a power of attorney. As a result, using it can often be cumbersome and cause serious delays. In addition, many people balk at signing a power of attorney, fearing that they have lost control. In fact, they have not lost control; a power of attorney can be withdrawn at any time by the signer. Furthermore, the power of attorney document can limit powers of the attorney-in-fact, depending on how much responsibility or authority the signer wants to hand over. That is why most attorneys recommend this method of giving children access to parents' assets rather than simply becoming a co-owner of accounts or other assets.

Access to Assets: Joint Ownership

A second way for you have access to your parents' assets is through joint ownership. For some reason, this method may not worry your parent as much, although most attorneys feel that it's *not* as good a method as a power of attorney is. As with a power of attorney, your parents must be willing to turn over the responsibility. In some families you'll meet resistance. But it's quite common for older people to feel comfortable entrusting a grown child with what they feel is "shared" responsibility, not taking over.

Simple Ways to Accomplish Access

Bank Accounts

Open a separate account over which both you and your parents have signature authority. You can usually open a new account yourself (if your parents cannot come to the bank with you) and take a signature card with you for your parents to sign later. You can designate either person as primary owner, which will affect who must claim any interest that's earned. If you meet resistance from others in the family, you can have multiple names on the account and require two signatures. Your parents can then transfer all or part of their funds as needed, and transactions can be handled through check-writing, or even through telephone or personal computer transfers.

co-owners. That means that any judgments against any one of the co-owners is a judgment against the asset, regardless of who contributed to the asset or account. Because of these considerations, joint ownership is usually not recommended by attorneys.

Safe Deposit Boxes

You should be able to go into your parents' safe deposit box so that important papers and assets are accessible. This is critical if your parent becomes disabled and is physically unable to go to the bank. Again, you can accomplish this by having a power of attorney. In practice, frankly, it's simpler for you to sign one before it becomes a problem.

Stocks and Bonds

Having easy access to your parents' stocks and bonds is not quite as simple as just signing a signature card. For you to have access to stocks and bonds means that your parent is actually required to transfer them to new owners, requiring a signature guarantee. Getting his or her signature guaranteed can be difficult if your parent is physically disabled. One easy way we found, other than having a power of attorney, is to open a new account at a brokerage house in both your names. Your parent can then deposit or transfer the stock or bonds into this account, giving you access. Since the new account has your parent's name on it, there's usually no signature guarantee required.

Important: Some brokerage accounts require signatures of all co-owners, so be sure to check when you open the new account.

Tax Returns

In many families, the person assuming more and more financial responsibility is often given the task of making sure that tax returns are filed and estimated taxes are paid (we'll cover more about estimated taxes in chapter 6, "Show Me the Money"). You don't need any special authority to prepare a tax return for someone. Furthermore, unless you're a paid preparer, you don't need to sign the return yourself.

Incompetence

Most people remain competent to make decisions for themselves until the day they die. Nevertheless, as the children of aging parents, we aren't always sure, and we want desperately to make sure, that they're making the best choices. The line between competence and incompetence is very unclear. Furthermore, people have the right to make their own choices, even if others consider them wrong. Again, don't you want that same right as you age?

But when your parents cross over the line and make choices that are harmful to them, you'll have to step in. The very last step you'll want to take is going to court to get your parent declared incompetent. Not only is it emotionally painful for everyone involved, but it can also be quite expensive. If this step is unavoidable, you'll want to discuss it with an elder law attorney who will be able to explain what will be involved and tell you about the costs.

Before your parent's competency is questioned, you and the other members of your family should discuss the situation openly. Pay particular attention to the actions your parents take, but try to look at them from their point of view. If, for example, certain medical treatment is refused, don't assume that the refusal was because of incompetence. It may be depression or, simply, your parent disclaiming, "I've had enough!"

Similarly, if only some behaviors are erratic, look at other possible causes (and be sure to discuss them with your parent's physician). Is it possible that the medication your parent takes is causing confusion? Is your parent in pain? Eating correctly? Dehydrated? Taking medication regularly? Many things can cause behaviors that appear abnormal, some serious, some easily taken care of.

When you consistently see behavior and decision-making that shows little reason, that will be the time to step in. Before that, discuss the situation with your parent's medical team, a geriatric manager, or a psychologist.

Elder Law Attorneys

As we said earlier in this chapter, elder law has become its own specialty. Those attorneys who practice elder law deal with a variety of laws and regulations that affect the elderly. These laws and regulations are constantly changing, and will continue to do so at a feverish pace as we baby boomers approach old age. For example, at the time of this writing the U.S. Department of Health and Human Services had just proposed a rule mandating that home health aides working for the roughly 9,000 agencies that provide Medicare home services would have to undergo criminal background checks. Other rules affecting home care will likely be proposed since home care is the fastest growing expenditure in the Medicare budget.

Elder law attorneys are generally familiar with most of the subjects elderly clients must face and bring to their practice a sensitivity to the afflictions of old age. But because the field covers so many areas, it's unlikely that any one particular attorney will be an expert in all phases of elder law. Nor does it really matter for most people, since you're not likely to need such an expert. What you do want is someone who has experience in the fields you're most concerned with and someone who has access to other experts as needed.

Finding an Elder Law Attorney

First, think about whether you or your parents need an elder law attorney (the National Academy of Elder Law Attorneys, Inc., advises: "Step back a moment and try to determine whether you actually have a legal problem in which an attorney needs to be involved.").

If you're not sure, ask a trusted friend, financial advisor, geriatric care manager, or health care professional for advice on whether you should see an elder law attorney.

If you decide that you need an elder law attorney, get a referral from your own attorney. Or get a list of elder attorneys *in your area* from various agencies, including your Area Agency on Aging; Children of Aging Parents; AARP; your state bar association; your parents' geriatric care manager, social worker, physician, or therapist; or the support group of those with certain diseases (for example, the American Diabetes or Alzheimer's Associations).

If you can't find a referral, buy a copy of the National Academy of Elder Law Attorneys (NAELA)'s Experience Registry, a list of 400 elder law attorneys nationwide. The registry costs $25 and may be ordered directly from:

NAELA
1604 North Country Club Road
Tucson, AZ 85716
520-881-4005

Narrow the list down to a few and call each one. You'll want to know:

- the attorney's specific areas of expertise within elder law
- how long the attorney has been practicing
- how much of the attorney's practice is focused on elder law
- how much it will cost for a consultation (many will waive the initial consultation fee)
- whether your particular problem is appropriate for this attorney

Go for the consultation and discuss your problem. Find out, specifically,

- ◆ how the attorney thinks it will be best to resolve the problem
- ◆ what other choices of action you have
- ◆ how long will it take to resolve
- ◆ how much will it cost
- ◆ who in the office, specifically, will deal with the issue (not all attorneys do trial work, for example, so you'll want to know about the trial lawyer's experience as well)

You should feel comfortable with and confident in the elder law attorney you and your parents select. Trust is the primary ingredient in an attorney-client relationship. If you don't feel good about this particular attorney, whether it's because of the attorney's attitude, experience, fees, or something intangible, look for another one.

In the next chapter, "I Got You Covered," you'll learn about Medicare, Medicaid, Medigap insurance policies, and prescription coverage. We'll also talk about long-term-care insurance and give you and your parents advice on how to select the right policy.

I Got You Covered

In this chapter we'll talk about medical insurance, for both short- and long-term care. We'll talk about Medicare, Medicaid, veterans' benefits, and private insurance plans, including Medigap policies. We'll review what constitutes long-term care and then examine the different definitions of coverage and levels involved with this type of care. Along the way, we'll clear up some of the misconceptions about long-term care. Then we'll give helpful tips to choosing a long-term-care insurance policy.

Disclaimer: Most of us, of course, are familiar with how much and how quickly Medicare, Medicaid, and private health insurance are changing. It's likely that by the time this book is printed, some of the specifics given about the governmental health and medical insurance programs will be outdated or inaccurate.

Medical Insurance

The goal of medical insurance, in general, is to defray the out-of-pocket expenses associated with acute care. Acute care is the care that is received for a short, definite time period. It requires the services of a physician, nurse, or other skilled professional. *The primary goal of acute care is recovery.*

The majority of individuals in today's society have access to some form of medical insurance. Most of our older citizens have access to all or some of the following:

1. *Medicare:* Most people age sixty-five or older qualify for Medicare, the government program designed many years ago to pay for the medical care of our older citizens.

2. *Medicaid:* Low-income people may also qualify for Medicaid, another government program for which strict guidelines on the amount of income and assets exist so that only those low-income people with few assets can benefit.

3. *Veteran's Benefits:* Veterans, of course, may qualify for veteran's benefits and can avail themselves of the care provided

by Veterans Administration hospitals. Much of that care is free or low-cost to qualifying vets.

4. *Medigap Insurance Policies:* Medigap insurance policies are plans that pay all or some of the difference between what Medicare will pay and what the health professional charges.

5. *Private Health Insurance:* Private plans, of course, are those plans available to anyone willing to pay the price.

   ◆ *Employer and Group Insurance Plans:* For those of us who are employed, many employers pay all or a portion of the insurance for us and our dependents. Of course, since most older adults are not working or are working part-time, they usually don't qualify for employee benefits such as paid health insurance.

   ◆ *HMOs:* HMOs, or Health Maintenance Organizations, are essentially groups of health care professionals that can provide all types and levels of care, all under the same roof (either figuratively or literally).

   ◆ *Managed-Care Plans:* Under the terms of managed-care programs, except in an emergency a patient must go first to a primary physician and then, if the case warrants it, is referred to a specialist.

Medicare

Medicare is administered by the federal government's Health Care Financing Administration. Payments to medical care providers are made through private insurance companies with which the government contracts. There are several contractors throughout the country, and the contractor for one state or region will be different from that for another state.

There are two parts to Medicare:

1. Part A, which is the part that handles hospital and long-term-care facility insurance

2. Part B, which is for medical services not performed in a hospital or long-term-care facility

Medicare Part B

Let's start our discussion with Medicare Part B since this is the part that handles most of the medical claims your parent will have, until and unless your parent is in a hospital or long-term-care facility. There is an annual deductible for Part B of $100 and, as of 1997, a premium of $43.80 per month, rising to about $67 by the year 2002. The premium is taken directly out of your parents' Social Security check.

Important: Even if your parents do not get Social Security monthly benefits, they are still eligible for Medicare once they are sixty-five years old. Make sure that they apply a few months before they reach 65, to allow time for processing.

Currently, Part B insurance is optional, although strongly recommended. However, if your parents are *fully* covered under another plan, they can elect to cancel their Part B insurance through the local Social Security office.

Because of the potential changes in the details of how the Medicare program will be administered, it's essential that you stay abreast of the changes and obtain the latest information. One change that was implemented in 1997 on a demonstration basis, and will likely be opened to more people once the success of the plan is proven, is the establishment of a Medical Savings Account (MSA). This will operate much like an IRA (Individual Retirement Account) in that people will be able to open a tax-free account to buy catastrophic illness insurance with a deductible as high as $6,000. Holders of these accounts would use the funds and the tax-free earnings to pay medical bills not covered by insurance.

Types of Medicare Part B Plans

Another change in the law passed in 1997 is the creation of a Medicare + Choice plan. Starting in 1999, Medicare beneficiaries would be able to choose their Medicare insurance coverage, selecting from among:

♦ the traditional Medicare plan (referred to as "fee-for-service")

♦ Managed-care plans, with a primary provider who refers the patient to other specialists as needed

- HMOs (health maintenance organizations)
- preferred provider organizations (PPOs), which give patients financial incentives to choose doctors who belong to the plan
- private fee-for-service plans, which allow doctors to charge more than allowed by Medicare (though not more than 15% above the standard Medicare rate for specific services and procedures)

What Medicare Part B Does Not Cover

- routine physical examinations (although the lab work, mammography, pap smears, and dental work are all covered)
- routine dental exams and prophylaxis
- prescriptions (unless the drug is administered by the doctor or nurse)
- eyeglasses
- hearing aids
- dentures
- most podiatric care (except if prescribed by a physician)
- chiropractic care

Approved Charges and Accepting Assignment

Medicare Part B pays up to 80 percent of the "approved" charges from doctors and other medical personnel. The key word here is *approved.* While doctors and medical care professionals can charge whatever they want for any service, Medicare will pay only 80 percent of what Medicare decides is a reasonable fee. This amount of course changes periodically. But it's important to keep in mind that it doesn't matter what the doctor charges. Medicare has a set amount for a particular medical procedure, office visit, etc.

Many doctors and medical providers, some two-thirds in fact, are willing to accept *assignment,* or whatever the Medicare-approved amount is. In that case, your parents will have to pay only the difference between the total approved amount and the 80 percent Medicare will pay. So for a $100 approved charge, your parents will be responsible for $20. (That's where Medigap policies come in, which we'll discuss later.)

If the provider does not accept assignment, and with the approved amounts so low about one-third of physicians do not, your parent is responsible for the entire amount charged minus the Medicare-approved amount. The amount Medicare pays will go toward the bill and your parent will have to pay the balance. So, using the same example as we used above, if the approved charge is $100 but the doctor charges $110, Medicare will pay 80 percent of the approved charge ($80), and your parent is responsible for the $30 that remains.

Doctors, outpatient clinics, and other medical care providers are required to file Medicare claims directly with the Medicare contractor. Some weeks or months later, depending on how quickly the doctor filed the claim and how efficient the Medicare contractor is, your parent will receive an Explanation of Benefits (EOB) letter from the Medicare contractor. If your parents paid the doctor directly, they'll also receive a check. The EOB details the date of the charge, the name and address of the medical provider, the amount charged, the amount approved by Medicare, the amount Medicare paid to the provider (usually 80 percent of the approved amount, unless some went toward the deductible), the amount of the deductible that this approved amount went toward, and an explanation of any details.

Important: Keep all EOB statements. They will be needed for Medigap claims, for appeals, and to reconcile accounts.

If your parents have a Medigap plan, they'll probably find that doctors who accept assignment usually don't require payment from your parent (which the combination of Medicare and Medigap insurance covers). For those that don't accept assignment, however, the doctors may require either payment from your parent of the complete charge or of the portion they know will not be covered by Medicare. Obviously, if your parent must pay anything directly to the provider, it's important that the provider submit a claim to Medicare so that your parent will get reimbursed quickly.

Medicare Part A

Part A is the portion of Medicare insurance that covers hospital bills and a portion of nursing home, in-home, and hospice care, although under strict conditions and up to a limit. We'll talk more about this when we discuss paying for long-term care in chapter 11, "You Don't Have to Go Broke."

When your parent is admitted to a hospital, Part A kicks in to pay a portion of the costs. There is an annual deductible that must be met which, in 1997, was $760 (again, with the changing political climate, it's likely that the Part A deductible will change, especially for older citizens who have higher incomes).

For the first sixty days in the hospital, Medicare will pay 100 percent of the costs of a semiprivate room (at least two beds), unless it's medically necessary for your parent to be in a private room. After the first sixty days, your parent is responsible for a portion of the bill, according to the following schedule:

- For days sixty-one to ninety in the hospital, your parents will be responsible for the first $190 *per day.*

- If your parents must stay in the hospital longer than ninety days, they must pay the first $380 *per day* from day ninety-one up to day 150.

- After the 150th day, Medicare will make no more payments, and your parents must pay the entire hospital bill.

Medicare Part A *does* cover the cost of prescribed medications while your parent is in the hospital since they are, by definition, administered by doctors or nurses. But it will *not* pay for private nurses hired for around-the-clock coverage (a fairly common practice for older people who are staying in hospitals with limited staffing, particularly after surgery), nor for any personal expenses like a TV rental.

Since the hospital must file claims to Medicare and will get 100 percent of the bill covered, you or your parent will not need to complete or send in claims to Medicare. At intake or admission, your parent will present a Social Security and/or Medicare card, as well as any other private insurance (Medigap) cards or IDs.

Important: Many people are covered under their spouse's Medicare, not their own. That means, for example, that your mother may be covered under your father's Social Security number, not her own. Make sure that your parent presents the Medicare ID card at admission so there's no delay in getting benefits.

It's likely that the hospital will also take care of billing the co-insurer as needed (for stays longer than sixty days). But you or your parent should double-check to make sure that's taken care of. If your parent has more than one Medigap policy (which we'll discuss later), you only need to give one number since it's likely the Medigap insurer will cover all the remaining charges. If not, you can always file with the secondary Medigap insurer later.

When you get the hospital bill, you'll go through shock at the length and detail of it (it will itemize every little expense, down to gauze pads or Band-Aids). It would be futile to say that you should scrutinize it—there's essentially no way you could keep track that on day eight an aspirin was administered, for example—but you should look at every itemized expense to make sure that it is, at least, reasonable.

If your parent underwent surgery, your parent might get multiple bills:

◆ from the hospital for room charges and all miscellaneous costs

◆ from the operating room if the OR is a subcontractor

◆ from the emergency room if the ER is a subcontractor and your parent entered through the ER

◆ from the surgeon

◆ from the anesthesiologist

◆ from a consulting physician whom it's possible your parent might not have even met (the consult could have occurred in the OR)

Each of these creditors must file a claim on your parent's behalf to Medicare. If a co-insurer will be paying the remaining portion (remember, not all physicians accept assignment, so it's possible the charges will be more than Medicare will pay), they will probably also file with the co-insurer. If they don't, you or your parent will be responsible for filing a claim.

Medicaid

Medicaid is a joint federal and state government health insurance program for low-income people. Much of the funding for Medicaid comes from the federal government (with some matching dollars from the states), but it's administered by the states. This means that there are differences between states in many areas. The key area, of course, is in eligibility requirements.

Since the eligibility requirements differ somewhat in each state, we won't go into the specifics. However, you should simply be reminded that Medicaid is a program for *low-income* people. This means, essentially, only people with very limited income and almost no assets qualify. A single person who gets the maximum amount of Social Security will usually *not* qualify, regardless of the amount of assets. That's how low we're talking about.

If your parent is eligible for Medicaid, you and your parent should become familiar with the specific rules governing the program, particularly, buying down assets in order to qualify. We'll talk more about this in the long-term care section of this chapter and later on in chapter 11, "You Don't Have to Go Broke."

Important: For most medical expenses, the combination of Medicare and Medicaid pay 100 percent of all the charges. However, *not all doctors and long-term-care facilities accept patients who are on Medicaid!*

Medigap Insurance

Medigap insurance is the term used to refer to all those private insurance plans that cover all or part of the "gap" between what the medical care provider charges and what Medicare will pay. A Medigap policy will cover the total difference *only if* the doctor accepts assignment, which means that the doctor charges exactly what Medicare allows (remember, Medicare will pay 80 percent of the allowed charge; Medigap policies then pay the remaining 20 percent). If the doctor or other medical care provider charges more, the Medigap policy will *still* pay only 20 percent of the Medicare-allowed charge. This means that there will be yet another gap, for which your parent is responsible.

Multiple Medigap Policies

Some people purchase multiple Medigap policies from different companies and, by filing claims with each, get reimbursed 20 percent of the Medicare-allowed charge from each insurer. The theory is, of course, that the total amount received from all Medigap insurers will equal the total charge from the medical care provider. Whether your parent does that will depend on two factors:

1. whether it is permissible by the insurers

2. whether the total reimbursement is greater than the premium charged

If your parent purchases multiple policies, the paperwork will likely be significantly more complex since you or your parent will have to be sending multiple claim forms along with copies of Medicare Explanation of Benefits (EOB) forms.

Suggestion: Before signing up with a specific insurer, you should check with the state agency on aging or the state insurance licensing agency to make sure that there are no problems with the insurer. You can also check with the Medicare Hotline by calling 800-638-6833.

A rule of thumb regarding the purchase of multiple policies (assuming that you're not prohibited from doing so—check the fine print of the policy) is: if a significant number of your parent's doctors and other care providers *do not* accept assignment, and your parent sees a great number of doctors each year, it will probably pay for itself. If most of your parent's doctors accept assignment, or if your parent sees very few doctors, the extra premium expense will probably *not* be a good investment.

Medigap insurance policies are heavily regulated and the companies are restricted by law. This means that there's essentially no difference between what one company offers and what another one offers. Obviously, then, the choice of which Medigap insurer to select will depend on the reliability of the company, not on the specific provisions of the insurance policy.

There are ten different Medigap policies offered by companies, conveniently referred to as Plans A through J. The range of coverage starts with the basic plan A, which covers the Medicare Parts A and B co-payments. Other plans cover the hospital deductible, Medicare Part B deductible, all or a portion of the fees charged by doctors who do not accept assignment, the cost of prescription medicines, and preventative medicine charges. Refer to appendix K for an outline of Medicare supplemental coverage plans A through J. Note the monthly premium in the last row; these figures were effective for 1996 for residents of the state of New Jersey.

For most older adults who have Medicare benefits, having a Medigap policy is a good idea. To decide which plan is best for your parent, you and your parent should consider the costs associated with each plan and decide whether it's a good idea to stick with the basic plan or to pay more for more coverage. The decision will be based on several factors:

- whether your parent has any other coverage, especially prescription or managed-care coverage, or belongs to an HMO

- whether your parent has any preexisting conditions that would eliminate coverage

- how often your parent sees a doctor and for what purposes: preventative exams, continuing care, etc.

- whether the doctors your parent sees accept assignment

- whether your parent also requires in-home skilled care

- how much money your parent is willing to spend on the possibility that the number of visits or the kind of care needed will change

Your parent will automatically be eligible for most of the Medigap plans (with no exclusions for preexisting conditions or no physical required). For some plans, however, the policy will require underwriting, which means that the insurance company must approve your parent (those plans that include prescription coverage, preventative medicine, and personal care when there's also in-home skilled care).

For more information about Medigap policies, you can check with most insurance agents and companies, as well as with AARP (you can call AARP at 800-523-5800).

> **Misconception 1:** Long-term care is primarily for old people confined to their beds in a nursing home.
>
> **Reality:** While nursing home care is certainly an integral piece in the long-term-care puzzle, it's not the only piece. Conceivably, long-term care could begin as home care and may progress, ultimately, into nursing home care or some other intermediate level of care.

Long-Term Care

Long-term care, by definition, is medical, social, and/or personal care services that are required over an extended period of time. The person receiving these services typically suffers from either a chronic illness or a disability. The *primary goal of long-term care is to help the recipient maintain as much independence as possible;* its timeline is indefinite (remember, the primary goal of short-term or acute care is recovery). Care is not restricted to a hospital or to any other long-term-care facility.

Specific Definition of "Long-Term Care": Long-term care is the daily care required because of a cognitive impairment or a continuous inability to perform basic functions ("activities of daily living") as a result of illness, disability, or old age.

The long-term-care services available are skilled nursing home care, assisted living, home health care, adult day care, and respite care.

Skilled nursing home facilities provide observations, medical care, and/or treatment under the direct orders of a physician and continuous twenty-four-hour nursing care under the supervision of a registered nurse.

Assisted-living facilities, sometimes referred to as residential health care facilities or board and care homes, provide assistance to older and more frail individuals who are not so impaired that they require the services of a skilled nursing home facility. Assisted-living facilities generally provide congregate meals, housekeeping, linen services, transportation, preventive health services, and help with personal care.

Home health care offers a variety of services either at home or in another residential setting. Services included under home health care are part-time skilled nursing care, speech therapy, occupational therapy, physical therapy, personal care by aides, and home care services.

Adult day care is a community-based, daytime program that offers several health, nutrition, social, and other related services. The program is generally conducted in a protective setting and it's usually available to those who are otherwise being cared for by family members. The goal of an adult day care program is to allow individuals to remain either in their homes or in the community while it provides family members with relief from the burden of constant care.

Respite care provides temporary relief to either family members or friends who are acting as caregivers for an older or disabled individual at home. This type of care is often provided by volunteers, home health care providers, adult day care centers, or skilled nursing homes. It enables caregivers to take a time-out for themselves, so that they can recharge their batteries, run errands, or just preserve their sanity.

Important: Less than 1 percent of individuals in nursing homes receive skilled care and less than 5 percent receive intermediate care. Some 95 percent of individuals in nursing homes receive custodial care.[1]

The type of care being received by an individual defines which long-term-care coverage is available and which is not. There are three levels of care: skilled care, intermediate care, and custodial care.

Skilled care is defined as twenty-four-hour nursing and/or rehabilitative care requiring the services of skilled medical personnel, under direct orders of a physician, generally provided in a nursing home.

Intermediate care is essentially the same as skilled care; however, it's provided occasionally as opposed to around the clock. This level of care is either provided by, or under the supervision of, skilled medical personnel, generally in a nursing home.

Custodial care is the third level of care and is defined as assistance with personal needs—for example, bathing, dressing, and eating. This level of care may be provided by individuals without medical training; however, it must be supervised and it must be administered according to a physician's orders.

Misconception 2: It will never happen to me.

Reality: Of all Americans who reached age sixty-five in 1990, 43 percent will require nursing home care at some point in their lives. Of that 43 percent, over half can expect to be there at least one year and another fifth will be in a nursing home for at least five years.[2] By the year 2000, over nine million Americans will require long-term care. And that figure is expected to double by the year 2040.[3]

Furthermore, a couple aged sixty-five or older has a 70 percent chance that at least one partner will require nursing home care.[4] The likelihood of requiring long-term care at some point in our lives is very high.

The Price of Long-Term Care

Obviously, long-term care is an expensive proposition. And, unfortunately, there's no way that most of us can pay its enormous expense.

So the likelihood that your parents will be able to pay for their long-term care out of their own money, as most Americans do now, is almost nil.

Caring for Our Own

Another common scenario for families is that children of aging parents have the aging parent move in with them and care is done in the grown child's home. Unless your family is like the "Walton" TV family, this is an impractical solution, for the following reasons:

- Most of us don't have the necessary medical expertise required for such long-term, comprehensive care.

- Even if we had members within our family unit who had the expertise, that places an enormous responsibility on them that they might not be able, or willing, to handle.

- The composition of the modern-day family unit, with fewer children, more single-parent households (or in two-parent

---

Misconception 3: I will be able to pay the costs of long-term care out of my own pocket.

Reality: The bottom line is that in 1993, 1.7 million individuals spent $53 billion on nursing home care.[5] That's an average of over $31,000. And this figure doesn't include expenses for all other types of long-term care and is four years old.

The current average annual per-person cost for nursing home care is about $36,000 per year (although, it may be $80,000 or higher in metropolitan areas such as New York City or Los Angeles). Adding in inflation, which has been averaging over 5 percent per year, means that in just twelve to fourteen years the cost will double. Therefore, a five-year stay in a nursing home, assuming a current annual cost of $50,000 and a 5 percent inflation rate, will cost approximately $275,000.

---

households, dual-income parents), and geographically separated generations, does not lend itself to this type of care arrangement.

So How Do You Pay?

The question is: How can we pay for the exorbitant costs of long-term care? There are four options available to people to pay for long-term care:

1. Medicare

2. Medicaid

3. private funding (from your parents' funds, from your funds, or from another family member's funds)

4. long-term-care insurance

As we said at the beginning of this chapter, Medicare is the government health insurance program that covers hospitalization and a large portion of regular medical bills. Medicaid is the government health insurance available to low-income people regardless of age.

> **Misconception 4:** Medicare and Medicaid are the two largest ways people pay for long-term care.
>
> **Reality:** The fact is that the majority of nursing home care and long-term-care patients currently rely on self-funding. In fact, about half of nursing home costs were being paid, out-of-pocket, by either the disabled/elderly individual or their families.[6]

What about Medicare?

Medicare is designed to provide funding for *acute care*. That is, it pays the expenses for a type of care whose main goal is recovery. While Medicare does provide some long-term-care benefits, they're very limited in their scope and they follow fairly restrictive eligibility requirements. In general, Medicare will cover the costs associated with nursing home care for a period of 100 days only after a prior hospitalization of three days. Also, your parents must be admitted for skilled nursing care within thirty days of their discharge from the hospital. Furthermore, the nursing home must be a government-approved facility. For the most part, Medicare pays only for skilled care. Unfortunately, *skilled care monopolizes only 0.5 percent of nursing home occupancy while custodial care represents 95 percent of the care received in a nursing home.*

As for the private Medigap insurance, it was designed specifically to cover the gaps in Medicare coverage (for example, deductibles, co-payments, etc.). It provides coverage for many services that Medicare does not cover. But *Medigap insurance does not cover long-term-care expenses.* Like Medicare, Medigap coverage is associated with acute care, not long-term care.

What about Medicaid?

About 40 percent of nursing home costs are covered by Medicaid.[7] On the surface, the statistics appear to tell a promising story. Here is a government program that appears to be doing what it's supposed to be doing. However, drawbacks do exist. Medicaid is a unique program because it is a joint federal and state program. While it's mostly funded by the federal government, it's administered and controlled by each state. As a result, programs vary significantly from state to state. In general, eligibility for Medicaid is based on one's level of prosperity. It bases its calculation on two elements: assets and income. For the most part, your parents must be impoverished before they become eligible to collect benefits under Medicaid. Medicaid was designed to take care of those who are not able to care for themselves (both financially and medically).

But even if your parents' income is low enough and they have "spent down" their assets enough to qualify, there are other restrictions: you or your parents will need to locate an "approved" facility and hope that there's an available bed. While some facilities maintain a specified allotment of "Medicaid beds," many nursing homes and long-term-care facilities will not accept any Medicaid patients. In heavily populated areas, it's extremely difficult to locate an available bed at a facility willing to accept Medicaid patients.

It has long been suspected, but never concretely proven, that those who occupy "Medicaid beds" receive treatment that's inferior to the level of care received by patients who are in the same facility under private funding. Obviously, if a Medicaid-eligible individual is occupying a bed that could otherwise be offered to an individual who has the necessary private funds, the facility stands to miss out on additional revenues. The monetary costs that are funded by Medicaid can be significantly less than what a facility could generate from private funds. Medicaid pays the facility a preset amount. Therefore, if a facility provides care to individuals covered by Medicaid and their expenses exceed what Medicaid pays the facility, then, obviously, the facility stands to lose money.

Medicaid will also cover most home health care services. However, restrictions do apply. If your parents are eligible for Medicaid and need home health care services beyond skilled care, you and they should talk with a Medicaid worker to determine what and how much home health care will be covered.

What about Veterans' Benefits?

For veterans, the Veterans Administration (VA) may be a source of funding. However, in general, VA medical benefits typically do not cover any long-term-care expenses that you have incurred. Within certain limits, the VA may pay for custodial care for "combat-related" injuries provided that there is space available. If your parent is an eligible veteran, you or your parent should contact the local VA office for more information regarding available services.

What about Long-Term-Care Insurance?

A relatively new way that people pay for long-term care is through long-term-care (LTC) insurance, which is specifically designed to pay for the extraordinary rise in the cost of long-term care and the number of people needing long-term care. The decision to purchase this insurance is very much like any other insurance decision—it has to do with *risk management.* Risk management encompasses all insurance products.

Most of us have health insurance. Many of us have life insurance, and an even smaller number of us have long-term disability insurance (coverage that we personally researched and purchased, not employer-provided coverage). We chose to purchase these insurance policies because we were not willing to assume the risk of not having coverage. The cost of most of these insurance products is low, and we feel justified since the potential cost of not being covered is enormous. Most insurance agents can offer specific guidelines as to who should be covered and for how much. It's almost formula-driven.

But long-term-care insurance is quite new and, therefore, our familiarity with the product is weak. It's not as clear, even to professionals, who should purchase the product, and for how much.

Is Long-Term-Care Insurance for You?

Who is a candidate for long-term-care insurance? Every situation is different and everyone's family environment may also differ. To prudently plan for long-term care, we need to approach this question just as if we were considering any other insurance product. The key to accurate risk management is to ask yourself these questions:

♦ Would the economic loss triggered by a tragic event (for example, becoming disabled and requiring long-term-care services) or the costs of long-term care be overwhelming and deplete everything you own?

- ◆ Is the probability of occurrence fairly high?
- ◆ Do you and/or your parents have ample assets to pay for all the costs of long-term care?
- ◆ Do you and your parents mind depleting your parents' estate?

If you answered no to these, you favor *self-insurance.*

If you answered yes, and especially if you're uncomfortable with the prospect of funding the expenses of long-term care with your own assets, then you may want to consider *transferring the risk* to an insurance company and purchasing long-term-care insurance.

The Top Reasons People Buy Long-Term-Care Insurance[8]

1. to avoid dependence on others (69%)
2. to protect their assets (67%)
3. to make long-term-care services affordable (66%)
4. to preserve their standard of living (59%)

Choosing the Right Policy

While there are over 1,000 insurance companies currently doing business in the United States, not all of them offer LTC insurance. However, as late as 1994, there were 121 companies selling long-term-care insurance products.[9] Determining which one is the right policy for your parents is difficult. You must consider not only the product, but the company as well.

Step 1: Begin the Search

Select a core group of insurance companies to choose from. One company, regardless of its reputation, does not provide a choice. And it would be impossible to choose from all the companies offering LTC products. The most important concern at this point is that the company will be around if and when the benefit is needed. Therefore, pick companies with the highest financial rating. There are four main rating companies within the insurance industry: A. M. Best, Standards & Poors, Duff & Phelps, and Moodys. A. M. Best is probably one of the most recognizable and one of the simplest to read. It uses a simple letter grade to rate companies: A++, A+, A, A–, B++, etc. Usually a safe bet would be to consider companies that are rated no lower than A by A. M. Best.

A caveat: There is no rule-of-thumb recipe used to select an adequately rated insurance company. If you or your parents have prior knowledge of some companies, by either name recognition or past experience, include them in your select group.

Step 2: Choose the Top Two or Three Companies

Examine the size of the company's asset holdings and investigate how long a company has been in operation, especially in the business of long-term-care insurance. Many insurance companies, while quite reputable, have very little experience in the long-term-care business. Therefore, it's best to select companies that have already built up a track record. Most insurance companies should be able to supply general information regarding their past claims experience. Calling individual insurance companies and requesting information regarding their long-term-care insurance products and services can be helpful. Also, call your parents' state superintendent of insurance to see if there are any problems with the company or the agent. If you or your parents already have an insurance agent or broker whom you trust, talk to that person about LTC insurance.

Step 3: Determine How Much Coverage Is Needed

Probably the most difficult task in choosing long-term-care insurance will be determining how much coverage, or *benefit amount,* to apply for. First, investigate the specific costs of nursing home and home health care in your parents' immediate area (which could range from about $100 to $250 per day). Find out how much full coverage would cost and how much lower percentages would cost.

Step 4: Determine the Length of Term

Determine how long your parents will receive the benefit, known as the *benefit period.* The most common benefit periods available are one year, two years, three years, five years, and lifetime (unlimited). A good general rule is: If you know that your parents will need long-term-care insurance and if you or your parents' finances can support it, purchase the lifetime benefit. Better safe than sorry. However, if money is a concern—and for most of us it is—then you need to be a little more pragmatic regarding your decision. Remember that 43 percent of people aged sixty-five and older will require nursing home care at some point in their lives; of the 43 percent, 55 percent will remain there for at least one year and 21 percent will be a resident for at least five years. As for couples aged sixty-five or older, there's a 70 percent chance that at least one of the partners will require nursing home care at some point in their life.

Family history can also play an important role in determining your benefit period. For example, if Alzheimer's disease runs in your family, then a longer benefit period is appropriate. Your parents can also mix and match benefit amounts with benefit periods to contain the overall cost of coverage. A policy that would pay $250 per day for three years may cost approximately the same as a policy that would pay $100 per day for life. Unfortunately, there's no magic formula. That's why education and seeking professional help are important elements in this process.

Choose a policy with "sharing" benefits. If the policy also provides the same benefit amount and benefit period for home health care services, some companies allow redirecting, or sharing, these fund pools to pay the costs of other services incurred. Typically, most companies offer long-term-care insurance policies that cover two forms of care: nursing home care and home health care. They almost appear to be two separate policies in one. Using the example in the side bar on this page in which your parents paid $80 per day for nursing home care, suppose that after three years and nine months your parents were still in need of the nursing home care services. If the insurance company offered a sharing provision, your parents would be able to tap into the home health care reserve, thus buying them an additional three years and nine months' worth of coverage, if needed.

Note: Benefit amounts and benefit periods work in tandem to provide the insured with a "pool" of funds. For example, if you purchased a three-year policy that pays $100 per day for nursing home care, the total maximum payout would be $109,500 (365 × $100 × 3 years). If your care only costs you $80 per day, then your coverage would last until your pool of funds were exhausted, or three years and nine months. This is what is known as *flexible benefits,* and you should choose a company that does offer this benefit.

Step 5: Choose the Plan That's Best for You

There is no "right" policy, just more appropriate ones for your parents. It's likely that several companies will offer excellent programs for pretty much the same price. The main thing is to consider the total premium (price) and all the considerations that follow in this chapter.

Premiums

There are several things you must consider when comparing premiums among policies:

1. basic price

2. guaranteed renewability

3. pre- and postdisability inflation protection

4. front-end and back-end underwriting

5. exclusions

6. nonforfeiture benefit

7. waiver of premium

8. deductibles

Basic Price

Naturally you'll want to make sure that the premium is the lowest of the companies you're comparing. But be certain that you're comparing apples to apples. The policies must cover the same level of care and for the same period of time.

Since the overwhelming majority of nursing home residents, 95 percent, receive only custodial care, and since custodial care is not covered by Medicare, you must be absolutely sure that the companies you research offer nursing home insurance coverage for custodial care. But don't forget to get coverage for the other levels of care as well, and in particular, coverage for home health care services.

Keep in mind, however, that there are different kinds of coverage for home health care. For example, some companies offer the insured the ability to pay a family member or close friend to provide the home health care services. The different coverages will affect the basic premium.

Guaranteed Renewability

Most long-term-care insurance policies are guaranteed renewable, meaning that the insurance company must renew your coverage as long as your premiums are paid in a timely manner. But guaranteed renewability also grants the insurance companies protection against adverse claims experience. This means that while a company cannot single you out and increase your personal premium, it can increase the cost of insurance across the board within a certain group. For example, if there are an inordinate number of claims among seventy-year-old women who smoke, the company can increase the cost of coverage for all seventy-year-old women who smoke. This enables the company to protect itself from the adverse effects of future claims.

Pre- and Postdisability Inflation

When you purchase a long-term-care insurance policy, there are three scenarios that could eventually play out. The first scenario, and the most favorable, is that you never use the policy. The second scenario is that you buy the policy and then submit a claim at some point in the future (for example, twenty years after the initial purchase). In this scenario, an option to consider when purchasing is the ability to increase your benefit prior to becoming disabled. So to protect yourself against inflation increases, you'll want to have the policy include *predisability inflation protection.*

The third scenario occurs when you buy a policy and you submit a claim shortly after the issue date and you're expected to be disabled for a number of years. In this scenario it's important that you own a policy that will adjust the benefit annually to account for increases in the cost of living that result from rising inflation. This provision is known as *postdisability inflation protection.* When you are researching companies, be sure that the company you choose offers a strong postdisability inflation rider.

There are three types of postdisability inflation riders that will effect your benefit and, of course, your premium: compounding, simple interest, and indexing according to the Consumer Price Index (CPI).

Compounding is the most comprehensive as well as the most desirable. However, it's also the most expensive of the three riders to purchase. The annual increases in benefits are heaped on top of the compound benefit amount; therefore, your potential to amass the greatest future benefit is optimized. The annual increase percentage is applied to the value of the current benefit on an ongoing basis.

The simple interest adjustment is the second-most-expensive rider. Its annual increase is based on the value of the initial benefit. Therefore, a fixed amount is added to the benefit year after year.

The index rider offers the least amount of benefit inflation protection and, therefore, is also the least expensive to purchase. The inflation index rider adjusts the benefit each year in accordance with the CPI. Therefore, since inflation rates are not predictable, neither is the increase in coverage.

Not all companies offer all three versions of this rider, so it may be difficult to compare the policies. Inflation riders offer room to compromise coverage in exchange for cost effectiveness (for example, if buying the compound rider is not in your budget, but you want some type of inflation protection, then you would explore the possibility of purchasing the index rider).

Front-end and Back-end Underwriting

Back-end underwriting means that the company spends little or no time determining the applicant's health and insurability during the application process (before a policy is issued), but when a claim is submitted, the company begins to scrutinize the responses on the original application and finds reasons to deny the claim. While not commonplace, back-end underwriting still occurs. Try to avoid companies that still practice back-end underwriting.

Instead, choose a company that practices only *front-end underwriting*—determining the applicant's health and insurability prior to the issuance of a policy. Companies that practice front-end underwriting tend to have better claims experience, healthier policyholders, lower premiums (thanks to their better claims experience), and less chance that there will be future premium increases under the company's guaranteed renewability rights.

Exclusions and Preexisting Conditions

Don't purchase a policy that fails to cover you for a condition that you were aware of at the time of the application. And be sure that you disclose all health information at the time of the application and are clear about what preexisting conditions may be excluded from coverage.

The same applies to the policy's exclusions, especially Alzheimer's disease. In the past, most policies did not provide coverage for Alzheimer's disease, so it's critical that the policies you're considering extend coverage for Alzheimer's disease.

The heated debate in today's long-term-care environment revolves around a distinction between Alzheimer's disease and cognitive impairment. By definition, cognitive impairment is manifested by problems with attention, memory, or other loss of intellectual capacity that require supervision to help or protect the impaired person. Depending on the cause, such impairment may be permanent or temporary. While Alzheimer's is an example of a cognitive impairment, the two are not synonymous. As a result, some individuals who suffer a cognitive impairment may never be diagnosed with Alzheimer's disease. Therefore, a policy that covers Alzheimer's, but not a cognitive impairment, would not provide any benefits. An example of someone who suffers from a cognitive impairment is an older person who is forgetful and, as a result, frequently leaves the gas stove on. Many of the better insurance companies are adding the cognitive impairment language to their policies.

Nonforfeiture Benefit

If your parent suffers from a cognitive impairment and is either unaware of receiving the premium bill or forgets to pay it, the policy coverage could lapse due to nonpayment of premium. With a nonforfeiture benefit, the policy would not be canceled. The amount of the nonforfeiture benefit depends on the insured's current age and the size of the existing policy.

As an additional guard against unscheduled termination, some companies allow the insured to specify that you or some other designated person are to receive duplicate policy statements and premium bills. Make sure that the company you choose will allow the insured to make that designation.

Waiver of Premium

Waiver of premium means that if you or your parent submits a claim against the policy, the company will waive all future premiums for a specified time while your parent is receiving benefits. The time period before the premium waiver is in effect varies from carrier to carrier: some offer a 90-day period, some a 100-day period, and others a 180-day period. Preferably, choose a policy with a waiver of premium that becomes effective after a short time period.

Waiting Period

The waiting period, sometimes referred to as the elimination period, is the period of time that your parent must be disabled or receiving insurable long-term-care services before the insurance coverage begins to pay benefits. Again, similar to the waiver of premium, the required waiting period can vary significantly from company to company. Given the extremely high costs of long-term care, the shortest possible waiting period would be the most preferable. However, the shorter the waiting period, the sooner the company begins to pay *its* money, and therefore the higher the policy premium. The waiting period can be as short as 30 days or as long as one year or more. The longer you wait to receive benefits, the lower the policy premium. Since Medicare will pay a large portion of the costs of nursing home care for a maximum period of 100 days, consider a 100-day waiting period, especially if keeping the premium down is a key consideration. On the other hand, the difference in premium between a 100-day elimination period and the next shortest waiting period may be minimal.

Deductibles

Some long-term-care insurance policies have a deductible that must be satisfied before any benefits are paid. The long-term-care insurance deductible operates in a similar fashion to the deductible on a regular health insurance policy. There are few policies with this provision, and it's best to avoid them.

Miscellaneous Services

There are a few miscellaneous services that you should consider when choosing the company from which to purchase long-term-care insurance:

Responsive Service: Positive consumer reports, toll-free phone numbers, and live voices on the other end of the numbers can be

Fifteen Questions to Ask about
Long-Term-Care Insurance

1. What kind of care is covered?

   ◆ skilled nursing care

   ◆ intermediate care

   ◆ custodial care

   ◆ home health care

2. How much will be paid for each level of care?

3. Is there a waiting period before benefits are payable?

4. How long will the policy pay benefits?

5. Is there a maximum policy benefit?

6. Will benefits increase with inflation?

7. Are preexisting conditions covered? If so, what is the waiting period?

8. Does the policy impose any eligibility requirements?

   ◆ prior hospitalization to receive skilled nursing home benefits

   ◆ need for skilled nursing care prior to payment of custodial-care costs

   ◆ prior coverage in a custodial-care facility or hospital to receive home health care

   ◆ coverage only in a Medicare-certified facility

9. Is Alzheimer's disease specifically covered?

10. Can the insurer cancel the policy?

11. Can the premium increase over the life of the policy?

12. Does the policy contain a waiver of premium?

13. Does the insurer have an A+ or A rating from *Best's Insurance Reports*?

14. Is the insurer experienced in handling health insurance claims?

15. Is the policy guaranteed renewable?

fairly reliable indicators that suggest that service is a high priority with certain companies.

Clear Contractual Language: An insurance policy is a unilateral contract that is legally binding. But it doesn't have to be full of ambiguities and legalese. Review a sample contract or policy to make sure that you understand the provisions (always ask if you're not sure).

Upgrade Privileges: Purchase a policy that allows upgrades because laws and regulations in the long-term-care field will change over the next several years.

Benefits Triggers: Most companies base a claim on an individual's ability to perform certain *activities of daily living* (ADLs). Usually, policyholders are eligible for benefits if they cannot perform a certain number of ADLs. There are five core ADLs—bathing, dressing, transferring (mobility), toileting, and eating—plus three additional ones: grooming, mobility, and continence. But some companies break these eight down into subcategories. In addition, cognitive impairment can be a benefit trigger. Most long-term-care policyholders become eligible for benefits when they're unable to perform two or three ADLs. This trigger will vary from company to company. Choose a policy that clearly spells out the position on cognitive impairment and Alzheimer's disease, the number of ADLs used, and the number of ADLs that trigger a benefit.

In the next chapter, "Show Me the Money," you'll learn about the various financial vehicles available to help you and your aging parents safeguard their future. We'll also discuss what you should know about their finances, how to know when they need your help, and how you can most effectively step in.

Notes

Portions of this chapter were written by William J. Gillett, a financial planner and president of Commonwealth Financial Services in Wappingers Falls, N.Y.

1. Harvard University survey for the U.S. House of Representatives.
2. Kemper, Peter, and Christopher Murtaugh, "Lifetime Use of Nursing Home Care," *New England Journal of Medicine,* February 28, 1991, pp. 595–600.
3. American Health Care Association, 1994.
4. *Wall Street Journal,* April 23, 1990.
5. "Long-Term Care," Dearborn Financial Publishing, Inc., 1993.
6. Health Care Financing Administration, 1990.
7. Health Care Financing Administration, 1990.
8. LifePlans, Inc., Survey of Buyers, 1994.
9. Health Insurance Association of America, Long-Term Care Market Study, 1995.

Show Me the Money

In this chapter we'll talk about your parents' finances. We'll discuss some of the vehicles to explore so that your parents can age with as much dignity and control over their lives as possible. We'll talk about setting up budgets, cash flow, and investments (of course, we won't give advice on where to invest). We'll review Social Security benefits, tax and estate planning, kinds of ownership, living trusts, and insurance. We'll talk about how to know whether your parents need your help—and ways you can step in. Finally, we'll outline what you have to do when the responsibility for your parents' financial affairs falls on your shoulders.

Talking about Money

At least four of the ten purposes of talking with your aging parent from chapter 2, "Tough Talk," deal with money:

1. to learn as much as possible about your aging parents' legal and financial affairs

2. to provide information to your aging parents about resources available to them and about their health, legal, and financial affairs

3. to help them make decisions about their affairs and their future

4. to help them maintain their dignity and as much control over their own lives as possible

If you've been able to have that conversation, or if you've already started to take over your aging parents' financial affairs, you should definitely put together the complete list of information required, as outlined in chapter 2. The information you'll need will include everything about bank accounts, assets and investments, tax information, retirement policies, credit cards, financial advisors, and household bills.

If you hit a stumbling block in your conversation, you're not alone. Your parents will always look at you as their child, regardless of your age. The idea of relying on their child for support is contrary to what they believe "should" be the way of the world. Furthermore, many people balk at revealing their financial state of affairs, not just your parents.

Even if your parents have not confided in you, you should continually try to have that tough talk, or at least find out some of the data. With each conversation you'll probably find out a bit more. If you wind up taking over their finances, you'll learn as you go along. Whatever you find out in advance will make it easier for you. And it will also help preserve your parents' estate.

If your parents absolutely won't confide in you, you should strongly encourage them to speak with a trained financial advisor (a financial planner, CPA, tax or elder attorney, etc.). Tell them how much is at stake (that they could lose everything they've worked all their lives for). Remind them that early planning, which includes letting someone else know what their situation is, will mean avoiding serious trouble for them as well as preserving their estate for their heirs. The more they confide in someone else who's knowledgeable about finances, the greater the chance they have of maintaining their wealth—and also the more control they'll have over their older years.

Seminars

You can also encourage your parents to attend one of the frequent financial planning seminars offered by local financial planners, usually for free (it's their way of advertising their services). Offer to go with them so they'll feel more comfortable (and so you'll be able to monitor what they're hearing, which will help you learn more about their financial situation and wishes). These seminars are usually advertised in the local newspaper and sometimes are sponsored by a seniors' council or agency. They'll usually cover such topics as:

- ◆ how to protect your assets from catastrophic illness and nursing home expenses
- ◆ how to increase your available income
- ◆ how to lower your income taxes

- how to eliminate paying tax on Social Security income
- the pros and cons of revocable living trusts
- property rights and ownership
- when to hire someone to help you
- record-keeping

A Chosen Confidant

Sometimes a parent will feel more able to talk to one child than another, or even to the spouse of a child (your parents may be of the age where many were brought up to believe that only men could handle money). This isn't a time to let your ego or politics get in the way. If your parents are more comfortable confiding in your spouse, or your sister's spouse, so be it. The point is, someone other than just your parents will be in on their financial situation.

When a major event occurs—the death of one of your parents or the sale of the family house, for example—it's especially important either to have the talk or to review the situation. That may also be a more vulnerable time, so you may have more success prying the information out of them.

Important: A big problem elders face is fraud. There are many con artists who specialize in taking advantage of elderly people by convincing them that their hard-earned money could be safely making much more than it is. If you suspect that your parents are being conned, step in. Speak to them and speak to the "advisor" (who may even be related to you). If you suspect fraud, make sure that you notify the authorities.

When to Step In

The short answer to the question "When do I step in?" is: yesterday. How much and when to get involved depends on five things:

1. how well your parents are managing their money
2. how realistic your parent's financial goals are
3. how focused your parents are in reaching their goals
4. how much your parents confide in each other or in others
5. how physically healthy your parents are

Keep in mind, once again, that your parents' assets, income, and financial decisions are theirs to make. How much they spend of their money, and on what, is up to them. They earned it and they own it, no matter how you feel about whether they're making the right choices.

Caution: It's entirely possible that your parents will be concerned that you're trying to learn about their finances so that you'll be better able to take their money. That could be one of the reasons they don't confide in you. While there's no sure-fire way of overcoming that hurdle, persistence and reasonability will probably prevail. If you reassure them that no decision will be made without their knowledge and consent, you may have better luck.

Because you care about them, about how financially secure they are, and how well taken care of they'll be later on, you'll probably want to get involved as soon as you see any decision made with which you don't agree. If you're unsure about whether to say something, our recommendation is: Don't wait. Erring on the side of more involvement at an earlier stage is safer than waiting until it's too late.

On the other hand, use prudence, particularly if your relationship is tenuous or if you feel that your parents will react strongly against you. If your parents are asking for assistance, it's an easy choice. If there are a few clues, such as stacks of unpaid bills lying around or large purchases made that make little sense for them, there are some good ways to begin to help out with their finances. For example, you might offer to help write out the checks for the bills, but they sign the checks. Or you might offer to organize their bill-paying procedures or balance their checkbook periodically. These are all ways to develop a trust without interfering with their dignity or with the control they have over their money (it's possible that a parent is not dealing with the bills because of failing eyesight, not confusion or some form of deterioration).

Social Security

We're all familiar with Social Security, and most of us contribute to it without realizing what it is. Here's a brief explanation:

Your parents' employers withhold (and self-employed individuals pay) taxes to the federal government under the Federal Insurance Compensation Act (FICA). This money is reserved for your parents' use when they reach the appropriate age. To qualify for Social Security benefits your parents must be at least sixty-two years old. There is no needs test for Social Security benefits; the amount your parents receive will depend on how much they contributed over the years and their age when they choose to begin receiving payments (your parents have a choice to start either at age sixty-two and get a reduced benefit, or to wait until age sixty-five and get the full benefit for which they are eligible. The age for full benefits will gradually increase until it reaches age sixty-seven in the year 2027 for people born in 1960 or later. Currently, retirees who choose to receive benefits before their sixty-fifth birthday receive $5/9$ of 1 percent for each month before their full retirement age. So at age sixty-two they'll receive 80 percent of their full benefit, at sixty-three they'll receive $86\frac{2}{3}$ percent, and at sixty-four they'll receive $93\frac{1}{3}$ percent.

People can also choose to delay retirement, which may be a good idea for those who are still earning a salary. Delaying the Social Security benefit has two advantages:

1. The extra income generated will increase their average earnings, which means they may qualify for a higher monthly benefit amount.

2. They'll receive a special credit added to their Social Security benefit. For those who turned sixty-five in 1997, an additional 5 percent per year will be added to the monthly benefit. This percentage will increase gradually and those who turn sixty-five in the year 2008 or later, and who delay receiving their Social Security benefit, will receive an additional 8 percent per year.

Important: You and your parents can get a complete, detailed analysis of their lifetime earnings and an estimate of their Social Security retirement benefit by requesting a "Personal Earnings and Benefit Estimate Statement" from any Social Security office. It's likely that by the time this book is published, you will be able to either get the statement, or at least request one, via the World Wide Web. You can visit the Social Security Administration at the following address: http://www.ssa.gov

The Social Security tax rate you and I (and many of our parents who continue to work) pay is set by law and is currently 7.65

percent of wages. Employers (and self-employed individuals) pay an additional 7.65 percent, meaning that the Social Security Administration receives a total of 15.3 percent of wages to pay those who are currently receiving Social Security benefits (those already age sixty-two and over).

How Much Social Security Will They Get?

The amount of monthly retirement benefits people receive depends primarily on how much they and their employers contributed while they were working. As a general rule, the benefit is based on average earnings over their lifetime, according to the following steps:

1. A base is established for the number of years of earning. This figure is thirty-five years for everyone born after 1928 and retiring after 1990, and fewer years for those born in 1928 or earlier.

2. The earnings are adjusted for inflation.

3. An average adjusted monthly earnings is established, based on the number of years of earning.

4. The average adjusted earnings is multiplied by a percentage specified by law. Currently, for those who had *average* earnings during their working years, their Social Security benefit will be about 42 percent of their earnings. For higher than average earnings, that percentage will be lower.

To apply for benefits, your parents can either visit one of the Social Security Administration offices throughout the country, or you can call 800-772-1213 and ask for an appointment. You will need to bring at least the following (and, if requested, additional documents):

 • Social Security card or a record of the number

 • birth certificate

 • proof of U.S. citizenship (if your parents were not born in the United States)

Table 6-1: Examples of Social Security Retirement Benefits

Approximate Monthly Benefits If You Retire at Full Retirement and Had Steady Lifetime Earnings

Your Age in 1997	Your Family	1996 Earnings		
		$20,000	$40,000	$62,700 or more[1]
45	You	$797	$1,229	$1,519
	You & spouse[2]	$1,195	$1,594	$2,278
55	You	$797	$1,226	$1,435
	You & spouse[2]	$1,195	$1,839	$2,152
65	You	$805	$1,205	$1,326
	You & spouse[2]	$1,207	$1,807	$1,989

1. Earnings equal to or greater than the OASDI wage base from age 22 through the year before retirement.

2. Your spouse is assumed to be the same age as you. Your spouse may qualify for a higher retirement benefit based on his or her own work record.

Note: The accuracy of these estimates depends on the pattern of your actual past earnings and on your earnings in the future.

Source: Reprinted from Social Security Administration publication no. 05-10024, January 1997.

◆ a marriage certificate (if they're signing up on a spouse's record)

◆ their most recent W-2 form (or tax return if they're self-employed)

If your parents don't have any of the above, they should try to get them, but at the same time, not delay in applying. The Social Security Admin-istration can often assist in obtaining certain documents.

Currently Social Security recipients can choose either to get a check in the mail or to have the money deposited directly into a bank account. Effective in 1999, *all* Social Security recipients will have to have the money directly deposited. Given the amount of money that will be deposited, the government expects banks to compete heavily and offer low-cost or free accounts to seniors. In areas with few banks, such as rural and low-income communities, the Treasury Department will contract with financial institutions to provide inexpensive, no-frills accounts. The government expects to save about $100 million per year by not having to print checks for the ten million recipients (18 percent of the total) who currently don't have accounts.

Financial Planning 101

The steps involved in planning for your parents' later years are not much different, really, than they are for planning your own. However, there are a few major exceptions that need to be spelled out because they'll have a large effect on what you and your parents do.

- ◆ Your parents have fewer years to prepare than you do.

- ◆ Your parents' income will probably be diminishing rather than being on the upswing like most baby boomers.

- ◆ Your parents can't afford as much volatility in their investments as you can because they have less time to ride out the lows.

- ◆ Your parents will likely need to live off the income their assets generate, rather than continuing to have them grow with deferred income.

- ◆ Your parents must make more provision for catastrophic illness or emergency.

- ◆ Your parents may be less able to manage their money on their own because of failing health.

So here are the five basic steps you and your parents need to go through to better manage their finances:

1. *Make a Reality Check.* Begin with a wake-up call as to the current state of their financial situation. Calculate their balance sheet; add up their assets and subtract their liabilities.

2. *Figure Out Their Costs.* Whether your parent will be living at home, in your home, or in a long-term-care facility, determine their monthly costs for at least one to two years (three or four is better). Use the costs they've had for the past year or two and then add 5 percent per year for inflation (you can adjust this inflation factor as needed, but 5 percent will give you a rough approximation of how their expenses will increase each year). Add in any anticipated expenses that will be incurred for home care or housecleaning. If your parent is in or entering a nursing home, use the figures the home provides, but don't forget to include the cost of "extras" that are not usually quoted in

the basic price (for instance, additional costs of incontinence, haircuts, nonprescription drugs they administer, etc.; see chapter 11, "You Don't Have to Go Broke"). And don't forget, also, to increase the costs about 5 percent per year.

3. *Calculate Their Income.* Add up all their outside income, including Social Security benefits, retirement plans, dividends, interest, and any wages. For Social Security income, use an inflation factor of 3 percent per year. Add in the expected income from assets, which you'll have to base on what these assets have earned in the past. If your parents' assets are invested in stocks or bonds, only consider dividends and interest. You're determining their budget, not their net worth.

4. *Determine the Shortfall or Surplus.* If there's a shortfall, determine how much will be needed to be taken from assets in order to meet your parents' budget. Then extrapolate how many months or years they can continue to reduce assets to meet expenses before those assets are totally depleted (remember, each year that they have to reduce assets means lower earnings).

5. *Learn About Other Sources of Income and Benefits.* Become an educated consumer. Explore the range of assistance programs that can reduce the shortfall (or increase the surplus). Include need-based programs (food stamps, SSI, "Meals on Wheels" programs, etc.) if your parents' are eligible, local assistance programs (including reduced or free rides for seniors, store and service discounts, etc.), life insurance benefits, Medigap insurance reimbursements, reverse mortgages, and any other benefits available.

When helping your parents create a budget, it's helpful to separate expenditures into fixed and variable. That way you can see more easily which expenses can be reduced and by how much. You can use the accompanying cash-flow budget worksheets for putting together your parents' budget.

Cash Flow

For many people, young and old, cash inflow does not match cash outflow. This is one reason that credit card use is so popular—it

Budget Worksheet: Expenses

Fixed Expenses

Household:	Rent/mortgage	_____
	Property tax	_____
	Gardner/lawn and tree service	_____
	Domestic help	_____
Insurance:	Homeowner's/renter's insurance	_____
	Life insurance	_____
	Automobile insurance	_____
	Medicare premium	_____
	Medigap insurance premium	_____
Loans:	Automobile	_____
	Other fixed loans or credit	_____
	Total Fixed Expenses	_____

Variable Expenses

Household:	Utilities (gas, electric, water, sewer)	_____
	Home repair	_____
	Telephone	_____
	Groceries	_____
Medical:	Doctors/dentists	_____
	Therapy	_____
	Prescriptions	_____
	Over-the-counter drugs	_____
Clothing:	Laundry/cleaning	_____
	New purchases	_____
Personal Care:	Toiletries	_____
	Haircuts/styling	_____
	Miscellaneous	_____
Transportation:	Auto licenses and registration	_____
	Auto gas and oil	_____
	Auto repair	_____
	Parking	_____
Personal:	Dining out	_____
	Entertainment	_____
	Gifts	_____
	Subscriptions and books	_____
	Donations	_____
Miscellaneous:	Bank charges	_____
	Investment expenses	_____
	Legal and professional fees	_____
	Taxes	_____
	Total Variable Expenses	_____
	TOTAL EXPENSES (fixed plus variable)	_____

Budget Worksheet: Income

Fixed Income

Social Security	_____
Wages	_____
Dividends	_____
Certificates of deposit	_____
Fixed-interest-bearing bank accounts	_____
Loans	_____
Rental payments	_____
Total Variable Income	_____

Variable Income

Capital gains/losses	_____
Variable-interest bank accounts	_____
Tax refunds	_____
Gifts	_____
Other benefits (assign monetary value)	_____
Total Variable Income	_____
TOTAL INCOME (fixed plus variable)	_____

allows people to continue their spending habits and pay off their bills at a later date. A situation like this for younger people, while not financially healthy, can be overcome through increased income (raises, cost-of-living increases, overtime, second jobs, new jobs, etc.) or through periodic belt-tightening.

When your parents' outflow is more than their inflow, the problem is more serious. The reason for this is that their income is not likely to increase significantly. Social Security will go up at a steady rate (to match inflation) and dividends and interest will remain relatively constant (and, therefore, may actually be losing out to inflation). Furthermore, as more and more money is needed to compensate for a shortfall, the only place it can come from is your parents' assets. This means that less and less income will be realized through investments, causing an even greater shortfall. So the shortfall problem is compounded. According to "How Boomers Save," an article in the September 1994 *American Demographics* magazine, "the average American household has saved only $13,000 for retirement. Yet to maintain their current standard of living after age sixty-five, boomers who are currently earning $40,000 to $60,000 a year will need to have saved over $200,000."

Preparing a budget with your parents is an excellent way to review their expenditures. It's likely that you or they will discover that they're paying for things they no longer need or use, like collision insurance on an eight-year-old car or a large life insurance policy.

How Much Do They Need from Assets?

First, you and your parents have to determine how much cash they would need from their investments to live on. Here's how that's done:

1. Determine how much is needed to live on per year (using the preceding budget worksheet).

2. Determine how much fixed income is received (Social Security, retirement, etc.).

3. Determine how much must be realized from investments to meet the remaining need.

4. Determine what return on investment is needed in order to meet their need.

Table 6-2: Projected Costs and Shortfall

Year	Costs + 5%/year	Total Assets	10% Yield	Social Security + 3%/year	Shortfall
1	$40,000	$150,000	$15,000	$15,000	$0
2	$42,000	$150,000	$15,000	$15,450	$1,550
3	$44,100	$148,450	$14,845	$15,913	$3,342
4	$46,305	$145,108	$14,511	$16,390	$5,405
5	$48,620	$139,703	$13,970	$16,882	$7,768
6	$51,051	$131,935	$13,193	$17,389	$10,469
7	$53,604	$121,466	$12,147	$17,911	$13,546
8	$56,284	$107,920	$10,792	$18,448	$17,044
9	$59,098	$90,876	$9,088	$19,001	$21,009
10	$62,053	$69,867	$6,987	$19,571	$25,495
11	$65,155	$44,372	$4,437	$20,158	$30,560
12	$68,413	$16,188	$1,619	$20,763	$36,031
13	$71,834	$0	$0	$21,386	$50,448

By looking at table 6-2, you can calculate the amount of your parents' shortfall for expenses. Let's say that your parents need about $40,000 per year to live on and that these costs will increase by 5 percent per year (while inflation may only be 3 percent currently, figure that your parents' costs may increase at 5 percent because medical costs continue to skyrocket). The second year's costs would then be $42,000. If your parents are receiving about $15,000 per year from Social Security and $10,000 per year from a retirement plan, the shortfall is $15,000 per year. If your parents' net worth is $150,000, then the return on this worth must be $15,000 from $150,000, or 10 percent. If your parents have sufficient assets to invest that would yield that amount, they'll be in pretty good shape. But remember, the second year's costs would be about $42,000, which means either that the investments would have to earn more (an unlikely scenario) or $1,550 would have to be tapped from assets.

For the third year, assuming all the same percentage increases, costs would be $44,100 and the income would be based on $1,550 less in assets. That means they'd either have to get a higher return on investment (again, an unlikely scenario) or the $3,342 shortfall will have to be taken from assets. Each year will see larger and larger shortfalls and more and more taken from assets to make up the difference—all compounded by increased costs and declining assets. If you work out the arithmetic, you'll see that in just 12 years your parents' assets would be totally depleted. This means that a sixty-five-year-old person, no longer working, and living off Social Security, pension, and return on $150,000 in invested assets, would be broke at seventy-seven years of age.

Table 6-3: Projected Costs and Shortfall

Year	Costs + 5%/year	Total Assets	8% Yield	Social Security + 3%/year	Shortfall
1	$30,000	$100,000	$8,000	$15,000	$7,000
2	$31,500	$93,000	$7,440	$15,450	$8,610
3	$33,075	$84,390	$6,751	$15,913	$10,411
4	$34,729	$73,979	$5,918	$16,390	$12,421
5	$36,465	$61,558	$4,924	$16,882	$14,659
6	$38,288	$46,899	$3,752	$17,389	$17,147
7	$40,203	$29,752	$2,380	$17,911	$19,922
8	$42,213	$9,830	$786	$18,448	$22,979

Table 6-3 presents a more realistic scenario: a sixty-five-year-old with $100,000 in assets that yield 8 percent per year, costs of $30,000 per year, and no pension other than Social Security. The first year's shortfall would be $7,000. With a 5 percent increase in costs and a 3 percent increase in Social Security benefits each year, by the eighth year all assets would be depleted. This sixty-five-year-old can only look to be financially secure until age seventy-three, a very frightening prospect.

This is why many financial advisors counsel their older clients to stay fairly aggressive in their investing plan and not simply put all their money in totally safe but low-yielding certificates of deposit or Treasury bills. Many advisors, for example, say that older people should invest as if they would be holding their portfolio for fifteen to twenty years, and they recommend holding about one-third of their capital in a short-term investment (often a stock mutual fund) and the rest in a long-term growth vehicle (often split between domestic and international stock funds). Of course, safety of principal is one of the most important aspects of investing funds for older people (because as we said above, they often need the cash to live on and they have less time to make up losses). They must feel comfortable knowing that their principal is safe. How high the return on the investment is will depend on how comfortable your parents are with risk and fluctuation in the markets. While many can tolerate a little fluctuation in the value of their portfolio, over the long term their investments need to grow in order to keep up with spiraling costs.

When the Home Is the Asset

For most people, the bulk of their net worth is tied up in their home, which they diligently paid off over twenty or thirty years and now own outright. That home may be worth $100,000 or $200,000 on paper, with nothing owed on it. (According to the U.S. Census data, the average home equity of people in the sixty-five to seventy-four age bracket is $48,000.) Clearly, the equity in your parents' home is available only if your parents sell the home or borrow against it. And without including the net worth of the home, most people don't have enough available capital to produce the amount of income needed to preserve the quality of life they've grown accustomed to.

Available Options

If your parents are in this situation, there are some options they should consider:

Sell the Home

There are many reasons people sell their home and move to more appropriate living quarters:

- smaller home
- easier to maintain
- one-floor living
- warmer climate
- more convenient to services
- more centrally located for family and friends

If this is an option, your parents will have significant resources to invest. Unless they're used to managing large sums, they should work with a financial advisor to make sure that their money is invested appropriately and that they're maintaining a well-balanced portfolio. Chances are, one of the main reasons they sold the home was to be able to live on the proceeds. You and they should make sure that the money is working for them as well as possible.

Note that under the tax law passed in 1997, the first $500,000 gain in the sale of your principle home is excluded from income. The amount above $500,000 is taxed at the capital gains tax, which is a maximum of 20%.

Refinance the Home

Home equity loans or lines of credit are very attractive options for many people. The interest paid on the loan is usually tax deductible and the interest rates are quite favorable. Home equity loans cost almost nothing to obtain (usually there's no application fee, although some lenders charge an appraisal fee of a few hundred dollars). With a line of credit, you borrow only what you need, up to a limit. Of course, the irony is that your parents diligently paid off the mortgage on their home so they wouldn't have to continue to pay for it in their later years. But chances are that the value of your parents' home has appreciated significantly beyond what they paid for it. Borrowing against the increase is an excellent way to realize the gain without selling the home and without paying any tax on the gain. Unfortunately, many older people cannot qualify for a home-equity line of credit because they have no visible means of repaying the loan, except Social Security.

Reverse Mortgages—Home Equity Conversions (HEC)

These financing mechanisms are in some ways a combination sale and home-equity loan. Essentially, a bank is paying your parents for an increasing interest in their home. The more the bank pays, the more it owns of the home. Most lenders will "lend" about 70 percent of the home's value, paying your parents a portion up front and the rest in monthly installments for five or ten years (some lenders will lend for an unspecified term, "your parents' lifetime"). At the end of the period, the homeowner—or the heirs—must repay or refinance the loan. For your parents, repaying will likely be difficult since they will have probably used a good portion of the funds they received to pay their living expenses. Refinancing the loan will also be difficult since, as with the home-equity loan, your parents won't have any visible income to qualify for a loan. A third drawback is that it's possible the value of the home will have dropped. On the positive side, this option allows your parents to stay in their home and take some of the equity out of it.

A similar Home Equity Conversion program that reduces your parents' expenses is the property tax deferral program. Under this program your parents can defer payments of their home property taxes until they either die or sell the home. There's usually an income cutoff to qualify for this benefit and you can get more information about it from the local taxing agency or the state office on aging.

Loans Against Retirement Accounts

Many supplemental or optional retirement accounts offer the opportunity to borrow against the value of the account. These are often offered at reduced interest rates and with little or no cost to the borrower. There's usually a limit of $50,000 or 80 percent of the value, whichever is higher, and the proceeds of the loan are forwarded within a few weeks of the application. The application itself is quite easy to complete and requires no proof of ability to repay the loan (since your parents are borrowing from their own money). A retirement account loan can be an excellent means of tapping some of the equity in the account when emergencies arise. But it should be *for emergency use.* The money in the account was meant to fund your parents' retirement years. Taking it all out now (and paying more than it's earning) will affect later years.

Loans Against Life Insurance Policies

Similarly, life insurance policies in which equity is built up through regular payments, such as a Universal Life policy, offer the opportunity to borrow against the equity. Again, this is an excellent source of emergency money but should be used cautiously. The purpose of the insurance policy was to protect the surviving spouse or heirs. Using the funds (and, again, paying more than it's earning) will deplete the protection.

Family Loans

A loan from a family member, particularly from a child of aging parents, is a very common way that older folks meet expenses. These loans have many benefits to both the parents and the child, but there are a few disadvantages worth mentioning.

On the positive side, for many the "loan" is an "advance" on an inheritance the child will receive. But keep in mind that it's very important that this loan be documented so that when the parent dies, there are clear records of how much is outstanding. Unless there's appropriate documentation, the executor of the estate will have no way to ensure payback. The obvious benefit to the parent is that the funds will be offered at low or no interest rates. This means, of course, a lower payback when the loan comes due (unfortunately, usually after the parent dies).

On the negative side, there's always that warning against doing business with relatives. While we don't necessarily adhere to that, we should make it very clear that loaning money is a business transaction. And in some families, that can cause serious problems in relationships. If you're considering loaning money to your parents, make sure you fill out loan papers (having an attorney draw up the papers may be a good idea). Also make sure your siblings or other close relatives know you've made the loan. We believe the more that's disclosed about the loan, the less chance there will be of intra-family fighting.

Family lenders might also consider loaning money against the parent's home equity, rather than just a signature loan. For one thing, that means that the loan is collateralized (with the home as collateral and the lender, then, more assured of getting repaid). Second, any interest payments your parents make would probably be tax deductible (although they would be taxable to you). Private home-equity loans like these should be well documented, particularly if a tax benefit is taken. There are strict IRS rules about the deductibility of family loans (they must be offered at an interest rate at least equal to the "applicable federal rate"), so you should probably seek the advice of a tax advisor. The current applicable federal rate is listed in the *Wall Street Journal* on or around the twentieth of every month.

Gifts

Tax rules stipulate that any individual can make a $10,000 gift to any other person without any taxable gain. That means, for example, that you, your spouse, and your two children can each give each of your parents $10,000 per year without their having to claim that amount as income on a tax return. Of course, if you can afford more, and if your parent's need more, the amount over the $10,000 per person would be taxed at your parents' rate (probably the lowest rate since they would probably have very little other income and their expenses would be high). A gift is a gift, and that means you don't expect any financial payback. If you do, you should probably consider a family loan as discussed above. Again, make sure that everything is documented in case either the IRS or a potential heir comes calling.

Claiming as a Dependent

When family gifts and loans start increasing to the point where you're supplying more than half the support of your parents, you can legally claim them as dependents. That means, of course, claiming them on your tax return as additional household members. A huge potential benefit is that all their medical expenses can be included in the family's expenses. And since it's often difficult for a family to claim medical deductions because the total must be more than $7\frac{1}{2}$ percent of the adjusted gross income, your parents' high medical costs may put you over that threshold.

Claiming your parent as a dependent also means that your parent will be covered by any insurance plan you have. Some employers have set up programs for the dependent parents of employees, and it's likely that more and more employers will do so as we boomers age (and, therefore, demand it). Check with your employer and weigh the benefits of claiming your parents as a dependent. Be careful, though, that you can document that you are providing more than 50 percent of their support. When considering support, you must count all sources of their income (including Social Security, retirement, interest, dividends, insurance reimbursement, etc.). If they're living in your home, you can certainly count the room and board you provide.

Note: If you and your siblings collectively provide greater than 50 percent of your parents' support, but no one individual provides more than half, you can rotate each year who gets to claim the parent on the tax return (make sure there's clear agreement on this since only one of you can make the claim each year).

Viatical Settlements

Under the terms of these programs, terminally ill patients can sell their life insurance policy to a viatical settlement company and receive a lump-sum benefit on which to live. (One such company is Viaticus, an affiliate of the CNA Insurance Company, which you can contact by phone at 800-390-1390.) If your parent's life expectancy is six months or less, a viatical settlement company will pay up to 80 percent of the face value of the policy; up to 60 percent if your parent's life expectancy is two years or less. Most companies will require that the insurance policy be in force for at least two years and that the beneficiary of the policy provide a waiver. It's a complex legal transaction and usually involves a great deal of documentation from physicians.

If you're considering this income source, you need to check that the viatical settlement company is licensed by the state and that there are no complaints against it (you can contact your state attorney general's office). Some viatical settlement companies are large enough to have the cash on hand; others are small and get private investors as needed. When working out the details of the settlement, make sure that the company either has the cash on hand or already has the investor. Insist on having an escrow account set up so that your parents are assured of timely payments.

Be sure you know the potential tax consequences of this program (the payout may be considered a capital gain under current tax law, although there is movement in Congress to change that). Also, if your parent is receiving public assistance (Medicaid), check with the Department of Social Service to make sure that receiving this payout won't affect your parent's eligibility for assistance.

For more information contact the Federal Trade Commission, Box P, Room 403, Washington, DC 20580. You can also access information on the Internet at:

http://ftc.gov/bcp/conline/viatical.htm

Kinds of Joint Ownership

There are four kinds of joint ownership. The one you and your parents establish will depend on their financial situation and where they live.

1. *Joint Tenancy.* Each of the parties has an undivided interest in the entire property, so that if one owner dies, the survivor or survivors own the property. If the property produces income, each party reports the income from his or her portion. Most ownership is joint tenancy unless otherwise stated.

2. *Tenancy in Common.* Each person owns a specified portion of the property. Upon death, that portion goes to his or her estate rather than to the surviving co-owners. There are some tax advantages for some people who have property owned in this manner (for example, if a surviving spouse is adequately provided for, a parent may want to leave an IRA account directly to a grandchild, thereby eliminating probate).

3. *Tenancy by the Entirety.* This form of ownership applies only to legally married couples and in some states applies only to real estate. Each spouse has an undivided interest

in the entire property, and on the death of one spouse, the survivor doesn't succeed to the decedent's right and title because he or she already had it. One-half the value of the property goes to the estate of the first to die, regardless of which spouse furnished the consideration for the property. Upon sale of the property by the couple, gain or loss is divided between the spouses.

4. *Community Property*. In those states that have enacted community property laws, each spouse is deemed to own one-half the property acquired by the other spouse after the marriage took place or after they moved into the state. Check to see whether your parents live in a community property state.

When You Must Step In

As we said earlier in this chapter, when you step in to help your parents with their financial situation depends on, among other things, how well they manage their money and how healthy they are. When you come to the point where intervention is necessary, here are some suggestions:

Credit: Each of your parents should establish credit in his or her own name so that when one of them dies, the surviving spouse will have a credit history. If they have only joint accounts, or if all credit is in your father's name, after your father dies, your mother may not be able to establish her own credit. This means that she may not be able to get even a credit card.

Credit Cards: Many organizations offer credit cards with no annual fee (*Money* magazine publishes a list each month). If your parents routinely pay off their balance each month, choose one of these, even if your parents have been using a different one. There's no reason to pay a fee when you can get the same service for free. Alternatively, if your parents usually carry a balance (which, of course, is not a good idea for anyone since the interest rate is so high), they should use a card that offers a low annual percentage rate. You might also consider closing all but a couple of credit cards. Usually, all that's needed are one or two Visas or MasterCards and an American Express card. The more cards, the greater the chance they'll get lost or stolen.

Affinity Cards: Airlines and other companies offer rewards for each dollar charged on certain credit cards. Using these is an excellent way to accumulate free flights for your parents. If you live far away, make sure that they choose a card that's aligned with an airline that flies between your home and theirs.

Senior Fares: Many organizations offer reduced rates for seniors, whether it's a discounted movie ticket, early-bird dinner, free banking, or special airline fares. If your parents travel frequently to your home or to a winter home, call the airline or your travel agent to get more information about these programs.

Check Writing: It's often a good idea for a second party to get signature authority on a checking account so you can be sure that all bills are being paid. Opening a joint account is one way, or having your parent complete a power of attorney is another (see the discussion of powers of attorney in chapter 4, "Blind Justice"). When you see a stack of unpaid bills on your parent's desk, that may be an indication that you need to step in. If you don't have signature authority, offer to write out the checks and envelopes and your parent can sign the checks. If your parent is bouncing checks, you may want to offer to balance the account (don't wait too long or it will get so involved that it won't be possible to balance the account without the bank's help). If your parent doesn't routinely enter checks into the register, use NCR checks that automatically produce a duplicate. Then you'll be able to enter the checks into the register yourself. Remind your parent not to use a felt marker when writing checks since it won't go through to the duplicate.

Bill Paying: Instead of having your parents pay their bills, you can arrange to have your parents' creditors send the bills directly to you. Contact your parents' utility company, mortgage holder or landlord, credit card institutions, etc. You can also ask these companies to notify you if they

Suggestion: In many communities, small businesses have started up that will help older people with their routine financial, legal, and medical paperwork. If you live some distance away or are unable to do the work yourself, check out these companies. To find a reputable one, you can call a local geriatric care manager, accountant, bookkeeping service, or social worker and get a reference. Compare prices and make sure that you check references before hiring the company.

don't receive a payment on time. You can then check with your parents to see if the bill was paid.

Safe Deposit Boxes: Only those with signature authority can access a safe deposit box. Make sure that someone other than a surviving parent has access to the box. That way, if your parent dies or is disabled, you can get into the box without having to go through probate. Also, it's probably better to store stocks and bonds at the brokerage house where they were purchased since valuables stored in safe deposit boxes are not necessarily protected against loss through burglary, flood, or fire.

Now that we've covered the legal and financial issues, in the next chapter we'll talk about the other ways you can help make sure that your parents' needs are being met. We'll discuss the things to look and listen for that indicate that there's a problem, visits, and long-distance caregiving.

Visiting Hours 7

As we've seen in the previous three chapters, staying on top of the many legal, financial, and insurance coverage issues is essential in making sure that your aging parent is being cared for. It also can be quite complicated and, therefore, we urge you to consider talking with the appropriate professional.

It's likely that you'll meet resistance from your parent as you take on more responsibility. Remember, although your intentions are good, it's your parent's life. Unless declared incompetent, he or she has the final say regarding how to deal with assets, what kinds of insurance coverage to carry, and, especially, how much and what kinds of medical treatment are desired. As we said in our opening remarks, you can try to influence, you can cajole, or you can even demand that you or someone else be involved in the decision-making. But never lose sight of your parent's autonomy.

That said, in this chapter we'll talk about some other things you need to do to make sure that your parents' basic needs are being met, that they are maintaining as much independence as possible given their medical and physical condition, and, essentially, that the quality of their lives is as good as it can possibly be. To do so means that you must use all your investigative prowess, being careful not to step on their sense of independence and autonomy. That's a fine line to walk. There will likely be times when you step too far and times when you don't step far enough. Both have their consequences.

Go too far and the relationship with your parent is likely to be strained or, if more serious, broken. In addition, the more you "take over," the easier it will be for your parent to become totally dependent on you. The burden will become increasingly severe, and your parent's ability to take care of him- or herself will diminish—likely having an effect on his or her health. The level of your involvement would then have to increase until your parent has lost all ability to take care of even the most minor things.

On the other hand, if you don't take on enough responsibility, the effects could be far more clear. They can even be harmful.

It is our opinion, therefore, that erring on the side of too much involvement is the safer road. At the same time, we urge you to be blatantly honest about your intentions. Many people who have not had the responsibility of paying bills will have to do so after their spouse dies. It can be difficult sometimes to make sure the cash flow is handled well and that all the bills are paid properly. If your parent is one that obviously needs assistance in this area, or if you've noticed a bounced check or two, you'll naturally want to be able to inspect their checkbook to see if you can prevent other checks from bouncing. Instead of just going through your parent's belongings to find their checkbook, it's a good idea to involve your parent with this task. You may say, for example, that you'd like to see their checkbook "because I know you've been a bit forgetful lately and I just want to make sure all the checks have been recorded."

Rule 1: The more observant you are, the better off your parent will be.

Five Things You Should Listen for When Speaking on the Phone

When you visit or even just talk on the phone, you'll want to keep a keen ear and eye to important signs that help is needed. Here are five things you should listen for when speaking on the phone:

1. How does your parent's voice sound?
   - Is it weak and breathy or strong and robust?
   - Do you hear any tremors in the voice?
   - Do you detect a difference from the last time you spoke?
   - Thinking back to six months or a year ago, is there a difference?
   - Do you have to speak louder or repeat more? (People who wear hearing aids often turn them down or off. Remind your parent to turn up the volume on his or her hearing aid.)
2. Is the conversation logical?
   - Does the conversation flow from topic to topic or jump around?

- Does your parent seem to get fixated on a particular topic?
- Does your parent seem to be overreacting to something?
- If so, has this always been the case or is it something fairly new?
- Does your parent seem to be underreacting to something that used to cause a bigger reaction in the past?

3. What sort of feeling is your parent expressing?

- Does your parent express despair?
- Does your parent continually talk about how difficult it all is?
- Does your parent talk about how confused he or she is?

4. How is your parent's health?

- Does your parent explain in great detail what's wrong with her?
- Is there a new problem every time you speak?
- Does your parent seem to be able to manage all the pills prescribed or do you feel there are dosages being missed repeatedly?
- Does your parent seem to be falling much?
- Does your parent complain about not being able to get up out of bed or a chair easily?

5. How is your parent eating?

- Can your parent tell you what he or she ate for dinner last night?
- Does the dinner sound well balanced?
- Can your parent tell you what's in the refrigerator and pantry?
- Can your parent tell you when the last time food shopping was done and what was bought?

When to Visit

The first thing you must decide is how often to visit. Naturally, that will be affected by the history of your relationship, the degree to which you feel responsible, your proximity, and your availability. There is no formula for determining how often to visit. In general, more is better (within reasonable limits), but not to the point where you are taking over the responsibility for daily activities or your parent is overly dependent on you for any interaction. When you visit, try to do so out of love and concern, not obligation. You'd be amazed how easily that's conveyed through body language and tone.

If possible, try to set up a regular pattern so that there's a sense of continuity. Of course, the more often you visit, the less time you need to spend taking care of the needs of your parent each time. When you're there infrequently, you'll likely find yourself doing a lot more work around the house, investigating how your parent is doing, going shopping, cleaning, organizing, and, probably, lecturing your parents on how they need to take better care of themselves or how they need to get out more.

Holidays and Special Occasions

Holidays, anniversaries, and celebrations are particularly difficult times for older people. This is especially true of the anniversary of a spouse's death or the first major holiday after a spouse dies. A visit, even a short one, on this special day will be highly appreciated. It will also give you insight into how your parent is *really* doing since emotions will likely be running high.

For many families, holidays are a time when the family gathers together, often at the parents' home. As your parents age, there will likely come a time when the site of this gathering shifts. Your parents may no longer be able to handle the chores involved or be the chief cook or host. This can be seen as a loss of

Rule 2: When you say you'll visit, do so (this is especially important if your parent is a resident in a long-term-care facility). If you must cancel, try to reschedule and be certain that you notify your parents that you won't be there. (For many older people, visits from family and friends are the only contact they have with another human being, possibly for days at a time.)

As a corollary to Rule 2, be careful that you don't promise too much. Don't say, for example, that you'll bring your children to visit every week when you know that that will be next to impossible.

Rule 3: If a decision has already been made about where to have the family gathering, don't pretend that the decision has not been made.

status, especially in families where there's competition. Before changing the venue, talk to your parents and explain the *facts* (your house is larger, more centrally located, easier for everyone to get to) and *your needs* (too much work for your parents, too much worry for you). You may find that your parents *want* the site to change, but they don't want to say so. And sometimes they may not even want to go to a family gathering but cannot say so.

Do You Bring the Kids?

Bringing along your children when you visit will have its pros and cons. Naturally, your parents will want to see their grandchildren, to see how they've grown, and to have the joy associated with grandparenthood. On the other hand, young children can be quite difficult for older people to contend with—the noise, bustle, and the children's boredom can be quite bothersome to your parents. Also, having to focus on your children's needs may interfere with some of the tasks you need to accomplish. If you know that you'll have a lot to do when you're there, and your parents are not able to mind the kids while you're busy, think about leaving the kids at a friends or bringing along a sitter.

Four More Things You Should Look for When You Visit

The things you should listen for when talking on the phone certainly apply as well when you're face to face. In addition, here are four more things you should pay attention to when you visit.

1. Check the refrigerator and pantry.

    ♦ Are the refrigerator and pantry well enough stocked?

    ♦ Will the items on hand provide a nutritionally balanced meal?

    ♦ How old are the items? (If they're too old, throw them away and be sure to tell your parent that you're doing so.) This would be a good time to make a grocery list.

2. Check that the bills are paid and the mail opened.

   ◆ Is there a stack of unopened mail piled up or still in the mailbox?

   ◆ Are bills repeatedly past due? (Many people get confused about billing procedures, and you may have to assist. Sometimes the problem is as simple as not having stamps or envelopes.)

   ◆ Is there a running balance in your parent's checkbook? (If not, you may have to help with balancing, which should be done as soon as possible. The longer you wait, the more difficult it will be.)

   ◆ Are all checks recorded?

   ◆ Is the checkbook legible? (Many older people have diffi-culty writing legibly in the confined spaces. If that's a problem, they should use two or three lines. There's nothing magical about using just one line.)

   ◆ Have there been bounced checks or repeated use of overdraft protection?

   ◆ Are some bills being paid twice?

   ◆ Is your parent paying medical bills when insurance should be covering it?

3. Are insurance premiums being paid and medical claims being filed?

   ◆ Medicare claims must be filed by the providers (that is, the physicians and other health professionals). But providers don't always have to submit claims for some Medigap insurers.

   ◆ How many Medigap policies does your parent pay for? Is that permissible? If so, is it cost-effective? (Remember, it often pays to have duplicate coverage since you're reimbursed only 20 percent of what Medicare allows.)

   ◆ Are there outstanding claims that have not been reimbursed for more than two or three months? (Most insurers pay their claims within sixty days.) If so, call the insurer's toll-free number and inquire.

Note: Keeping track of medical claims and reimbursements can be an extraordinarily time-consuming task, especially if your parent has multiple insurance policies in addition to Medicare. Some people have chosen to hire out that service to a private company to ensure that claims are filed and reimbursements received. For more information about this service and for a list of medical claims assistance companies, contact the National Association of Claims Assistance Professionals, 4724 Florence Avenue, Downers Grove, IL 60515.

4. Does your parent appear to be deteriorating physically?

   ◆ How does your parent look to you? Sudden weight loss or gain can be an indication of a more serious problem.

   ◆ Is your parent able to get around easily or is some form of assistance (for example, a cane or walker) necessary?

   ◆ Can your parent get in and out of bed or a chair easily? If not, there are many devices available to help. Or will physical or occupational therapy help?

   ◆ Do you notice that your parents are not reading the paper or magazines as much as before? If not, it's possible that their eyesight may have gotten worse. When was their last eye exam? (There are many large-print books and newspapers available now.)

   ◆ Do your parents' eyeglasses appear to fit properly and are they clean? Having a small eyeglass screwdriver available can be a great help.

   ◆ Do your parents seem to have the same sense of balance? Are they falling more? Check that there are no loose rugs, slippery or uneven floors, areas of poor lighting (especially stairs), or telephone and electrical extension cords in walkways.

   ◆ Check the medication bottles. Does it appear that the correct number of pills has been taken since the last time you checked?

   ◆ Do your parents appear to have any problems chewing? If they wear dentures, do they fit? Are there sores around the mouth and gums? Dental problems are very common among the elderly and should be taken care of immediately.

◆ Do you notice changes in your parents' behavior?

◆ Does the house appear to be as clean as usual? (If not, you may want to work out a system where either you clean it or you hire someone to come in and clean periodically.)

◆ Are your parents staying at home much more or not going to places that used to be rituals (for example, to church, an activity center, shopping, etc.)? If so, it may be because of a simple transportation problem or something more serious.

◆ Has your parents' ability to drive gotten to the point where it poses a danger? Many older people continue to drive well after their reflexes, eyesight, and agility make it dangerous for them and others on the road. If so, help to arrange transportation to the extent possible (check to see what community services are available). If your parents refuse to stop driving, you can try to get them to take another driving test.

◆ Does a particular health concern keep coming up? That may be a clue that something is wrong. Or it may be a subtle way your parents are reaching out for help. (Sometimes checking with someone with whom your parents talk freely may give you more insight.)

◆ Are your parents constantly feeling down or showing lack of interest in things? Older people are often losing friends and associates which can lead to less social interaction. These feelings can also be a sign of depression.

◆ Do your parents seem to be drinking more? Alcoholism is much too common a problem with older people.

What to Do When You Visit

As your parents age, visiting them, whether in their home or in a long-term-care facility, brings with it some responsibility. In addition to making sure that your parents are taking caring of themselves properly, you also want to be able to make the visits

Fifteen Danger Signals That Your Parents Are in Distress

1. Sudden weight loss or gain

2. Marked change in personal habits

3. Burns or injury marks on the body

4. Pronounced forgetfulness and misplacing items

5. Repeated falling or dizziness

6. Consistent disorientation

7. Difficulty performing familiar tasks

8. Problems with language

9. Increased number of accidents

10. Medications not taken as prescribed

11. Extreme suspiciousness

12. Unexpected mood swings

13. Loss of initiative

14. Major personality changes

15. Repeated bizarre behavior

enjoyable and productive. Later on, in chapter 10, "Ugh, I Hate Going There," we'll talk about specific things you should do when visiting your parent in a nursing home or other long-term-care facility. Here, we'll talk only about visits to their home or apartment. If you're visiting with a spouse or relative who may be sharing the responsibility, you can split up the tasks. For example, one of you can take your parent shopping while the other cleans and straightens up. Or one of you can "visit" while the other takes care of paying the bills (remember, both are equally important).

Forty Things to Do When You Visit

1. Straighten up and clean the house (or arrange to have someone come in). Pay special attention to the oven, where grease fires can occur when there's build-up.

2. Clean out the refrigerator.

3. Fill out a food shopping list together.

4. Go food shopping together.

5. Prepare meals together (make some extra so there'll be leftovers). Many older people can no longer lift heavy pots and pans, so you may want to buy some inexpensive lightweight ones. Make sure that they have fairly large handles.

6. Prepare meals that can be easily warmed up or cooked later in the week. Be sure to mark them clearly.

7. Rearrange the pantry and cupboard so that the items most often used are within reach.

8. Label all chemicals and cleaning agents in large letters.

9. Prepare meals for later use.

10. Wash your mother's hair or take her to a beauty salon.

11. Review and balance the checkbook.

12. Make sure that all bills have been paid.

13. Review the medical claims forms and reimbursements.

14. Go over financial concerns and do cost projections.

15. Make a list of all credit cards, their numbers, and their expiration dates.

16. Cancel all credit card accounts that are no longer used and cut up the cards. To cancel, you must write the company and your parent must sign the letter.

17. Do the laundry.

18. Make a list of all your parents' medications and when they're to be taken.

19. Mark the medicine bottles appropriately or set up a system (make sure that your parent is not getting the childproof bottles—many older people find that they no longer have the strength in their hands to open them).

20. Throw away all outdated medications.

21. Check that the toilet is accessible. (Many older people have difficulty getting up from a toilet seat. Consider buying an extension seat that makes it easier to sit or get up.)

22. Install handrails near the toilet and in the shower.

23. Check that the shower and/or bathtub are accessible. (There are many products available that can make it easier. A particularly helpful item is a waterproof seat that extends across the bathtub.)

24. Change the temperature on the hot water heater to 120 degrees to prevent accidental scalding.

25. Check that all smoke and carbon monoxide detectors are working. Replace batteries as needed (many people change these batteries when the clocks change).

26. Make a call to a friend or relative.

27. Make a large-print telephone list for your parent.

28. Replace low-wattage lightbulbs with a slightly higher wattage if your parents are having difficulty seeing. (Be careful not to exceed the manufacturer's suggested wattage for the lamp; going from a sixty-watt bulb to a seventy-five-watt bulb is usually fine.)

29. Use a marker to highlight where the "off" position is on the stove dials.

30. Program your parents' telephone for quick or one-touch dialing (including 911 or the local emergency number, your number, and other often-called numbers). Make sure that your parents understand how to use the quick-dial feature.

31. Install extension phones so that your parents can easily answer the phone regardless of which room they are in.

32. Install a deadbolt on all outside doors.

33. Buy a phone with extra-large numbers and an adjustable volume.

34. Help your parents write a letter to a friend or relative.

35. Put together a gift list.

36. Go clothes shopping (or if your parent is unable to do so, go make-believe clothes shopping).

37. Browse through a catalog, or visit one of the stores specializing in adaptive equipment for people with disabilities or arthritis (see chapter 8, "I've Fallen and I Can't Get Up").

38. Go through photo albums and label pictures with the names of relatives and places.

39. Talk about your parents' family and get help in putting together your family history.

40. Ask your parents to talk about their early lives.

Long-Distance Caregiving

Caring for aging parents is difficult. Caring for aging parents when you're not in the immediate vicinity will feel to you like an impossible task. "After all," you'll say to yourself, "how are we going to know what's going on when we're so far away?"

The fact is, long-distance caregiving is not all that different from caring for parents who are just down the street. The problems are the same. It's the solutions that may be different.

One of the biggest problems you'll face is poor communication. Telephone conversations can reveal only so much, and letters almost nothing, about how they're really doing. There's nothing like face-to-face talking to get a good sense of reality. Face to face, you'll see problems that are masked when you only have verbal communication. On the phone you won't see whether there's been any weight loss. And you won't see whether mobility and agility are problems. From afar you'll only know what your parent chooses to tell you, or what another person can tell you.

Another obstacle you'll face is guilt—guilt that you should be doing more, that when you're visiting your parent your family back home will resent your being away, and that you're relying on siblings, other relatives, and friends to do your work. There's not much anyone can say to you that will convince you not to feel guilty. All you can do is try to minimize those feelings and recognize that there are many things you can do for your parents when you're far away, and many tasks you can take on from afar that take away some of the burden left to those who are nearby.

There is one aspect of caring for your parents that benefits from your being far away. That is, when you visit, you're better able to see changes in your parents' condition. When you see your parents every day or every week, you're liable to miss the subtle changes that occur incrementally. Visiting only once in a while will give you a better perspective on any physical or mental deterioration your parents experience.

Ten Tips for Long-Distance Caregiving

1. Communicate as often as you can by phone.

   ♦ To minimize your phone bills, enroll in a long-distance plan from one of the long-distance carriers.

   ♦ If your parents have difficulty dialing the phone, pre-program your parents' phone for one-touch dialing.

   ♦ If your parents' eyesight is failing, or if arthritis or another physical condition make dialing difficult, buy a phone with extra-large numbers.

   ♦ If your parents don't want to call because of the cost of long-distance calls (or is in a long-term-care facility and can't dial long distance or only have access to a pay phone), have your parents use your calling card. If using a calling card is too difficult, set up a toll-free 800 or 888 number for which you pay the charges (collect calls can be much more expensive, especially if your parent goes through the operator).

   ♦ Use all your listening skills to find out as much as you can from them. The more open and direct you are with them on the phone, the more open they will likely be with you. You don't have the luxury of giving or receiving subtle hints, so pay close attention to what your parent is not saying.

2. Use all possible ways to communicate.

   ♦ Use e-mail—you can communicate electronically several times a day for as little as $5.00 per month, or even free for a limited time. If your parents don't have a computer, you can pick up an old 386 or 486, with a modem and monitor, for just a few hundred dollars.

   ♦ Write letters and send cards—they're excellent ways of conveying that you care. Unfortunately, this is one-way communication, which means that you won't learn much about them. To help your parents use this medium, be sure to give them pre-addressed envelopes or labels. If your parents reside in a long-term-care facility, you might also provide stamped envelopes, since obtaining stamps can be difficult for some people (the post office will deliver stamps for a small handling charge).

3. Make the most of your visits.

   ◆ Pay attention to the list of things to do when you visit.

   ◆ Schedule ahead of time any meetings that you plan to have with agency personnel, doctors, therapists, or other professionals.

   ◆ Make sure that your siblings are aware of your visit and can make some time for all of you to talk things through.

   ◆ If you don't know certain people who are key to your parents' care, make sure you find out about them and try to visit them while you're in town.

   ◆ Visit your parents' neighbors and friends to get their perspective on how your parents are doing and what care is needed.

4. Try to identify your parents' needs and what they may be willing to accept.

   ◆ Just because you know that they need a specific service doesn't mean that they'll accept it. They'll want to preserve their control and independence.

   ◆ Similarly, don't make decisions behind their backs, either from afar or during a visit (if you arrange for a service, be sure they know about it).

5. Investigate all resources available.

   ◆ Check with the local Area Agency on Aging (see appendix A for a list of state agencies).

   ◆ Check with county, city, or regional agencies that can help provide services for your parent.

   ◆ Get a copy of the yellow pages for your parents' area (you can call your parents' local phone company and request one). Having one at home will make it easier to find resources for your parent.

   ◆ Make sure that you have a current list of all the key contacts—primary physicians, geriatric care manager, therapists, clergy, financial advisor, attorney, etc. (see chapter 2,"Tough Talk")—and update it regularly.

   ◆ If your parents can't get out easily, arrange with the local pharmacy and grocery store to have goods delivered (most pharmacies will deliver free of charge and many grocery stores offer the service to seniors for a small charge).

◆ Find service providers (for example, a hair stylist) who will go to your parents' home or locate someone or an agency that will provide a ride for your parents.

◆ If you'll be handling the finances, arrange to have all bills and statements sent directly to you (banks, utilities, phone, charge cards, etc.).

◆ Use the Internet to access Web sites that can give you information about local resources (a partial list of related Web site addresses is in appendix L). You can usually find some help through your Internet service provider.

Note: Using one of the search engines—Lycos, Yahoo!, Alta Vista, etc.—to look up elder-care resources will yield thousands of citations. Be very specific when using a search engine (for example, if you're investigating legal issues, start your search with "elder law in Virginia" rather than just "law").

6. Establish a local network to help your parents and to help you keep up-to-date.

◆ Know who to call in an emergency.

◆ Know who you can call who will be willing to help out even when there's no emergency.

◆ Call one of the contacts on a regular basis to get an update on how your parents are doing.

◆ If your parent is housebound and alone, check with a local senior center about companion calling (volunteers who call or visit those who are alone).

◆ Set up a system and network of people who can help your parents with some tasks, such as shoveling the sidewalk, raking the leaves, mowing the lawn, taking out the garbage, bringing in the newspaper or mail, etc.

Important: Ask the letter carrier and newspaper delivery person to notify you if the mail or paper hasn't been picked up in a couple of days.

◆ If your parents have a dog that needs to be walked, but your parents cannot do so easily, hire a neighbor teenager or professional service.

7. Work out as fair an arrangement as possible for sharing all the tasks among your siblings and other close relatives.

◆ Many tasks can be handled from afar (for example, financial responsibility, legal issues, etc.). By splitting up the tasks, you can do your share and reasonably expect that those who live close by are doing what they can to ensure that your parents are cared for.

8. Hire a local geriatric care manager or surrogate who can take care of dealing with all the local arrangements and services (see chapter 8, "I've Fallen and I Can't Get Up").

◆ If you're hiring various caregivers, some of the early screening can be done from afar. However, the final choice should be made after a face-to-face interview.

◆ If your parents need some homemaking care, you can hire someone to come in periodically (see chapter 8 for more about hiring practices).

9. If you and your parents decide to rent the extra bedroom in your parents' home to someone who will provide some service for your parents in exchange for reduced rent or board, be especially vigilant about whom you hire. Notify neighbors and friends that you have worked out this arrangement and ask them to check up periodically. If you have even the slightest suspicion that there's a problem, follow up on it. These situations can have serious consequences, or can be wonderfully synergistic for both parties.

10. Consider moving your parents closer to you.

◆ Moving should be a mutual decision by you and your parents.

◆ Before a decision is made, your parents should come to your house or to the community for extended visits so that they can begin to set up a new social and resource network.

◆ Make sure that their new home has been adapted to their physical needs.

Minimizing the Cost of Visiting

Naturally, you'll want to minimize the costs of visiting. Here are a few suggestions to save you money:

♦ Purchase your airline ticket(s) fourteen days or more in advance and stay over a Saturday night (that will qualify you for a "supersaver" fare).

♦ If you're not going to stay over a Saturday night, you can still purchase "supersaver" tickets by buying two at the same time and using half of each ticket for each trip, or "back-to-back" ticketing. So if you plan on staying only one day, buy a round-trip ticket leaving Monday the third and returning Wednesday the twenty-fifth, and a round-trip ticket *in the opposite direction*—that is, leaving from your parent's hometown—for Tuesday the fourth and returning Tuesday the twenty-fourth. (Check with your travel agent about doing this.)

♦ Use "frequent flyer" mileage to qualify for free trips.

♦ Ask the ticket agent about special sales. Often airlines try to fill empty seats at the last minute (within three days) by offering very low rates.

♦ Check the Internet for special fares for specific destinations or last-minute discounts.

♦ If you must rent a car, take advantage of club memberships, "frequent flyer" clubs, and credit card discounts (membership in AAA qualifies you for 15 percent discounts, often in addition to the company's discount rates).

♦ If your parent is suddenly hospitalized or when there's a death in the family, when you obviously can't plan ahead, speak to the airline about special rates (they're called "compassion rates," "bereavement fares," or emergency travel). You'll likely have to provide documentation, but the fare will generally be about 40 percent off the regular no-advance-purchase fare.

In the next chapter we'll talk more specifically about what you can do when your parents need assistance. We'll talk about purchasing or renting special equipment and hiring home caregivers, home care agencies, and geriatric care managers.

I'VE FALLEN AND
I CAN'T GET UP

In the previous chapter we focused much of our attention on the various aspects of visiting your aging parent. We talked about the frequency of your visits and what you can do to make the visits both enjoyable and productive. We were particularly concerned about the signs you should look for that suggest that your aging parent is experiencing distress.

In this chapter we'll look at the business side of the visits and talk about what you can do when you realize that your parent needs assistance or when your parent is discharged from a hospital. We'll start with the most basic of their needs. Then we'll talk about home care and end with a discussion about overseeing your aging parent's overseer.

Medical Alert Tags

Millions of people have some sort of medical or physical condition that warrants wearing a special tag to alert emergency personnel. If your parent is allergic to a particular medicine or is diabetic, for example, these facts must be known so that the proper treatment can be administered in an emergency. Coming across an unconscious person is a common occurrence for emergency medical personnel, particularly when the person is elderly. Many factors could have caused a fall or lapse into unconsciousness. If the person in distress is a diabetic, then one likely scenario causing the unconsciousness will be insulin shock, a potentially serious condition but one that's quite easily treated. Wearing a special bracelet or necklace can be a lifesaver. Medical alert tags can be ordered from various companies. In your local pharmacy you can usually find a bracelet or necklace for any of several conditions or allergies. If you need to have a special one printed, you can call the National ID Company at 800-525-1982.

While these tags can be extremely useful, many people don't wish to wear this kind of "jewelry" because of how they look. These people should, at a minimum, keep a card in their wallet that explains their condition. Emergency medical personnel are trained to look in wallets for clues to a medical condition.

Registering with an On-Call Service

Some wallet cards and medical alert tags list a phone number that can be called in case of emergency. Your parents must sign up with this service and give them a medical history and a list of their conditions, allergies, etc. These services can be quite helpful, but it's essential they be kept up-to-date on your parents' condition.

Panic Buttons

Emergency response services can be excellent protection for elderly people living alone. Your parents wear a necklace that has a panic button they can press if they fall or are stricken. Pressing the button alerts a monitoring service that telephones the person to see if everything is okay. If no one answers the phone, the service will call various people to see to the ailing person. The service may contact the local police, a neighbor, a relative, or whomever it has been instructed to call.

Some systems also offer in-house radios and receivers so the distressed person can actually talk with the monitoring service without using a phone.

Some hospitals and local police forces offer these services on a limited basis—as long as they don't have to show up too often. The police service is free, and the hospital service is offered at a reduced price. Generally, medical insurance doesn't cover the expense, and the cost of the service must be paid privately. So you'll have to make your own judgment as to whether it's appropriate for your parent.

We recommend that if your aging parent lives alone and has a medical condition that could cause falls or blackouts (for example, diabetes, or frequent transischemic attacks or "TIAs"), and if the cost of one of these systems is not too much for you, it's a good idea to invest in one of these services. It's likely that you won't rely on this system for very long, particularly if your parent ends up having to press the button often. At some point you'll decide that your parent can no longer live unsupervised for long periods of time.

Appendix M lists a number of emergency medical response systems you can contact for more information, courtesy of the Children of Aging Parents Society.

Neighbors, Friends, and Relatives

For aging parents, particularly those who are frequently housebound, a key element in ensuring that they're properly taken care of is for you to make good use of their neighbors, friends, and close relatives. Even if you stop in every day to see your parent, it's always good to have someone else who checks up periodically. For one thing, you can't always be there. Second, your parent will probably want contact with some other people.

The Key Is *Not* Under the Mat

It's essential that a close neighbor have a key to your parent's home and that the local police know that the neighbor has access to the home. But leaving a key under the mat, on the door frame, or in a fake rock are not good ideas. Burglars know all about these hiding places. One alternative is to purchase a keyless entry system. These are available in hardware stores for under $100 and look just like regular doorknobs. With these systems you can use either a combination or a key to open the door. They're quite secure—they won't allow more than three wrong guesses before shutting down. Some have special security devices that allow two combinations to be used—one that works all the time and one for hired help that can be turned off with a flip of a switch.

Keep Their Local Police Informed

Even if the local police don't offer a designated on-call check-in service, it's a good idea for you to let the local police know that your parent is living alone and may need special assistance or monitoring. In addition to potential medical crises, older people living alone are more susceptible to crime. Local police offices may offer special services for the elderly, or may simply check the area more often. Either way, if they know that your parent lives alone, they're in a better position to prevent a crisis or handle one if one should occur.

Cabs, Transport Services, and Ambulances

Older people tend to need a great deal of medical attention and, as a result, make frequent visits to doctors, therapists, and other medical personnel. Older people are also less likely to be able to drive themselves or take public transportation to get them there. This means that they must use cabs, private transport services, or, too often, ambulances. These three means of transportation are quite different, yet are often used interchangeably. Transport to a hospital or medical care facility by ambulance is often covered by medical insurance whereas using a cab or private transport to get your parent to a doctor will certainly not be covered. And the expense may be significant, especially if your parent is wheelchair-bound or worse.

The first rule is, if it's an emergency, an ambulance with emergency medical personnel should be called. Usually, this happens automatically when you, your parent, or a third party calls 911 and explains the situation. If your parent doesn't live in an area with 911 emergency calling, make sure that he or she knows the local emergency number. Also, most push-button telephones have speed-dial capability in which you program the number and the caller merely presses one button. We strongly recommend this for people who don't have a local 911 emergency number. While dialing "0" (zero) for the operator is still in use in many places, it's much less efficient than a designated emergency number where the respondent is trained to handle emergencies.

In non-emergency situations, such as appointments with doctors, you must use a totally different approach. Transportation for the elderly is often a significant problem for families, both for financial reasons and lack of availability.

Ten Ways to Handle Non-Emergency Medical Transportation Needs

Here are a few suggestions for you if your parent needs non-emergency medical transportation:

1. Make sure that there's one person whose role includes responsibility for *coordinating* transportation for your aging parent (coordinating—not necessarily transporting).

2. To the extent possible, doctors' appointments should be arranged with the designated transportation scheduler.

3. Try to arrange appointments an hour or two apart if the doctors' offices are close to each other or in the same building. When you and your parent select a specialist, you might consider convenience to the office an important factor.

4. Avail yourself and your parent of free or reduced-price transportation services offered by local agencies, clubs, day-care centers, and even municipalities.

5. If public transportation is available, and if your aging parent is both familiar with and comfortable with the system, encourage him or her to use it. (Don't forget about reduced fares for seniors.)

6. Many of your parent's neighbors, friends, or relatives may not be able to drive but may be willing to accompany your parent using public transportation. Offer to pay the fare (and buy lunch) in exchange. Or set up a swap system where your parent does the same for the other person.

7. Set up a carpool system, just as you do for your children. Work with friends and relatives whose aging parents have a similar need for non-emergency transportation, and arrange for group transport to doctors' offices, optometrists, therapists, and even for shopping trips.

8. Arrange with a pharmacy to have medicines delivered (or use a mail-order prescription service).

9. Negotiate rates in advance with a local cab company, promising that your parent will use the company exclusively (you might even want to set up a monthly billing rather than having your parent pay for each individual ride). If you can have several of your parent's friends and neighbors do the same, you might get an excellent group rate even when there's only one passenger. Don't forget to make sure that the driver is tipped appropriately.

10. Contact a local medical transport service and try to work out the same arrangement. For parents confined to

wheelchairs, this may be the only method of transportation available for non-emergencies. These services can be expensive, so working out a group arrangement could save a great deal of money.

Renting and Buying Special Equipment

If you've ever broken a leg or sprained an ankle, you got to spend some time using crutches. You also got to know how expensive they are to buy.

If crutches are so expensive, imagine the cost of walkers, wheelchairs, self-raising chairs, hospital beds, or other specialized equipment that so many of our parents need on a daily basis. The rising popularity of new supermarket-like stores that carry this kind of equipment should indicate how much of a market there is, and also how many different products there are available to help your aging parent get along more efficiently. There are devices and gadgets to help people with daily living; safety and adaptive devices for the bathroom; back supports, braces, and orthotics; ostomy and incontinence supplies; automatic chairs and beds that help people get in and out; and, of course, sophisticated wheelchairs with just about every bell and whistle you or your parent could want. Biomedical engineering is a huge field, and new products are coming out every day that will make your parent's life better and easier. Manufacturers and distributors put out 600-page catalogs of products, selling just to pharmacies. And there are now several large retail stores—that are not affiliated with pharmacies—which specialize in these products. Three such examples are "Health and Home Care," located in five states; "JoAnnes Bed & Back," in the mid-Atlantic region; and "take-goodcare," in New Jersey. Check the yellow pages under "wheelchairs" or "hospital supply."

If you've hired a home care agency (see below) to help your parent, the staff can assist you with obtaining the appropriate devices and equipment.

You could spend a fortune on some of these products and, in some cases, medical insurance will pay for all or part of the cost. For the most part, though, unless the device is prescribed by a doctor, you or your parent will have to pay for it with no help from insurance. The key is, of course, to have your parent's doctor prescribe the device.

Chances are that your parent will start out renting a wheelchair, not purchasing one. There are many ways to deal with this, usually by phone. The chair will then be delivered. Your parent's doctor, therapist, local pharmacy, or hospital supply company can help you get a chair. They can also help in selecting the right one. You'll have to consider not only price, but comfort, size, ability to maneuver, ability to take apart for storage in car trunks, and weight. If your parent is not totally confined to a chair, and if you ever plan to take your parent somewhere (including your home), we can't emphasize enough how important it is that you be able to lift the chair and put it in your car. We've often found it easier to put wheelchairs in the back seat of a car rather than lifting them into the trunk.

Many older folks who are shaky on their feet start out with walkers. Again, pharmaceutical supply houses and physical therapists can help you and your parent select the right one. One major question is whether to have wheels on the front two legs. It's easier for your parent to move the walker with wheels, but at the same time there's a greater chance that he or she will fall since the walker can move when not expected. This decision is one best left to your parent and his or her therapist or doctor. You may feel strongly that you want your parent to push for more mobility, meaning that a walker with wheels would then be better. But your parent may feel quite insecure about a disability and would prefer one without wheels. Encourage all you want. But our advice is that it's your parent's decision.

Professional Helpers

Prior to needing full-time supervision or residency in a long-term-care facility, your parent may start out needing occasional assistance in some daily tasks while remaining at home. These tasks can include food shopping and meal preparation, bathing and toileting, mobility and transport, or even skilled nursing care and physical therapy or rehabilitation. You and other relatives, friends, and neighbors can pitch in. But it may be too much work and far too many hours for you to rely on volunteer assistance or just yourself (don't try to be Wonder Woman or Superman—it's essential that caregivers take care of themselves as well as those they're caring for). Therefore, you may have to consider hiring a home care aide, also known as a "home caregiver." According to the National Association for Home Care, more than three million older Americans (over age sixty-five) receive formal home care, and probably another three or four million receive informal home care from family members, friends, and neighbors.

There are two approaches you can take to hiring aides. The simpler, but often more expensive method, is to contract with one of the almost 20,000 home care agencies in this country. You can locate these services in the yellow pages. A few are nationwide companies with branches in many locations (for example, Kelly Assisted Living and First American Home Care), but there are also many local companies and agencies that are quite reliable. A home care agency can provide personnel to handle a comprehensive package of services ranging from personal care and light housekeeping to skilled nursing care or physical therapy. Some home care providers have set up networks to provide social workers, dietitians, occupational therapists, physicians who will visit patients in their homes to diagnose and treat illnesses, and even companions for people who, for medical or safety reasons, should not be left at home alone.

The advantages of using a home care agency are fairly obvious. You don't have to deal with recruiting and hiring workers and various professionals; you'll have access to a wide variety of services, often with twenty-four-hour, seven-days-a-week on-call service; and you don't have to be an "employer," with all the paperwork and time that it requires. The main disadvantages are: cost; lack of control over who is selected to care for your loved one; the turnover of staff (aides you hire tend to be paid more so they also tend to stay longer); and the lack of loyalty and bond established between you, the employer, your parent, and the individual hired to care for your parent.

Choosing the Right Home Care Agency

When selecting an agency, you must be diligent about choosing the right one for you and your parent. Here are some suggestions to help you:

1. Determine if the agency has the appropriate state license (not all states require one).

2. Check to see if the agency is accredited by one of the following national organizations:

   ◆ Joint Commission on the Accreditation of Healthcare Organizations (One Renaissance Boulevard, Oakbrook Terrace, IL 60181; 708-916-5600)

   ◆ National Association for Home Care (1320 Fenwick Lane, Suite 100, Washington, DC 20910; 202-547-7424; Web site: http://www.nahc.org)

3. Contact your local Better Business Bureau to make sure there are no serious complaints against the agency.

4. Find out how many years the agency has been in business (there are no rigid guidelines, but the more years the agency has operated, the greater the chance that it's reliable and in good standing).

5. Ask your doctor or your parents' doctor, social worker, or geriatric care manager for recommendations.

6. If your parent is being discharged from a hospital, ask the appropriate hospital personnel for a recommendation (many hospitals have specially trained discharge planners or social workers).

7. Check with your local Area Agency on Aging (see appendix A) to see if there's any information on file about an agency or if they can refer you to one or several.

8. Ask your church or synagogue, local senior center, or social service organization for recommendations.

9. Ask friends, colleagues, and relatives who have used agencies to give you their recommendations. Make sure that they tell you about ones that were *not* acceptable too.

10. Determine the range of services the agency offers, the price of each service, and whether these services are clearly spelled out in their literature.

11. Determine whether the agency is Medicare-certified.

12. Talk with several agencies and visit their offices (or have their staff come to your or your parent's home). Make judgments about the friendliness and efficiency of the personnel you meet and the general appearance of the office.

13. You probably will want to choose an agency that's willing to visit your or your parent's home to do an evaluation of the services needed (some agencies will also want to interview your parent so they can determine the kind of personality that would work out best).

14. Evaluate the costs of the services and, if the agency is Medicare-certified, make sure that it is knowledgeable about what costs can be paid by Medicare.

15. If possible, try to meet one or more of the aides that the agency employs.

16. Make sure that you understand what services are being offered and at what price, what your rights are, and what the agency does when a particular aide doesn't show up or is unacceptable.

17. Ask how the agency handles emergencies and whether it can handle twenty-four-hour-a-day, seven-days-a-week service if needed.

18. Find out if the agency has a supervisor overseeing the treatment being offered, and ask how often this person visits homes to check on the quality of the treatment.

19. Ask to see a sample of a patient/client course of treatment (if the agency balks because of confidentiality, ask to have photocopies made with the patient's identification not visible). Make sure that the report details the specific tasks to be carried out by each professional caregiver.

20. Ask the agencies to provide you with a list of references and be sure to contact each one.

When There's a Problem with a Home Care Agency

Problems with a home care agency *do* occur, no matter how diligent you've been in selecting it or how reputable the agency appeared when you contracted with it. When problems occur with a particular provider, first try to solve the problem directly with the agency—notify the agency supervisor or administrator. If the problem persists, you should notify your state's health department, the state Medicare hot line (if all or a portion of the fees are being paid by Medicare), the Better Business Bureau, and the Office of the Inspector General hot line (the toll-free number is 800-HHS-TIPS).

The Price to Pay

The cost of hiring a home care agency will depend on the kind of services it provides, the region of the country in which your parent lives, and the agency's policies. Compare the costs of the agencies you've selected, making sure that you're comparing the same services. This can sometimes be difficult since different agencies have different payment options and link some services with others. You don't have to worry about every dollar as long as you're roughly comparing costs for similar services.

Self-Directed Home Caregiving

Many people choose to be personally involved with selecting home caregivers, particularly when the level of care needed is basic and nonmedical and when they are both physically and emotionally close to the parent's home (or when your parent is living in your home). If you choose this option, you'll have much more work and responsibility. But you'll likely save a good deal of money and have considerably more control over who takes care of your aging parent. Hopefully, this control will serve to improve your parent's quality of life through greater loyalty of the aides and by maintaining more of your parent's independence.

Home Caregivers' Tasks

Here's a listing of the key tasks and responsibilities you will assign your parent's aide. We suggest that you use this chart when explaining the duties of the aide you hire.

1. Personal Care
    - bathing and washing
    - brushing teeth
    - washing hair

- combing/brushing hair
- makeup and skin cream application
- shaving
- toileting
- dressing

2. Food Care
   - food shopping, or accompanying your parent on food shopping trips
   - putting away groceries
   - meal planning and preparation
   - assistance with feeding

3. Housekeeping
   - dusting and vacuuming
   - cleaning bathrooms
   - changing bed linens
   - straightening up
   - washing floors
   - laundry

4. Household Help
   - record-keeping/secretarial paperwork
   - assisting with bill paying
   - assisting with health insurance forms

5. Supervision
   - monitoring your parent's physical and health status (This is critical. The aide should observe changes in your parent's eating habits, diet, weight, mobility, comfort level, confusion, etc., and all changes should be reported to you immediately.)
   - making sure your parent's personal hygiene is taken care of (especially if your parent has bowel or bladder problems or is incontinent)
   - making sure your parent takes all medications at the right time (By law aides cannot administer any

medication. But they can provide the water, remind your parent of the time, make the medicine easy to get to—even open the container if necessary—and monitor that the medicine was taken.)

6. Mobility

   ♦ assisting in getting in and out of bed

   ♦ assisting in getting in and out of a wheelchair, if appropriate

   ♦ assisting in getting to and from the bathroom (including on and off toilet)

7. Transportation (personally driving or accompanying your parent)

   ♦ to and from doctors' offices/clinics

   ♦ to and from supermarkets and/or restaurants

   ♦ to and from stores for other shopping

   ♦ running errands (pharmacy, post office, bank, etc.)

8. Companionship

   ♦ conversation

   ♦ listening to music or watching TV together

   ♦ reading aloud

   ♦ assisting and participating in activities your parent enjoys

Hiring Home Care Aides

The process of hiring the right home care aide is very similar to hiring any other person who will work in your home. With a few important exceptions, it will be the same as if you were hiring a nanny, au pair, or baby-sitter. You're looking for someone who will be reliable and conscientious.

But working with older persons is quite different from working with children, and the aide you hire will have to understand those differences. The aide you hire will not be "baby-sitting," but assisting an adult. And he or she should not view or treat your parent as a child (then again, neither should you). Your elderly

> ### Home Care Workers Should *Not*:
>
> ◆ administer medications, even aspirin (All medications must be self-administered, but it's a good idea for an aide to monitor that medications are taken correctly and timely.)
>
> ◆ care for any wounds, except for emergency first aid
>
> ◆ cut toenails
>
> ◆ monitor equipment
>
> ◆ perform anything that could be construed as providing medical or paramedical assistance (including taking blood pressure, pulse rates, etc.) except for emergency first aid

parent won't be "cute," and may even be downright obstinate or nasty at times. There may be some physical strength required to lift or guide your parent in and out of chairs, beds, toilets, and cars. And, for the most part, disciplining your aging parent is not part of the job description.

Recruiting

The best way to find a home caregiver is through word of mouth, from someone who has used or is using a reliable person or, more likely, from a friend of a friend, a co-worker, or a colleague. This means, of course, that you must let people know what you're looking for. The more people who know, the greater the chance you'll find someone (just like a housecleaning person).

Second, you'll want to speak to your church or synagogue administration and any other club or service association with which you're affiliated. These organizations often have referral services. In addition, using these organizations spread the word quickly.

A third way to find a home caregiver is through a recommendation from a professional in the field: a geriatric care manager, elder law attorney, hospital social worker, etc. Sometimes these people can supply you with a list of agencies or individuals they've worked with. They can be excellent sources of information.

If those methods fail, you'll need to advertise, through flyers and want ads. Local papers and small-circulation newsletters or journals can be very cost-effective and reach a particularly widespread population. Look, for example, at your hometown "weekly" newspaper, your church or alumni newsletter, etc. Put up a flyer in the local supermarket and any other local store that will allow you to do so, in your town library, and in local churches and synagogues (you usually don't need be a member). If you live near a college or university, you might put an ad in the campus newspaper or post an ad on the job placement office bulletin board. You should also consider putting a flyer on college kiosks and in dorms. The ad should explain what you're looking for, the basic requirements, a way to contact you, and the best time to reach you. You don't need to include the salary at this point. Try to make the ad as personal and appealing as possible (see the example below). *Important:* For security purposes, do *not* include your address or even your last name.

```
HOME CAREGIVER WANTED: Looking for
a caring person to help my aging
mother with daily tasks, including
light housekeeping, some cooking,
personal care, and local trans-
portation. 4 hours/day, M-W-F.
Nonsmoker. References required.
Call 555-1212 evenings.
```

If you put together a flyer, you'll want to explain more about the responsibilities—not necessarily the complete list on the preceding pages, but a reasonable summary. Make the flyer as visually attractive you can, but you needn't use a professional service. If you have access to a computer at home or at work, any word processing software can do a reasonable job by using different fonts and inserting graphics to help it look more appealing to the eye. Naturally, if you have access to a color printer, that will help make your flyer stand out from the others (consider tear-offs with the phone number at the bottom of the flyer to help those who may not have something to write with when they see the flyer).

Screening by Telephone

The first thing you must do is screen your applicants, and the best way to do that is over the phone. Explain the responsibilities to the caller and the requirements—the number of hours required, days of the week, whether the aide must have their own transportation, and the general (but not the exact) location. Be sure to paint a good picture of what they'll have to do, but be brief. Say what you're willing to pay and ask if they're interested. If they say yes, ask them to tell you about themselves and why they would want the job. Make sure that you take notes about each person, including their name, phone number, and current employer. You can also ask them to describe any other job they've had, or currently have, in which they've had similar responsibilities, and whether they've worked with any older people before (even a relative—you're looking for someone who will care for your parent, and a person who has helped his or her own parent or relative could be exactly the right person for you, even if it wasn't a paid position).

If you feel that this person could work out, we recommend that you say you'll get back soon (try to give a time frame) to schedule a personal interview. That will give you time to evaluate all the candidates and eliminate some. Getting back to them will also mean that you'll get a better read on how interested they are. If there is still interest the next time you speak, often several days later, there's a better chance that it will work out. Try to set up at least three people to interview. Arrange to meet in some public place (a restaurant, coffee shop, park, etc.), not your home or your parent's home (be ever vigilant about security). Ask them to bring identification, a summary of their employment, proof of address, their driver's license (if they'll be responsible for driving), and a list of references (with phone numbers). You may also ask them to be sure to call you if they change their mind or can't make it. Unfortunately, that may happen all too frequently.

Interviewing

Good interviewing skills are learned, often through practice. If you've had experience interviewing someone for a job before, you'll have an advantage over those who have never conducted an interview. Still, you'll likely be just as nervous as the person being interviewed. We believe it's important that both people feel comfortable at the interview, but you must be clear about what your role will be.

The purpose of an interview is for you to learn as much as you can about the person and for the interviewee to learn about the job. We strongly recommend you have each applicant complete a job application (see appendix F for a sample). This form will give you much information and also allow you to check the applicants' references (make sure they've signed the statement permitting you to do so).

Usually, the subject of salary will come up during the interview. If you know how much you're willing to pay, you should state it during the interview so that there are no surprises. If the ad listed the salary, or if it was discussed in the initial phone interview, you may not even need to bring it up again, although it never hurts to be sure.

Ten Interview Questions

1. Are you available the specified hours and days? If not, what hours and days of the week are you available?

2. Are you available for extra hours if something comes up?

3. What are you doing now? And what made you call about this job?

4. What are your longer-term goals, say, in the next two or three years?

5. Have you had any experience caring for an older person? If so, please describe what you did, for whom, and for how long.

6. What is it about caring for an older person that you enjoy or find particularly rewarding?

7. What is it about caring for an older person that you don't enjoy or are uncomfortable performing?

8. Do you have an alternative means of getting to work if your car breaks down or if the public transportation mode you use is out of service?

9. What would you do if you came to work and found the person you're caring for lying on the floor unconscious? What about if he or she was lying on the floor conscious?

10. How would you handle a situation in which the person you're caring for starts to scold you or is particularly nasty?

Ask any other relevant questions and try to allow for an open exchange. You're trying to find out as much as you can about the applicant: how he or she will react in various situations, whether a bond will form between the applicant and your parent, what his or her motivation is, and whether this can be a long-lasting relationship. You're also trying to find out about any potential risks. So you may decide to pose a question about discovering a piece of jewelry or some household money missing.

Driving

If the person will be driving your parent, you might want to take a test drive (you can ask the applicant to drive you to the store or your office). You should also ask for a copy of his or her driving record, which can be obtained from the Department of Motor Vehicles. (If you try to get it yourself, you'll need a letter of permission, the person's full name, address, license number, and the reason for the request.) The turn-around time for this may be several weeks, so you may have to make continued employment contingent upon receiving a clean record. Also, explain that if the applicant is hired, you'll want a copy of his or her car insurance, showing a paid-in-full policy with sufficient liability coverage. If the caregiver will be driving your parent's car, you must make sure that your parent's insurance will cover other drivers.

Physicals

Many tasks performed by caregivers require physical strength or agility. Therefore, you might want to require a physical or medical clearance before the person begins work. If so, you should be prepared to pay for this examination. But at the very least, be sure you know of any physical limitations the caregiver has, especially if your parent has difficulty with mobility, bathing, or toileting.

Checking References and Background

This is a *must!* Check all references given (at least three), including personal and employment references. Some professionals even recommend doing a complete background check, including a credit report, police record, medical record, and driving record.

If you decide to do one or all of these, you must have written permission from the applicant. A sample general-purpose permission letter you can adapt to the specific background check you'll be conducting is included in appendix J.

When checking references, if one has moved or the business is no longer there, call the applicant and ask for another reference. Make sure that you verify all information provided by the applicant. Explain to the reference that the applicant has applied for a job as a home caregiver, and try to get the reference to talk about the applicant, specifically, whether the applicant will be suitable for this job. Don't hesitate to call personal references. They can provide you with a great deal of information. Remember, you're hiring someone to care for your parent. The more you know, the easier it will be to decide who will be the right home caregiver.

Making Your Choice

If you're comfortable making a choice at this point, do so. Call the person, make a specific salary offer, and if it wasn't mentioned in the interview, be sure to discuss when raises and reviews will occur and how often he or she will be paid (we recommend every two weeks). Also decide on a starting date (obviously, you'll want the sooner the better, but you should expect that he or she will have to give two weeks' notice to any current employer). Be sure to say that the offer is contingent upon the receipt of satisfactory background checks.

If the person says that he or she would like some time to think about it, that's common. Generally give no longer than a week for a decision. Be sure to call the other candidates you've interviewed to inform them that the position has been filled after you've actually hired someone and that person has started work. You may need to hire them as a backup or if your first choice doesn't work out.

If you're not comfortable with any of your options, don't pick someone unless you're really in a bind. Instead, reopen your search. You'll likely have a new pool from which you'll be able to select the "right" person, not just what you could get. You might also consider raising the pay if you think you may be a bit low.

How Much to Pay

There's no set amount you should pay. The general rule is "more than what they could make if they worked for an agency." In fact, about 20 percent more is recommended! Since you're looking for a quality person who will feel loyalty and stay a long time, you don't want to underpay your caregiver. Pay rates vary regionally, so you might want to check with some local agencies to see what they pay. And, of course, different jobs require different levels of expertise and responsibility.

At the very lowest level, an agency worker is likely to make a little more than minimum wage. So if in your area the lowest-level home caregiver could earn about $6 per hour, you should consider paying about $7 (see table 8-1 for other rates). If you're reimbursing your worker for transporting your parent in the caregiver's car, you'll want to pay about 35¢ per mile, plus tolls and parking.

You'll also want to be sure to include bonuses and merit pay increases. For example, you may want to give an extra paid vacation day for three months' perfect attendance or pay a bonus for one or two months' perfect attendance (and be sure to mention this incentive in the beginning). A reasonable amount is an additional 50¢ per hour for a level-one home care aide. You may want to offer a shift differential for those workers who work nights or weekends. Again, a 50¢ per hour increase is a reasonable amount. You might also pay a birthday or holiday bonus. And don't forget positive feedback. It won't cost you anything but will go a long way in building loyalty and commitment.

Table 8-1: Average Hourly Compensation of Home Health Agency Caregivers, October 1995

Caregiver	25th Percentile	Median	75th Percentile
Homemaker	$5.39	$5.70	$6.52
Homemaker/Home Health Aide	$6.28	$7.25	$8.50
Home Health Aide	$7.14	$8.00	$8.67
Licensed Practical Nurse (LPN)	$10.14	$11.74	$13.05
Registered Nurse (RN)	$15.74	$17.50	$19.04
Occupational Therapist	$20.00	$21.82	$25.00
Physical Therapist	$20.90	$23.16	$25.89

Source: National Association for Home Care, *Homecare Salary & Benefits Report, 1995–1996,* Hospital & Healthcare Compensation Service, October 1995.

Contracts and Forms

On the caregiver's first day, have him or her fill out all the necessary papers and sign an employee contract (see appendix N for a
sample). Of course, be sure to go over the job description and
responsibilities you expect him or her to take care of, as well as
any other expectations you may have.

As an employer, you will have certain legal responsibilities that
must be taken care of (remember Nanny-gate, where a U.S.
Supreme Court Justice nominee was eliminated from consideration because she had not paid Social Security taxes for her child-
care worker?).

First, you'll need a Federal Employer Identification Number
(EIN), which you obtain through the Social Security Administration (any of the local branches) or the IRS (call 800-829-1040). You
must have the employee's Social Security number, and you'll
be responsible for paying Social Security and unemployment
taxes. You can find out how much you must subtract and get the
proper forms from the Social Security Administration (you can
reach it at 800-772-1213). You may also be required to withhold
federal income tax (it's up to the household employee if he or she
wants federal taxes withheld) and state taxes (check with your
state department of labor for more information about state taxes).
When hiring a new worker, you must also have him or her complete a U.S. Immigration and Naturalization Service (INS) form
I-9, which you can obtain from the INS, 425 I Street NW,
Washington, DC 20536.

Geriatric Care Managers

More and more families are deciding that dealing with their aging
parents' multiple conditions and growing need for services is
more than they can handle by themselves. So they're turning to
geriatric care managers. Essentially, these professionals, who
usually have degrees in social work or human services, act as
your parent's personal health and services manager. Typically,
after assessing your parent's condition and needs, and making
suggestions that you and your parent can take advantage of,
the geriatric care manager will coordinate and monitor all the
medical, transportation, legal, and financial services involved.
Geriatric care managers work with community services, home

care agencies, long-term-care facilities—even acting as a referral to particular nursing homes and respite care centers or working with the staff to ease the transition from home to the facility. They use their expertise and training to provide counseling to family members and make referrals to other professionals as needed (physicians, lawyers, financial advisors, insurance agents, etc.). A geriatric care manager can be particularly helpful when the children of the aging parent live some distance away and have difficulty managing the local arrangements.

Fees

The services of a geriatric care manager are usually paid for by the family since insurance does not cover this expense. The fees are hefty and can run anywhere from $50 to $150 per hour, depending on the manager's experience, credentials, and location (figure an average monthly charge of $400 to $500, plus the costs of the supportive services). An initial assessment will range in price from $150 to $350.

Despite these high fees, geriatric care managers can often save money for the family because they're highly knowledgeable about taking full advantage of Medicare, Medicaid, and private insurance (including making sure that the correct diagnosis is made so that coverage is provided), finding free community services, and referring to other professionals who optimize care versus cost. You often can negotiate a rate with a geriatric care manager based on your financial situation and need.

Ten Ways for Finding the Right Geriatric Care Manager

1. Ask for a referral from the National Association of Professional Geriatric Care Managers (1604 North Country Club Road, Tucson, AZ 85716; 602-881-8008). A directory costs $35 but you can get a referral for one state for free.

2. Contact Aging Network Services (4400 East West Highway, Apt. 907, Bethesda, MD 20814; 301-657-4329).

3. Get a referral from the U.S. Administration on Aging's free Eldercare Locator (800-677-1116).

4. Ask your or your parent's doctor for recommendations.

5. If your parent is being discharged from a hospital, ask the appropriate person (a specially trained discharge planner or social worker) for a recommendation.

6. Check with your local Area Agency on Aging (see appendix A) to see if there is any information on file about a geriatric care manager, or if it can refer you to one or several.

7. Ask your church or synagogue, local senior center, or social service organization for recommendations.

8. Ask friends, colleagues, and relatives who have used geriatric care managers to give you their recommendations. Make sure that they tell you about ones that were *not* acceptable too.

9. Look in the yellow pages under "social worker."

10. After you've located one or more potential geriatric care managers, have an interview and choose one based on the following:

   ♦ previous experience with families

   ♦ licenses and professional degrees held

   ♦ years in the profession

   ♦ what kind of initial assessment is done (and the charge)

   ♦ services provided and whether or not outside providers are used

   ♦ fees charged

   ♦ provisions for backup during the manager's vacations or illnesses

   ♦ references (be sure to get two or three—and check them all)

   ♦ if you live some distance away, find out how—and how often—you'll be kept informed

In the next chapter, chapter 9, "For the Long Haul," you'll learn about the long-term-care options for your aging parent. We'll discuss the different levels of care available, review the steps to choosing the right facility, and provide suggestions for dealing with the various people who will have input on where your parent will live.

FOR THE LONG HAUL

You've now arrived at that sensitive time when you'll have to make one of the biggest and most difficult decisions you've ever made. If you're lucky, it will be the most obvious decision imaginable. For most of you, though, it will be a torturous time. Nevertheless, some sort of decision must be made and this chapter will help you make the right one.

Note: A common scenario is one in which an aging parent is discharged from a hospital and now requires long-term care. This gives you very little time to select an appropriate facility. For most people, this need for long-term care should not come as a complete surprise. Therefore, we urge you to start thinking about an appropriate facility before this occurs. An appropriate time to begin a search may be when you begin to see your parent requiring assistance with daily activities.

Day by day, or more likely week by week, you'll notice changes in your parents. The daily routine of eating, sleeping, dressing, and even going to the bathroom will become just too much of a struggle, even if someone is there to assist them. The mechanical devices your parents have been using—canes, walkers, self-rising chairs, porto-potties, etc.—won't be enough. When they have their good days you'll feel optimistic, but they'll have setbacks and your hopeful attitude will wither.

Ideally, before you realize that your parents' part-time aide needs to be there full-time, you should seriously think about a permanent long-term-care situation. Most people don't until it's too late and are then thrown into turmoil, having to make a quick decision without the benefit of research.

More than likely, neither you nor your spouse, siblings, or anyone involved will want to discuss a long-term-care solution for your parents. The fact is, however, that you have very little choice, unless you have unlimited resources and unlimited time to manage the around-the-clock care your parent will need.

A nursing home is one of the options. But it's just *one of the options*. You need to investigate all the possible options, and that means learning as much as you can about your parents' condition, their needs, and their prognosis.

Nursing Homes Are Not the Only Solution

People often use the term "nursing home" in a generic sense, that is, to refer to all the different kinds of long-term-care arrangements. But there are many kinds of housing and living arrangements available for long-term care, and we'll describe them in this chapter. Before we begin, though, let's define what we mean by nursing home care so that we can dispel the myth that all long-term-care facilities are nursing homes.

Options/Levels of Care

Once you've made up your mind that your parent can no longer live at home (or your home), or

Definition: Nursing home care is a special kind of care and support for people who need long-term nursing care or help with daily living. It includes a variety of services: medical and twenty-four-hour nursing care; help with personal care, grooming, and getting around; social services; and recreational activities.

that adult day care and visiting help are not enough, you need to look at "long-term-care" facilities. You don't necessarily need to send your parent to a nursing home. You should consider what kinds of care and help are needed now and what kinds will be needed later. It may seem like a daunting task, but finding the right place *can* be done. Knowing your options and the levels of care available will make your decision easier. Also, keep in mind that there isn't just *one* right place. There are several places that will work well for your parent. You just have to be able to find one of them.

The housing arrangement you decide will be best suited to your parent will be determined, in part, by the degree of functional loss he or she is experiencing. When insurance companies determine whether or not a person is entitled to long-term insurance benefits, they frequently rely on an index of Activities of Daily

Living (ADLs) consisting of six functions: bathing, dressing, toileting, transferring (mobility), continence, and feeding (see table 9-1, "How Independent Is Your Parent?"). You can use the same definitions to judge your parent's degree of independence and the level of care needed. You might also take into account some other functions that, although they're not included in ADLs, research has shown are good predictors of the need for home care assistance, hospitalization, and institutionalization. These additional functions are: shopping, driving, preparing meals, cleaning house, managing medications, and managing personal finances.

Table 9-1: How Independent Is Your Parent?

An individual is judged to be independent in the activity if he or she successfully performs the functions without supervision, direction, or active assistance.

Independent	Dependent
Bathing: able to wash oneself in either a tub or a shower, including getting into and out of the tub or shower, or able to take a sponge bath without the aid of another person	*Bathing:* needs assistance in bathing more than one body part; not able to bathe self; needs assistance getting into and out of the tub or shower
Dressing: able to get clothes from the closet or drawers, put on clothes, and attach necessary braces or prostheses without the aid of another person	*Dressing:* not able to dress oneself or only able to partly dress oneself
Toileting: able to get to and from the toilet, get on and off the toilet, and perform associated hygiene without the aid of another person	*Toileting:* unable to get to and from the toilet, get on and off the toilet, or perform associated hygiene by oneself
Eating: able to feed oneself by any means without the aid of another person	*Eating:* requires feeding by another person
Mobility: able to walk, with or without the assistance of a mechanical device such as a wheelchair, braces, walker, cane, or other walking aid and move between bed and chair without the aid of another person	*Mobility:* requires the aid of another person in walking, with or without the assistance of a mechanical device, and in moving between bed and chair
Managing Medications: able to take medications in the prescribed amounts and at the prescribed times without the aid of another person	*Managing Medications:* requires the aid of another person in taking medications in the prescribed amounts and at the prescribed times
Meal Preparation: able to prepare complete, well-balanced meals without the aid of another person	*Meal Preparation:* requires the aid of another person in preparing complete, well-balanced meals
Housekeeping: able to do all routine housework, such as washing dishes or removing garbage, without the aid of another person	*Housekeeping:* requires the aid of another person (not including a maid) in doing all routine housework

Long-Term-Care Options

Assisted-Living Facilities

- ◆ Boarding houses
- ◆ Residential-care facilities
- ◆ Continuing-care community centers
- ◆ Mental health care facilities

Nursing Homes/Full-care Facilities

- ◆ Level 1 Nursing Facilities
- ◆ Level 2 Skilled Nursing Facilities

Note that continence, one of the ADLs, is not necessarily a measure of a person's need for long-term care, particularly since the availability of Depends and similar products.

The degree of independence your parents demonstrate and the level of care they need will determine what sort of long-term-care facility will be best suited for them.

Assisted-Living Facilities

Boarding Houses

These are unlicensed and unregulated homes that house elderly people. The situation is similar to your parent's living in your home or sharing a home with a bunch of roommates. The "staff" will usually provide some assistance in daily living (group meals, housekeeping, and social/recreational activities) and other services for an additional fee. There is no skilled or unskilled nursing care, coordination of services, medication maintenance, or health monitoring (except that when residents don't show up for a meal, someone will usually look in on them). These homes don't have to adhere to the same stringent fire safety rules that nursing homes do. We recommend that you *stay away* from these boarding houses unless cost forces you to consider them. If you do decide to have your parent live in one, monitor the house closely and often. Take nothing for granted. Visit at random times and spell out your concerns in writing.

Residential-Care Facilities

These facilities are similar to what you think of as a nursing home, but the focus is on the residents' social needs, not their medical needs. They also don't offer skilled nursing care. They're usually state licensed and provide:

- twenty-four-hour oversight
- shelter
- dietary services (three meals a day in a group dining room)
- housekeeping and maintenance services
- medical monitoring
- medication administration
- transportation
- coordination of services that promote quality of life (social services, therapy, etc.)
- social, recreational, and spiritual opportunities (including exercise)

What You See When You Walk Around: Most residents are alert, mobile, and in relatively good health; speak with each other and staff; have visitors on a regular basis; talk on the phone with friends and family; play cards and board games; participate in arts and crafts; go on field trips; and watch TV regularly (in the common room as much as or more often than in their own room). The primary role of the staff is to ensure that residents remain active. At the best places they take special care to make sure that residents are happy and healthy and that families and physicians are notified of problems as needed. These places also take residents on as many field trips (often just to the local mall) as is feasible.

Continuing-Care Community Centers

These centers provide help with daily living activities to residents in private housing units. Often semiskilled assistance is available on a limited basis. When skilled care or professional services are needed, residents must go to a hospital, infirmary, or have a visiting caregiver.

What You See When You Walk Around: Most residents are alert and mobile, though often with walkers or even wheelchairs; speak with each other and staff; have visitors on a regular basis; talk on the phone with friends and family; participate in activities; go on field trips; and watch TV regularly (in their own rooms more often than in a common room). The primary role of staff is to ensure that residents remain functional.

Mental Health Care Facilities

These facilities provide psycho-social services with therapeutic intervention and remedial education. They differ in the kinds services offered: some have close monitoring while some have little. They're licensed facilities (or at least the therapist is licensed) that offer group support and activities, basic living assistance as needed (meals, housekeeping, etc.), and some social and recreational activities. The staff will monitor the residents' medical conditions but cannot provide medicine maintenance or any skilled or semiskilled nursing care. These facilities can be helpful for a parent undergoing high degrees of mental disability such as severe depression, even in the short term. The facility is not appropriate for residents with Alzheimer's or a pathological disorder.

Nursing Homes/Full-Care Facilities

Level 1 Nursing Facilities

These are licensed nursing homes that provide skilled nursing, rehabilitative, and health-related services. Nursing care is available twenty-four hours a day with an RN always available, though not necessarily on the floor. The emphasis in these homes is on maintaining a practical level of functioning. Services include:

1. Medical, Nursing, and Rehabilitative Care

   ◆ assessment by a physician who visits periodically (usually at least once a month unless more frequent visits are judged to be medically necessary) and is either on staff or on call

   ◆ treatment, injections, and coordination of health care by RNs

- service coordination (physical therapy, occupational therapy, speech therapy)
- dietary consultation and special diets
- dental, laboratory, and X-ray services
- pharmaceutical dispensary
- medicine administration

2. Personal Care and Residential Services

- help with walking, getting in and out of bed, dressing, and eating
- bathing and assistance with toileting
- preparation of special diets as prescribed
- general supervision of environment and health condition
- social activities
- transportation coordination
- housekeeping and maintenance
- laundry and linen service

What You See When You Walk Around: Most residents are relatively alert, but their condition could be called failing. They're mobile, either in wheelchairs or with the use of walkers; speak with the staff often but not so much to each other; often have hearing and/or sight disabilities that make communication difficult; have visitors on an irregular basis; talk on the phone with friends and family periodically; participate in activities in a common room; eat most of their meals in the common dining room; go on field trips on good days; and watch TV a great deal of the time (almost always in their own rooms and at very loud levels). The primary role of staff is to ensure that residents remain functional. They monitor residents' health and generally attempt some rehabilitation or improvement.

Level 2 Skilled Nursing Facilities

These homes provide all the services listed above but with increased emphasis on rehabilitative therapies for convalescent patients. These facilities are eligible to participate in Medicare and may also provide subacute care. Beyond that level of care, residents must be taken to a hospital.

What You See When You Walk Around: Most residents are not very alert and not mobile except with a wheelchair or walker; may be hooked up to IVs; speak pretty much only with the staff; often have hearing and/or sight disabilities that make communication difficult; have infrequent visitors, usually just family; will talk on the phone with friends and family but pretty much only receive incoming calls; rarely if ever participate in activities; don't go on field trips; and the TV is on almost all the time (at very loud levels, and they may or may not watch or pay attention). The primary role of staff is to ensure that residents are comfortable, clean, fed, and free of disease.

This is the level of nursing home one often sees pictured in movies and discussed in conversation. The best ones do everything they can to preserve the dignity of the residents. They offer the level of care just short of hospital care, which, for many people, is just on the other side of that fine line separating the two.

Ten Steps to Choosing the Right Living Arrangement

1. Determine the kind of care that's needed
2. Decide how far away the home should be
3. Identify potential homes
4. Decide how much you can afford and eliminate those that are too expensive
5. Telephone the homes on your list
6. Visit as many homes as you can
7. Narrow down the list to three to five homes
8. Equate the services so you can make appropriate comparisons
9. Revisit the top choices
10. Make your final choice and set up the arrangements

Step 1: Determine the Kind of Care That's Needed

The first step in choosing the right housing arrangement is identifying the kind of care your aging parent needs now, and what kind of care you anticipate he or she will need in the foreseeable future. You should discuss this with your parent's personal physician, any specialists your parent has been seeing, a social worker, visiting nurse, aide, physical therapist, and any other professional currently assisting your parent. You may even talk with your friends, but remember that everyone is different. Your neighbor's mother who had Alzheimer's when she was just sixty-five and was otherwise in perfect health had needs very different from your widowed father who is extraordinarily alert but has adult-onset diabetes and never learned to boil water by himself.

Step 2: Decide How Far Away the Home Should Be

There are thousands of nursing homes in this country. Obviously, most of them will be inappropriate simply because they're too far away. You have to draw the line somewhere so you must consider your own convenience. It will be hard enough to continue to visit, or to get your children, spouse, siblings, or your parent's friends to go, without making it totally inconvenient for everyone. While you won't want to compromise the quality of the home, proximity will be a critical element in making the right choice. If your parent lives nearby, you can get a map and draw a circle around your home, trying to limit the commute to less than half an hour. Given the kind of mobile society we live in, however, it's more than likely that you don't live anywhere near where your parent has lived for the last several years. So you'll have to make your first decision here: Does your parent move into a home near where *he or she* lives (so friends can visit), near where *you* live, or near where the bulk of the relatives live? You can probably rule out the first option since for most residents of nursing homes, friends are not the primary visitors. The choice between near you or near the other relatives is based on who will carry the prime load in decision-making and care (see chapter 2, "Tough Talk").

Step 3: Identify Potential Homes

This exercise is the easiest. You're not eliminating any yet (other than by location from step 2), you're just putting together a list of possible places. You can develop this list using the phone book (your public library will have phone books from other localities), talking with your parent's doctor(s), social workers, other professionals, friends, neighbors, etc. You can contact the state affiliate of the American Health Care Association (see appendix B), the state or local office on aging (see appendix A), the American Association of Homes for the Aging (901 "E" Street NW, Suite 500, Washington, DC 20004), or even your church or temple. Write down the name, address, and phone number of the home; who, if anyone, referred you to it; and any comments that person made about it. You might want to put the list on your computer so you can continue to add relevant comments easily.

Step 4: Decide How Much You Can Afford and Eliminate Those That Are Too Expensive

The next step is to evaluate the cost and whether you and/or your parents are able to manage it. The reality is, many nursing homes will be out of the realm of financial possibility. Remember that not all homes accept Medicaid patients, so if you're planning on having Medicaid pay for the home, you need to know right away whether the home accepts it or not. Also, Medicare won't pay for the bulk of the costs, only the medical costs incurred. If your parent has private long-term-care insurance, you'll also have to take that into consideration when calculating how much you can afford. Sit down and figure out how much your parent has in income and assets, how much you and the other responsible parties can contribute, and how much your parent's insurance, including Medicare and Medicaid, will contribute (see chapters 5, "I Got You Covered," and 11, "You Don't Have to Go Broke," about insurance and advice on paying).

Step 5: Telephone the Homes on Your List

Call all the homes on the list. Talk to the administrator, head nurse, and/or social worker, if they're available, and discuss your parent's needs. Find out about the levels of care available, what happens when your parent needs more (or less) care, and the basics about the facility. Chances are, the person you talk with will provide you with quite a lot of the important information without your even asking. But be sure you at least find out:

- ◆ whether it's state licensed
- ◆ whether it's certified for Medicare/Medicaid coverage (even if you won't be relying on it)
- ◆ the kinds of care available
- ◆ the kinds of special services available
- ◆ whether your parent's current physician is allowed to be the physician of record
- ◆ the size and number of residents
- ◆ the number of staff
- ◆ whether there's a dietitian on staff for special diets
- ◆ the basic costs (private, semiprivate, and four-person room)
- ◆ the costs of extras (for incontinence, laundry, etc.)
- ◆ buy-in costs and deposits required

After you've described your parent's condition, ask the administrator, head nurse, and/or social worker whether they feel the home is an appropriate place. If so, ask them to send you material for you to evaluate. Ask them to include: brochures, a list of residents' rights, a sample newsletter or weekly activities sheet, and recent sample menus for at least two consecutive weeks to make sure they don't keep repeating the exact same menu.

Step 6: Visit as Many Homes as You Can

This will likely be an emotionally draining experience and so you should not bring your aging parent along for the time being (you can bring him or her along for the final choice if you want). For this visit you should bring along at least one of the other responsible parties—your parent's spouse, your spouse, your sibling, etc. Before you visit, set up a time for a tour and meeting with the administrator, the head nurse, and the social worker.

It's a good idea to start with one of the homes that's *not* at the top of your list. As with any interview, you need to warm up a bit and get some experience. But don't waste your time visiting a home that you know won't be a possibility.

You should also make copies of the questions you'll want to ask or be able to answer yourself after the tour. A complete list of questions appears in appendix H. While you don't have to have every one of them answered at this point, be certain you ask the ones that you feel are most important

Step 7: Narrow Down the List to Three to Five Homes

After each visit, sit down and write up your visit. This isn't a formal report, but it should convey the key points you saw and, most important, your impressions. It's both a subjective and an objective report (hopefully, the checklist of questions will provide the objective answers; the subjective part can just be free association).

After you've visited all the ones on your list, start narrowing. First, eliminate those that are really easy to eliminate (too expensive, too far away, disgusting, etc.). Include those that are really easy to include. If you're down to three to five possible places, then you've accomplished step 7. If not, start whittling away at the list until you get to just three to five.

Step 8: Equate the Services So You Can Make Appropriate Comparisons

You want to equate the same services and costs at different homes so you can narrow the list down to, at most, two or three possible homes. You'll have to identify the arrangements your parent will need, determine whether all the services are available, and at what cost. Then you can make objective and subjective measures on each of the homes on your list. Since your aging parent may come along for the second visit, you don't want to have more than two or three places.

One way to narrow down your list is to talk about your three to five possible places with others.

If you can easily rank the homes, you're lucky. If not, make some hard choices and remember that any of your top choices will likely work out fine.

Step 9: Revisit the Top Choices

Go at a different time of day from the first visit. This time, you might bring along your aging parent if it's possible and practical. Bringing your parent along to participate in the final decision may help ease the transition. If there's strong resistance, it's not absolutely essential for your parent to be included in this visit. But we recommend that you ask. For this second visit, be sure to bring along any other key decision-makers. If you were not able to meet with the administrator or head nurse on the first visit, insist on doing so on this visit. If the administrator cannot accommodate you when you're considering the home, chances are that he or she won't be any more accessible when your parent is a resident and there's a problem.

Note: Be careful about anecdotal information. It reflects one person's experience, not necessarily the norm. On the other hand, more than one incident may indicate a problem.

When speaking with your parents, it's extremely important that you be firm with them that the decision of moving to one of these homes is *not* negotiable. The only question is, which one.

Step 10: Make Your Final Choice and Set Up the Arrangements

Call the administrator at the facility and say you've made the decision that your parent will move in there. Set up a date for the move, making certain (if possible) that the administrator, head nurse, social worker, and dietitian will be available to greet your parent and meet with you. Ask the administrator for any advice for moving in. If your parent needs to be transported to the facility by ambulance, arrange with the ambulance or transport company.

Then, inform all the people involved and make sure they're either in agreement or at least support your decision.

Who Makes the Big Decision: The Players

Deciding that your parent needs to be housed in a nursing home is an extremely difficult decision to make. In most families it's a group decision made by several key people. The following are the people who will participate in the big decision to send your aging parent to a nursing home and some suggestions for dealing with them.

Your Parent's Spouse: Usually the aging parent's spouse is the ultimate decision-maker, but not always. You may have to intervene, despite resistance. A spouse may feel that sending a husband or wife to a nursing home is abandonment and that it's selfish to do so. In that case the decision may be made long after it should have been. Second, the spouse may not be able to listen to or understand what the doctors and other trained professionals are saying. You may have to interpret technical jargon or be a reality check to the spouse who has difficulty admitting that professional help is needed. Since the spouse is usually also your parent, you'll have to be conscious of the parent-child roles that have developed over the years.

You: You are obviously one of the major players—but you're not the only one. Deciding to place a parent in a nursing home should, if possible, be a group decision, so it's wise to seek consensus among the other family members.

Your Sibling(s): Depending on the arrangements you've made (see chapter 2, "Tough Talk"), your siblings are also key players. Try to reach consensus.

Your Spouse: Traditionally, a daughter, rather than a son, takes on the primary caregiving role. After her, it's often a daughter-in-law who assumes the responsibility, even before a son. So for many women, your spouse may have a more secondary role in dealing with your parents than either your parent's spouse or your siblings. However, depending on the arrangements you've made, and what responsibilities your spouse has taken on, he or she could have significant involvement in the decision.

Your Parent's Siblings: While your aging parent's siblings may have been inseparable for more than sixty or seventy years, ultimately they're not the decision-makers. They won't be the ones taking care of your parent on a daily basis, hiring professionals to assist, making sure that they show up, or handling finances. Also, like your aging parent's spouse, they'll be saddled with guilt over their abandonment and terrified that their time, too, will be coming.

Your Parent's Doctors: Their advice will likely carry a great deal of weight with you and the other participants in the decision-making. After all, your parent's medical condition is probably the most critical factor in the decision. You should also be aware that your parent's doctors may be the key to getting your parent into the right nursing home and providing assistance in financing the expense. If your parent is given the "right" diagnosis, your parent's insurance (including Medicare and Medicaid) will cover all or part of the cost. With the "wrong" diagnosis, insurance covers little or nothing.

Trained Professionals: By the time you face the decision to place your aging parent in a long-term-care arrangement, your parent will likely have been involved with many trained professionals. These include therapists, nurses, lawyers, social workers, gerontologists, and aides. No matter what they tell you, they're not the decision-makers. At the same time, their input is invaluable to you and the other decision-maker(s)—in particular, their knowledge of your parent's current condition and prognosis for the future.

Your Friends: Your friends will be most concerned about you, not your aging parent. They love you, and sharing with them the struggles you're going through will bring you closer. You may even find out that they've been there. If they offer advice, it will be for what they perceive is in your best interest. Having someone on your side will help you get through this difficult time.

Support Groups: See "Your Friends," above.

In the next chapter you'll learn about what it's like in a nursing home. We'll dispel some of the myths and legends about them, talk about residents' rights, discuss ways you can ease your parent's transition to a nursing home, and give you guidance on what you can and should do when you visit. Then in chapter 11, "You Don't Have to Go Broke," we'll discuss specific methods of paying for the nursing home or assisted-living facility.

UGH, I HATE GOING THERE

The title of this chapter expresses something that many people feel, at some point at least, when their parent or grandparent is in a nursing home. We all have preconceived notions of what these homes are like, despite what we may have read in the previous chapter or in other books. But, in fact, the range of long-term-care facilities—which we'll collectively call nursing homes to make it simpler—will vary enormously.

There'll be those homes in which you feel depressed just walking through the front door and where there's a distinct, unpleasant odor throughout the building. More often than not, these are the Level 2 Skilled Nursing Care homes that house severely ill patients, most of whom are bedridden, not very alert, and hooked up to IVs.

But not all Level 2 Skilled Nursing Care homes are depressing and, certainly, not all have that distasteful odor. There are, indeed, many that make life for the residents as good as it possibly can be. Keep in mind, however, that many of the people who live in these homes are severely disabled. You're probably not going to find it joyful going to any Level 2 Skilled Nursing Care home, even an attractive one. This is particularly true early on when you haven't had much experience with nursing homes. None of us wants to picture our loved one so ill and needing to be placed in a home. Again, many of these Level 2 Skilled Nursing Care homes cater to those who are just short of needing hospital or hospice care.

When your parent is living in a long-term-care facility, you'll likely be spending a great deal of time visiting. In this chapter we'll talk about how to ease the transition into a nursing home (including dispelling some of the myths), some of the specific things you can do when you visit, things you should look for to make sure that your parent is being cared for properly, and ideas for you to pass the time pleasantly so that you don't always feel *"ugh, I hate going there."*

What Do the Residents Feel?

First, let's explain a little about what many people feel about nursing homes. Some of these comments are sheer myths. Some, sadly, have a bit of truth to them.

How People Feel About Nursing Homes

1. Once I go there, I'll die there.

2. I'd rather die than have to go into a nursing home.

3. I'll go broke paying for a nursing home.

4. After I go broke from paying for the home, I'll be on welfare and left to rot.

5. I'll never see anyone anymore; people won't visit me.

6. They'll drug me so I won't know what I'm doing.

7. They'll steal everything from me.

8. I'll starve because the food will be so terrible.

9. Nursing homes are gross—they all smell from urine and death.

10. They'll tie me up so I can't move.

Dispelling Some of the Myths

1. Since Level 2 Skilled Nursing Care homes cater to the severely ill, many of those who enter leave only to go to the hospital. And while some residents die in a nursing home (less than 5 percent, according to the American Health Care Association), most die after they've been taken to a hospital. But the point is, few nursing home residents ever return "home." So there's some truth to the statement "Once I go there, I'll die there."

2. The statement "I'd rather die" is based on the notion that nursing homes are disgusting places. Again, there is some truth in that. Nursing homes are for those who cannot care for themselves. It's depressing, and many of us do feel that we'd rather die than suffer the indignities of being totally dependent for our most basic bodily functions.

3. Nursing home care (not to mention in-home care, medical care, and all other care) is extraordinarily expensive. Unless your parents have long-term-care insurance or are taking other steps to preserve their capital, their assets will either be diminished or depleted.

4. Once their assets are depleted, your parents qualify for Medicaid, which is, indeed, "welfare." However, being on public assistance doesn't mean being left to rot. People are only left to rot when their family and friends do so, not because of the nursing home staff. The fact that you're reading this book is assurance to your parents that they won't be left alone.

5. Sadly, as time goes by, visitors to nursing homes become fewer and fewer. The fact is, many of your parents' friends can no longer get there, are ill themselves, or have died. There's no indication that family visits drop significantly, except as normal activities and obligations come up for families. Then again, ask yourself how many visitors your parents get now, when they're not in a nursing home!

6. Many older people are on several medications. Some are very strong medicines. Some are tranquilizers, pain relievers, sleeping pills, or mood changers. And some may have side effects or a combined effect that leaves the patient "a bit out of it." But everyone, including residents of nursing homes, has the right to know what medications are being prescribed. Your parent also have the right to refuse any medications, unless he or she is declared "incompetent" (see chapter 4, "Blind Justice"). If your parent is "out of it" all the time, check with the doctor to make sure that the proper and appropriate medications are being prescribed.

7. Again, sadly, crime does occur in nursing homes. But it's the exception not the rule. Many residents complain about losing various things or being robbed. Often those things are misplaced or lost (we know of a case when a ring fell off in the bath, went straight down the drain, and was never recovered). As a precaution, residents should have no valuables and as little cash as is necessary.

8. Institutional food is rarely "as good as Mom's cooking." And sometimes what's served in nursing homes is pretty bad. Nursing home food is almost always bland, which, for

many, is tasteless. Salt and other spices are not used to any extent, since most older folks can't tolerate spiciness. Also, your parent may have been placed on a restricted diet with limited salt, fat, or sugar (the things that taste good). Furthermore, there's also very little "snacking" and almost no drinking. So the parent used to raiding the refrigerator or pantry, or having a nightly cocktail, will likely feel deprived, though many homes allow a glass of wine before and during dinner. If your parent has a particular request, be sure you talk with the dietitian. More important, if after some time your parent is losing weight, be certain that you discuss the problem with the administrator. It's unlikely that the weight loss will be from not liking the food. It's more likely to be caused by illness, depression, or inability to handle the utensils.

9. Most nursing homes don't smell. If nothing else, the strong cleaning products will mask any unpleasant smell (you'll want to avoid one that does smell all the time since that will indicate that it's not being cleaned as often as necessary). The truth is, many nursing home residents are incontinent. But if the home and resident are cleaned promptly, there should be no lingering odor.

10. Some residents are indeed strapped to a bed, chair, or wheelchair. Those with paralysis, often from a stroke, may be tied in so that they don't fall or so they can be propped up. If restraints are used in bed, they're most likely there to protect the resident from falling out. If a resident is restrained, it must be on a physician's order. Furthermore, restrained residents must be moved at least every two hours and should be checked on much more frequently. If your parent is being restrained for no apparent reason, is uncomfortable with the restraint, or is not being checked on as often as necessary, make sure that you talk with the administrator, doctor, or nurse.

Easing the Transition

Since many people feel (or at least say) they'd "rather die than go to a nursing home," making the transition to a nursing home would seem like a Herculean task. In actuality, while it's not easy, it's also not as difficult as you'd imagine. Yes, your parents are likely to feel angry with you and any others who contributed to the decision. But it's also possible that they'll have a sense that around-the-clock care is a necessity for them and will feel a sense of relief knowing that they'll be taken care of properly. And while you may feel guilty about making the decision, especially if you're one of the many who promised you'd never place your parents in a nursing home, you can rest easier knowing that the decision was made after careful thought and a great deal of research.

If your parents have lived with you in your home, you and your family may feel sadness at the loss of their daily presence. Visiting a nursing home, no matter how conveniently located, will not replace the everyday contact you had. On the other hand, the great relief of having the enormous burden you've shouldered finally lifted somewhat could make visits easier and your relationship closer.

What to Expect from the Nursing Home

Even after all the hard work and deliberation that went into deciding the right home in which to place your parent, your work has not ended. You must remain diligent in order to preserve the quality of your parent's existence at the home. Whenever you visit you must keep a sharp eye so that the standards you expect are maintained. If you're some distance away and can visit only sporadically, you'll have to rely on telephone conversations with your parent, the nursing home staff, and friends and relatives who visit.

Suggestion: It's a good idea periodically to call or visit various members of the nursing home staff to get their perspective on how your parent is doing. You'll get an update from them and also have the chance to air some of your concerns.

Quality and Commitment

You selected this particular facility because you felt that it was a quality operation. Now you'll want to make sure that the management and staff continue to honor their commitment to quality service. Naturally, there will be some problems that come up—a surly staff member, a lost item or two, your parent's complaint that no one comes after ringing the call button, etc. You should expect these and try to keep them in perspective. When too many problems surface, or when the same problem occurs several times, you should have a talk with the administrator (that's one reason why it's a good idea to have periodic meetings with the management). For the most part, and in most nursing homes, the management is committed to good service. The same can be said of most staff members, even the aides, many of whom are poorly paid. But problems do occur and you must keep on top of them.

Staff Turnover

A major problem in most long-term-care facilities is the turnover rate of the staff, in particular of the aides. That's to be expected, since the pay is low, often little more than minimum wage. Unfortunately, while the nurse's aides have the least responsibility in the home, they also have the most direct contact with your parent. How they treat your parent will affect his or her daily life greatly. Very often, your parent will talk about one of the aides in very endearing terms or, conversely, complain about one vehemently. Again, unfortunately, there's little you can do to stabilize the staff turnover. What you must do is make sure that you get to know the aides who have the primary responsibility for your parent and make sure that they know about your parent's particular idiosyncrasies and needs. When one of those aides leaves, you'll have to start all over with a new person.

Suggestion: Being extra nice to your parent's aides, befriending them, and even giving them little treats (not tipping, since it's usually prohibited, but letting them share the treats you bring your parent, for example) will prove to be an excellent investment.

Language Barriers

One problem worth emphasizing is the language barrier. Many aides are recent immigrants. Therefore, English may not be their native language (or their accent may be difficult for your parent to understand). Couple that with the fact that your parent's hearing may be failing and you wind up with communication problems. Again, the aides are the ones with the most direct contact, so communication is critical—not only to make your parent's quality of life better, but also because the aides need to be able to pick up on subtle clues that something serious may be happening. If there is a problem, explain to the aide that your parent is having trouble understanding her, and ask her to be extra careful. That should be sufficient. If the problem persists, make sure that the administrator knows.

Medical Care Availability

Every nursing home must have a physician on call at all times. In addition, there must be an RN available on-site (not necessarily on your parent's floor, but in the building). Your parent's personal physician, who may also be the facility doctor, must visit your parent at least once a month. If any of these are not the case, there's a problem and you should speak with the administrator. Many residents will claim that the doctor hasn't visited in months (or that the visit lasted thirty seconds, with no examination). Sometimes this can be true. But time and days are not visible in nursing homes. More than likely, the doctor did visit, and indeed may have spent what seemed like only seconds with your parent.

Suggestion: Physicians usually visit their patients in a nursing home on the same day each month. Find out what day that is and check in a day or two afterward to see what the doctor learned. Also, ask the doctor or nurse to mark on your parent's calendar when the visit occurred.

Recreational Activities

A major part of the services offered in nursing homes is recreational activities. When you selected this home you certainly looked over the activities schedule. You may also have spoken with the person in charge of this function. But offering activities doesn't mean that your parent is taking advantage of them, or that the facility is still offering them. On a regular basis, ask your parent which activities he or she attended. In addition, check with the activities coordinator periodically. You could find different stories about your parent's level of enjoyment. You may also find out that your parent wasn't able to attend because no one came to wheel her to the activities room. That's a problem that should not occur. If it does, make sure that you speak with the administrator.

Food

Many residents complain that the food is awful, even inedible. It will likely be bland—salt, sugar, fat, and spices are kept to a minimum, even for those who aren't on special restricted diets. Let's face it, nursing homes serve institutional food, not Mom's home cooking or culinary treats.

If your parent is mobile, you might want to take him or her out to a restaurant (or your home) periodically. You can also bring in some food and picnic on the grounds or in the common area.

Suggestion: Make sure that you visit around mealtime and can at least observe what's being served. You can usually have a meal too if you want, although many homes will charge your parent for guests.

Check with the staff to make sure that you know the rules and that you bring in or serve foods that will agree with your parent, which may not necessarily be what he or she wants. Also, after eating just this bland food for some time, your parent may not be able to tolerate what he or she may have enjoyed in the past. Keep the spices to a minimum.

Guidance

Another service you should expect from a nursing home is family guidance. There will likely be a social worker on staff, hopefully on-site as well. Furthermore, your parent's physician, the nurses, and the administrator are all professionals. They've studied gerontology and should be familiar with the issues you and your parent are facing. Take advantage of their expertise—for your parent as well as for yourself and your family. Ask all the questions you have. And expect answers. That's what they're there for, and that's what you're paying for.

On the other hand, you have to be realistic about how much guidance you can expect from the nursing home staff. Periodic counseling sessions may be available, both individually and in groups. When that's not enough, the social worker should recommend that you see other professionals. This is not a time to let pride stand in the way. The stress of being in a nursing home—or having a parent in a nursing home—is enormous. Getting answers from those with experience, and having a chance to talk through the difficulties with a professional, could be extremely beneficial for you and your family. Some families are literally torn apart when a parent is placed in a nursing home. Others are brought closer. How you and your family cope with this crisis may depend on the quality of your family communication, how much you can rely on others, and how much you take advantage of professional expertise.

Twenty Suggestions for Making the Transition to a Nursing Home Easier

1. Have your parent be a part of the decision-making process, or at least have a say about which home he or she will enter.

2. If your parents can visit prior to the decision's being made, bring them. If they cannot, describe the top choices in detail before a decision is made.

3. Make sure that your parent meets the administrator, admission director, head nurse, social worker, and activities director.

4. Talk to the administrator about what kind of roommate would be best suited for your parent.

5. Emphasize that the arrangement is not permanent—your parent is not being "committed." You'll continue to make sure that this is the right alternative, and if a switch or transfer is appropriate, you'll arrange it.

6. Reassure your parent that there will be many other residents at the facility with whom new friendships can be formed, many of whom will share interests and outlooks.

7. Reassure your parent that you and others will visit often, arrange to go places together, and, if possible, schedule times when your parent can visit your home.

8. Have your parent participate in packing for the move and be the one to decide what personal belongings should be brought along (try to bring as much as possible, at the same time being aware that space is probably quite limited).

9. On moving day, spend some time arranging the room, touring the facility, and meeting some of the staff and residents, especially the roommate. If possible, stay for a meal or activity.

10. Contact your parent's friends and relatives and ask them to write or call often, especially in the beginning.

11. Make certain that the staff and other residents do what they can to welcome the new resident (many homes have a resident welcoming committee).

12. Ask the resident social worker to monitor your parent's emotional progress.

13. Discuss with the staff your parent's routines (putting it in writing will be even better), such as preferred mealtimes, special diets (and preferred foods), bathing habits, bedtimes, time to be awakened, and religious preferences.

14. Discuss with the staff your parent's desires about privacy, knocking on the door before entering, etc.

15. Have a "going away" party or shower for your parent.

16. Buy a few small, appropriate gifts (see the discussion later in this chapter about what to bring).

17. Arrange to have the telephone and cable TV already hooked up before your parent arrives.

18. Become familiar with the procedures for taking your parent out (many homes require that you sign in and out).

19. Arrange to have the doctor pay a visit once your parent is settled.

20. Talk about how often you'll visit—and be prepared to keep your promises.

Roommates

In most nursing homes, two or more people share a room. For the first time in many years, except for short hospital stays, your parent will have a roommate other than a spouse. Think back to when you first met your college roommate, or a similar experience. More important, remember those anxious days before you first met. Now keep in mind that that's just one tiny piece of what your parent will be facing. In fact, given all the other emotions you and your parent are going through, the anxiety about a roommate may not even come up. Don't get fooled into thinking that because nothing is said there's no problem. Your parent's room-mate will be one of the most important people in his or her life in the nursing home. That's one of the reasons most nursing homes try to pay close attention to compatibility. They know that pairing the right people can make life considerably better both for the roommates and for the staff.

But also don't think that when your parent is about to enter the home, the management evaluates and examines the personali-ties, idiosyncrasies, and wishes of potential roommates. The fact is, usually your parent will be placed in the only bed that's available. Who the assigned room-mate is will be the luck of the draw. The only thing guaranteed will be that the two roommates will be of the same gender. Interests, states of mind, even physical conditions will not count unless there happens to be more than one bed available (already not a very common phenome-non and likely to be even rarer in the future). If the nursing home, or this particular floor or wing, caters to some of the most severely ill res-idents, your parent's roommate could be uncon-scious or significantly worse off physically. That will likely have a strong negative effect on your parent's state of mind.

Suggestion: One key to making your parent's stay in the nursing home as good as it can pos-sibly be is to move your parent when the right bed, with the right roommate, becomes available. Speak to the administrator and/ or social worker if you feel that a change is needed.

Family members can be an important cog in helping to strengthen the tie between room-mates. You should try to get to know the room-mate by taking an interest in what he or she has to say and trying to find common interests between the two. But the most important thing you can do is to reassure your parent that it will take some time to adjust to hav-ing this new person so close. Four to six weeks is typical. Try to get your parent to agree to that length of time before any change would be made. If you're lucky, things will work out and your par-ent and the roommate will find a way to at least coexist. Don't expect them to become friends. Friendships, as we think of them, are not that common in nursing homes for a variety of reasons (physical limitations like hearing loss, wanting to maintain pri-vacy, anger and depression, and wanting to distance yourself from all the "old people," to name a few).

Changing Levels of Care

Most nursing homes separate residents based on the level of care needed, either on different floors or in a different wing. This allows those residents who are mobile to see and interact with other residents easily. It also means that those residents requiring only semi-skilled care won't see those who are significantly worse off. Your parent will likely talk about those other people, expressing fear that it will happen to them too.

Suggestion: If you can afford to wait to make the decision to move, do so. It may cost you a few more days of paying for the home, but it may also keep more of your options available. Given how difficult it was to find the right home in the first place, you'll probably not want to have to go through the search again.

If your parent's condition worsens, he or she may have to be moved to the area for those needing a higher level of care, or if this particular home doesn't have multiple levels, to a new nursing home. Any move will be difficult for all of you. Moving to a totally new facility will be especially hard. That's one of the reasons that we strongly suggest choosing a home that offers multiple levels of care.

When your parent needs to be moved, he or she will usually have to give up the current room. In many ways it will be like starting over with a new roommate, new staff, etc. Review the list of "Twenty Suggestions for Making the Transition to a Nursing Home Easier" earlier in this chapter. In addition, all of you will have to face the fact that your parent's condition is deteriorating. Again, remind yourself, and your parent, that better care will be available.

While it's uncommon for a resident to move back to a lower level of care, it does happen. Despite the change, that kind of transition is obviously much easier. You'll still have to reconnect the phone, update the new aides, meet a new roommate, etc. But, of course, the psychological uplift will make all those tasks a lot easier.

In and Out of the Hospital

Many nursing home residents are taken to the hospital for extensive periods. One question that will come up is whether to keep the rights to your parent's nursing home room (and continue to pay for it), or to give it up and find a new room when your parent is discharged from the hospital.

Each circumstance is different. For short hospital stays, there's no question (unless it has become obvious that your parent will need to move to another facility anyway). For lengthy hospital stays, it's not as clear cut. Rooms in good facilities may already be difficult to find (and your parent may have paid a great deal of money to "buy in" to the home). As we all age, rooms will become even more scarce.

A second consideration is whether the hospital stay and nursing home expenses are paid for by insurance. Obviously, if it's paid for, it's best to keep your options open.

Third, you'll have to get good advice from the doctors about how long your parent will be in the hospital and the level of care your parent will need after being discharged. This can be somewhat of a guessing game, particularly early on. The longer your parent is in the hospital, the more obvious the choice will be.

Suggestion: If your parent doesn't have friends and family who can visit, you should speak with a local senior center or the Area Agency on Aging. Many communities have an extensive network of volunteers who visit residents of nursing homes on a regular basis. Some nursing homes have set up their own volunteer programs for residents who they see are visited infrequently. Speak to the social worker or administrator to see if the home has such a program.

Visiting

There are two kinds of visitors: those like you who have responsibility for caregiving and casual visitors who care but are not involved. As an involved visitor, one of the things you'll want to do is encourage the casual visitors to continue visiting, and, if possible, at regular intervals. That will take some of the burden off you and your family. It will also give your parent a great deal of encouragement. Regularly scheduled visits give your parent something to look forward to—a scheduled visit will probably be the highlight of your parent's day. Schedules also help to prevent a logjam or long periods of time with no visitors.

In most nursing homes there are distinct visiting hours and curfews. You shouldn't feel that you have to adhere to this tight schedule, particularly if your own schedule conflicts. You should also tell others who might visit that they should try to follow the schedule, but should not let limited hours stand in their way. If a particular friend or relative can only make it before or after visiting hours, let the administration know this so that no one will say or do anything to discourage the visitor.

Thirty Ways to Make the Most of Your Visit

If you live close to the nursing home, you'll likely be visiting often. If you're a long-distance caregiver, much of what we say here will be relevant. But you'll also have to rely on those close by. Here's a tip: You'll never visit often enough! That's true from both your parent's viewpoint and from your perspective as caregiver. The key will be to make every visit count. Here are some ways you can do that: things you should know about and suggestions of things to look for when you visit.

1. If possible, set up a regular visiting pattern. It gives your parent a sense of continuity in the timeless world of nursing homes. Even short visits (ten to fifteen minutes) are effective and worthwhile.

2. Regular visits are what your parent looks forward to—they're the highlights of his or her day. Most nursing home residents feel isolated from the outside world. It's the shared bond among residents. When they talk with each other, or with the staff, they usually talk about an upcoming visit or the people who just left.

3. In addition to your regular visit, try to stop in unexpectedly. Not only will this be welcomed by your parent, but it will also help you find out how your parent is being treated by the nursing home.

4. Visit at different times of the day and on different days. That way you'll meet all the aides who take care of your parent, not just the weekend or evening aides.

5. Mark all your visits on your parent's calendar (which you've given when he or she first entered the home). It will help your parent keep track of the days (again,

nursing homes are timeless) and prevent feelings of abandonment.

6. Whenever you visit, be as observant as possible. You'll have a lot to keep track of: your parent's health and state of mind, and also what's going on in the facility.

7. If you see, hear, or smell anything that doesn't seem right, tell someone about it and ask the administrator, head nurse, or social worker about it. On your next visit, look for it again. If the problem persists, you may have to find a long-term-care ombudsman through the Area Agency on Aging. If there's a consistent problem, notify the National Citizens Coalition for Nursing Home Reform, 1825 Connecticut Avenue NW, Washington, DC 20009.

8. Do a visual medical checkup of your parent's health. If you notice any of the following, notify the nurse or physician:

   ◆ weight loss

   ◆ changes in appetite

   ◆ sores around the mouth

   ◆ trouble chewing food

   ◆ dentures that don't fit

   ◆ eyeglasses that don't fit (do they fall off? are they your parent's? are they clean?)

   ◆ any bed sores, black and blue marks, or scratches

   ◆ bunions, ingrown toenails, and infections (don't cut your parent's nails, especially if he or she is a diabetic)

9. Do a visual inspection of how well your parent is groomed. How your parent looks will reflect the level of care in the nursing home. See that your parent's hair is clean and brushed, nails trimmed, makeup applied, and clothing clean and pressed.

10. Listen to your parent's complaints (and there are likely to be many). If you hear the same ones over and over, other than about the poor quality of food, follow up to see if there's really a problem. As for the food, well, there are some things you can do (like making sure your parent realizes that he or she can ask for something special or for seconds on dessert) and some things you can't do (like

changing the basic menu or the amount of salt used in the cooking).

11. Nurse's aides are the people who have the most contact with your parent. They're usually underpaid and often underappreciated. Praise and thanks will go a long way in making your parent's daily life a little better. In addition to taking care of your parent, many nurse's aides serve as caring listeners. Many nurse's aides are recent immigrants and English may be their second language. Make sure that your parent is able to understand the aide when he or she speaks.

12. The turnover rate of nurse's aides is usually pretty high. Nevertheless, you should expect some degree of continuity. If you meet a new aide on every visit, you should speak to the administrator. An unusually high turnover rate could be a sign of a serious problem in the home. It's certainly not good for your parent.

13. Not every visit will be pleasant. Your parent may be angry, hostile, or sullen, and there may not be anything you can do about it right away. Don't be discouraged. Many residents feel this way at times. If you continue to visit, at least your parent won't feel abandoned.

14. Every nursing home will have a resident's bill of rights. Read it and make sure that your parent's rights are being respected (appendix G lists the Nursing Home Resident's Bill of Rights that every nursing home must meet in order to participate in the Medicare or Medicaid program).

15. Most residents like to have their grandchildren or young nieces and nephews visit. Family is a great source of pride. On the other hand, children will likely get bored quickly, unless they can be kept busy with an activity or watching TV. Both the child and the resident feel a strong bond if they work on a project together or if the child provides a service for your parent. For example, a young child may be able to read to a resident whose eyesight is failing.

    Suggestion: Some nursing homes will let your young child sit in on a crafts class where the resident and your child can do something together.

16. Some nursing homes allow the family pet to visit with you. Check to see if this is possible, even if the pet must stay

outside. If your parent likes animals, check with the nursing home or the local animal shelter to see if they will set up a visitation program.

17. Touch your parent as often as possible. Residents report that the most rewarding visits are those that include a lot of touching. It relieves feelings of isolation, even for residents who don't appear to be affected. Touching also seems to lessen the anxiety felt by visitors who feel depressed about the quality of the visit.

18. Sit close to your parent. Being close physically increases the "contact" between two people. If you have to stand, touch your parent in some way: hold hands, squeeze a shoulder, pat a foot or back, etc.

19. If your parent sometimes gets confused, it's a good idea to introduce yourself when you first arrive by saying something like, "Hi, Mom, it's me, Bart" (be sure to say your name). If your parent cannot see well, it's even more important to say who you are. It may seem odd at first, but there have been many instances in which a parent in a nursing home wasn't absolutely sure who was visiting and was very embarrassed (and later depressed) to find out that it was a son or daughter. Avoid potential embarrassment by simply stating your name in context.

20. Bring a small gift every time you visit: a magazine, flower, toothbrush, book, etc. It will be a tangible reminder that you were there. These gifts should be small—there's very little room to put anything in your parent's nursing home room. If you're bringing food, make sure it's okay with your parent's doctor. Candy is usually *not* a good idea. Food is frequently shared, and there are many diabetics in nursing homes.

21. Label everything that's there. For clothing, use indelible markers or sewn-on name tags. On other items, write your parent's name using a marker. Rarely are things stolen. More often than not, things get misplaced, put away into storage closets, or are accidentally borrowed. One of the most lost items in a nursing home are dentures. So make sure they're labeled too.

22. Don't leave cash with your parent; there's no need since almost everything is paid for or billed. However, many

residents like to have some change or a few dollars around to make themselves feel more independent. And in some facilities there are vending machines available to residents.

23. If possible, take your parent out of the room. If your parent is mobile and/or you can manage to get him or her in and out of a car, short excursions are terrific for a resident's state of mind (reminder: wheelchairs and walkers are more easily stored in back seats than in trunks of cars). Malls make excellent destinations because there's a great deal of activity and a number of places to rest. But the trip can be just to a local drugstore or your home if nearby. If possible, take a picture of the excursion, which can be another reminder of the visit.

24. If you've taken your parent out of the home, be prepared to hear him or her say "I want to go home," meaning the nursing home. And don't be surprised if your parent nods off in your living room. Residents are used to very little activity, and going out, even to your home, can be a significant effort and will fatigue him or her quickly.

25. If you can't manage an excursion, try to visit with your parent in the designated visiting room. These rooms are set up to be warmer and more like a living room. If the weather is nice, sitting outside will make an excellent change of pace for both of you.

26. If you're coming from a long distance, set up a specific time to visit. This gives your parent the chance to look forward to the visit, prepare, spruce up, etc. It also ensures that your parent won't be taken for a bath or to the hairdresser when you arrive. And it means that you won't be interrupting your parent's favorite activity or TV show! These events become very important to residents. Interrupting them can lead to a less-than-satisfying visit.

27. At every visit, make sure that you speak with someone about your parent's progress or state of health. The conversation can last just a couple of minutes, or if there's something significant going on, a lot longer. Rotate the person you speak to: the administrator, social worker, head nurse, activities director, etc. The more often you speak with someone, the more you'll find out about the little things affecting your parent.

28. Take your parent out for lunch or dinner. If that's not possible or practical, bring in a catered meal or some special favorite dish. Make sure that the ingredients are appropriate for your parent. Heavy spices after a regimen of bland food can be disastrous. And salt, fat, and sugar may not be on your parent's diet.

29. Check that the furnishings of the home aren't deteriorating and are being updated periodically. Furniture that looks bad will make the atmosphere depressing. More important, it may indicate some neglect.

30. Check your parent's closet and drawers to make sure that everything is there. If there appear to be some clothes missing, ask about it. They may be in the laundry. But they also may be missing. The longer things are missing, the harder it will be to find them. Depending on how you and your parent feel about privacy, it may also be a good idea to rummage through things just to see what's going on. You may find pills that should have been taken, rotting candy bars, another resident's set of dentures or eyeglasses, checks that were sent to your parent but never cashed, etc.

Suggested Gifts for Residents of Nursing Homes

Bringing or sending small gifts is important. They serve as reminders of visits or contact. And they meet the resident's needs. Of course, many of the gifts you bring will depend somewhat on the activities your parent enjoys or can do alone. But here are some suggestions of things to bring or send:

Clothing

- ◆ housecoats that close in front and have pockets. Residents don't carry purses; pockets give them someplace to put things.

- ◆ leg warmers or a lap afghan. Most nursing home and hospital gowns are short.

- ◆ bobby socks and socks to sleep in.

- T-shirts (many men like to sleep in them), and you might label it or have it personalized with a silkscreen.

- lightweight shoes with Velcro fasteners. If your parent can't get to a shoe store, trace the outline of your parent's foot and bring it to the store. Inexpensive jogging shoes are excellent for nursing home residents—they're lightweight, flexible, provide good traction, and are stylish.

- a terry-cloth robe for the bath, which is often down the hall. Many residents are simply wrapped in a sheet when brought for a bath.

- pajamas or nightwear.

- a warm-up suit.

- a fanny pack to carry around small items.

Personal Items

- an extra blanket. Make sure it's washable and labeled clearly.

- wallets (but with no money). Men are used to carrying them and they can put pictures and business cards in them (your business card, for example).

- toiletry items (toothbrush, toothpaste, new comb or brush, powder puff, lipstick, baby wipes, etc.).

- massaging oil or lotion.

Entertainment Items

- letters from other people—even if your parent can't read them. You can read the letters aloud. Or later, when you're not around and your parent wants to look them over again, there's often someone around to ask. Correspondence is one of the treasures in a nursing home. Letters from grandchildren are especially appreciated.

- photos or clippings (though you may need to bring them home with you so they won't get lost).

- junk mail. As strange as it seems, many residents like junk mail since they don't get any themselves. Junk mail always makes interesting reading while watching TV.

- a magazine (old ones are perfectly okay). Women's magazines, *National Geographic,* and *Life* are very popular. Consider buying a gift subscription as a present.

- a large-print book. But try to make sure it's not too bulky. Many residents can't hold heavy books.

- a foreign newspaper, magazine, or phrase book

- a book on travel. This gives those residents who have traveled a chance to remind themselves of places. For those who have not traveled, it gives them a vicarious experience. Rarely does a travel book cause sadness about the inability to go anywhere. But you should keep an eye out for that.

- tapes or CDs. Again, be sure they're labeled clearly.

- a tape of a family gathering with children, grandchildren, and friends.

- a subscription to the hometown newspaper.

- board games and playing cards.

- jigsaw puzzles.

- greeting cards.

- a magnifying glass.

- a bird-identification book. Some homes also allow birds in cages.

For the Room

- a wall calendar. Numbers should be clearly visible. Get your parent to mark important dates on the calendar with a crayon. You can mark your visits together.

- a wall clock with large numerals. Watches are not good items because they're often lost (or stolen). Also, the numbers are usually hard to read. A desk clock is also not a good item to bring because of the limited space on the night table.

- cassette or CD player.

- framed photos of the family.

What to Talk About

Most visitors complain that there's nothing to talk about and the minutes seem like hours. Remember, not every moment needs to be filled with conversation. Shared silence can be effective in bringing people closer. Also, you're there to visit your parent, not the other way around. If your parent is uncomfortable with the silence, that's one thing. But many residents just like the idea that there's someone else around. They may be used to sitting in a chair with a spouse nearby and miss that feeling. They may like to watch a TV program with someone to have a similar, shared experience. Or they may want to do all the talking and have you serve as a passive listener.

Unless you have something specific you must discuss, let the topic of conversation be your parent's choice. Listen carefully and with a kind ear. Try not to argue, but never condescend. To repeat what was said early on in this book: Your parents are not your children, no matter how much you're taking care of them. Don't treat them like children.

Because many older people experience memory loss, a popular thing to talk about is the distant past. Talking about the past jogs your parent's memory and is fun. Together you can come up with a family tree or just a complete list of relatives. Take the time to have your parent describe the various people and tell an anecdote or two about each one.

Visits to nursing homes can be difficult and depressing. They can also be rewarding and beneficial. You'll probably experience both kinds of visits. The key will be to keep a watchful eye to make sure that your parent is being treated as well as possible and that the quality of your parent's life in the nursing home is as good as it can be.

In the next chapter we'll talk about ways for you to pay for your parent's nursing home care. We'll review some of the rules of Medicare, Medicaid, and long-term-care insurance. We'll talk about buy-ins, deposits, guaranteeing payment, and some of the extra charges that will appear on the bill.

YOU DON'T HAVE TO GO BROKE

If you or your parent think that nursing home care will be paid by medical insurance, you're in for a big surprise. Hopefully by now you've learned that Medicare won't pay for much—only that portion of the nursing home charge that is directly medical-related. And, of course, since Medicare doesn't pay, neither will your parent's Medigap insurance policies since they only cover the difference between what Medicare pays and what the doctor or other medical personnel charge.

You've also learned that Medicaid will pay, but only after most of your parent's resources are tapped out. And your parent will have to be in one of the nursing homes that accepts Medicaid patients (remember, not all do, and some impose a limit on the number of Medicaid patients they will accept).

But let's say for the sake of argument that your parent is one of the few who has purchased long-term-care and/or nursing-home-care insurance that we discussed in chapter 5, "I Got You Covered." You're both now assuming that the coverage will be enough. Again, you're in for a big surprise. The fact is, even long-term-care insurance in conjunction with Medicare and a private Medigap insurance policy doesn't cover the full costs of nursing homes. Sure, it will pay for a big chunk. But it won't cover the whole thing. And equally important, it's likely that with nursing home costs escalating so dramatically, insurance will cover a smaller and smaller percentage of the total cost. That's one reason why it's so important to have an inflation rider in any long-term-care (LTC) insurance policy.

In this chapter we'll talk about the costs of staying in a nursing home, and we'll review Medicare, Medigap, private long-term-care insurance, Medicaid, and "spending down" assets to qualify for Medicaid. We'll discuss the extra costs that insurance doesn't cover, including personal expenses and the extra cost of "dignity." We'll talk about down payments or buy-ins, guaranteeing payments, and payment plans. We'll mention a few sources of assistance that your parent may be eligible for and that will help pay the cost of nursing home care. Finally, we'll go over some of the main features of financial and estate planning that you and your parent need to keep in mind so that your parent's estate is preserved to the extent possible.

Who's Paying the Bill?

The person living in the nursing home is the resident, and therefore is responsible for all charges, even if Medicare or some long-term insurer will be assisting. While most homes handle billing of third parties, including Medicare and Medicaid, ultimately it's your parent who is held liable. So if for some reason the case is reviewed and Medicare decides that your parent is not eligible, or if the long-term-care insurance doesn't pay for any reason, your parent is responsible. That's one reason, of course, it's critical that your parent choose a reputable insurance company when selecting a long-term-care insurance policy.

If the nursing home charges will be paid by the resident, not Medicare, Medicaid, or LTC insurance, many nursing homes will require a guarantee from the family or a third party. Of course, if you're the guarantor in this case, you're then assuming responsibility in the event your parent cannot pay or if the LTC insurance is denied.

Often, cash flow is a problem with nursing home charges. It has been our experience that, within reason, nursing homes are understanding about short delays, as long as there's a history of on-time payment. Many homes realize that such large sums cause major difficulties for families and are willing to work out arrangements as needed. For example, a nursing home may charge a new resident a deposit equivalent to one month's room and board charges (similar to a rental deposit). Some of these homes may be willing to work out a payment arrangement in which the deposit is paid out over two or three months, rather than all up front. Also, if your parent is covered under an LTC insurance policy, there may be some delay in payment. Many homes will work with you so that they're paid on a timely basis without causing undue problems for you and your family. The key will be to keep the home informed about any problems you have.

There are some homes that will accept credit card payments, which, of course, allows you to defer your payments. As a rule, we strongly caution you about using this method since you'd be paying interest on the unpaid balance, and from the date the charge is posted. On the other hand, if you pay off your balance, you've had a few weeks' use of the funds for free. And you may have acquired a lot of "frequent flyer" miles.

The Costs . . . The Real Truth

According to the American Health Care Association, the *average* cost of a nursing home stay is about $30,000 to $35,000 per year (in 1996). The first thing to point out is that this figure from the AHCA is the average throughout the country, in both rural areas and in cities, for nursing homes that accept Medicaid and those that don't, and for all levels of care. And while that average includes the many homes that are excellent, it also includes those you wouldn't consider for your parent. The average cost, therefore, according to the AHCA, comes to about $75 per day.

Well, the real truth is, in larger metropolitan areas, and for the most complete level of care, that's just a bit over half of what the cost really is. For a bed in a semiprivate room in a skilled nursing home, either in or near a major city, the charge will more likely be about $120 to $140 per night. That comes to roughly $50,000 to $60,000 per year. And for some homes you may have to pay $75,000 per year or more. These are not the cream-of-the-crop, exclusive nursing homes. They're just good homes, in high-priced areas of the country, that offer complete service. Your parent won't have a suite for that price, just a normal semiprivate room.

What's Included

The basic per diem charge generally includes:

- ♦ a bed in a semiprivate room (with at least one roommate)
- ♦ three meals a day in the group dining room (including some special diet preparation, but no supplements)
- ♦ a snack or two during the day (maybe even a glass of wine if the resident wants and the doctor permits)
- ♦ complete skilled nursing service

- complete nurse's aide service (unskilled care)

- linen changes (but not if your parent is incontinent)

- weekly bathing (usually in a separate room, although some homes have showers in the guest rooms)

- in-house activities

- limited family and individual counseling with a social worker or trained specialist

And What's Not . . .

Note what is *not* included in the quoted cost:

- extra per diem charges for residents who are incontinent (usually $5 to $10 extra per day, just for the linen changes)

- special meals and snacks

- occupational, physical, and speech therapy (which may be reimbursed through Medicare or a private insurance program)

- podiatric care

- prescription drugs (which may be reimbursed through a private insurance program)

- nonprescription drugs, which will certainly *not* be reimbursed, and for which the nursing home will charge an extraordinarily high price (for example, one aspirin may cost close to $1 because a nurse must administer the aspirin—residents are not permitted to take any drugs themselves)

- other medical incidentals (for example, Band-Aids, like aspirins, will cost a lot and because your parent can't get to the drugstore, will be administered by a nurse)

- "diapers" for residents who are incontinent (the charges by the home are not as exorbitant as they are for other incidentals, but you can certainly save a great deal by purchasing your own disposables at the supermarket)

- telephone charges

- TV cable hookup and monthly fee (although in some homes that's included)

- optional activity fees for materials (for example, ceramics)

- optional activity fees for excursions outside the nursing home

- transportation to and from doctors' offices

- laundry and cleaning

- haircuts and styling

- eyeglasses (which, sadly, are often lost or broken in nursing homes)

- eye exams

- routine physical exams or checkups (which may or may not be covered by insurance)

- dentures and routine dental care

These extras, most of which will *not* be reimbursed by medical or prescription insurance, could add another $20 per day to the cost, or another $7,000 per year!

Level 1 Care

If your parent doesn't need Level 2 Skilled Nursing Care, there are many homes that offer less-skilled care, and at a lower price. (With Level 1 care, nursing care is available twenty-four hours a day and an RN is always available, though not necessarily on the floor.) It's possible, for example, that for a Level 1 nursing care bed, your parent may only have to pay $60 to $85 per night. That's a significant reduction.

Suggestion: When you're speaking with nursing home administrators about costs, be sure to ask what most residents pay, not just the basic per diem charge.

But at the same time, it's important that you and your parent be prepared in the event that skilled care is needed. Many homes may offer multiple levels of care, with residents moving from one floor or wing to another as greater or lesser care is required.

There are some homes that offer not only Level 1 and 2 care, but also day care, assisted-living, or residential care. Some homes require that residents start out at the lowest levels and, as the aging process takes its toll, move to higher care areas. Many of these homes also require that a resident "buy in," that is, purchase a space for a significant sum of money ($10,000 to $25,000 or more). In some places this is more like a deposit that's refunded when your parent moves to a higher level and his or her lower-level room is taken by another resident.

When you're investigating nursing homes, be sure to ask about the different levels of care offered and whether there's any difference in price.

Medicare

As we discussed earlier, nursing home coverage by Medicare is very limited. For the most part, if nursing home charges are covered at all, it will be under Part A, the hospital insurance part.

For a resident to qualify for any Medicare payments, first the home itself must meet certain requirements—namely, the home must be a skilled nursing facility that provides twenty-four-hour nursing care to post–acute care patients. The facility itself, then, will be considered "Medicare-certified."

Second, patients must meet certain requirements. And you should note that we now refer to residents as "patients," since Medicare only covers medically necessary expenses.

- ◆ A physician must certify that your parent requires skilled nursing care or skilled rehabilitation services, as defined by the federal government.

- ◆ A physician must certify that your parent requires this care *on a daily basis.*

- ◆ Your parent must have been in a hospital for at least three consecutive days.

- ◆ Your parent must be admitted to the nursing home within thirty days of discharge from the hospital following the three consecutive days.

- ◆ A physician must certify that the skilled care required is for *the same or a related illness* for which your parent was hospitalized.

Those are a lot of conditions and, you'll note, custodial care or chronic illnesses such as Alzheimer's disease or dementia are not covered—only acute illnesses and rehabilitative services.

Medicare Benefits

Even if all the conditions are met and your parent is covered, there are limits to the amount Medicare will pay and the services it will pay for:

1. Medicare will pay the costs for the first 20 days.

2. For days 21 through 100, Medicare will pay the costs *minus* a patient's co-payment, which is set each year (in 1997, this amount was $100 per day, which may even be more than some homes charge).

3. After the 100th day, Medicare will pay nothing.

Furthermore, Medicare will pay only for covered services, which include:

- ◆ expenses for a semiprivate room
- ◆ all meals
- ◆ nursing services
- ◆ rehabilitative services
- ◆ drugs furnished by the facility
- ◆ medical supplies
- ◆ medical appliances (wheelchairs, walkers, canes, etc.)

Medicare will not pay any of the other expenses associated with a nursing home (except Medicare Part B, which essentially covers medical expenses by doctors and therapists, as outlined in chapter 5, "I Got You Covered").

Medicaid

Medicaid is a joint program between the federal government and each state. The program is designed to assist low-income people with medical expenses. Since it's inception in the mid-1960s it has grown enormously and now pays the bills for over 40 percent of nursing home residents. Many people liken Medicaid to "welfare" since it's need-based, with very strict eligibility requirements, and is usually administered by the state's department of social services.

Suggestion: When you're looking at nursing homes for your parent, you should find out whether they accept Medicaid patients, even if your parent is not currently a recipient. If your parent eventually does apply for Medicaid, you'd want your parent to be able to stay in the same facility.

Individuals must apply to be eligible for Medicaid. And nursing homes must be "certified," which means that, like those homes certified for Medicare eligibility, they must meet a strict set of government standards. However, many nursing homes don't accept Medicaid patients since the reimbursement they receive is considerably less than the amount they charge full-pay residents. Some other nursing homes have a limit on the number of Medicaid patients they accept.

To qualify for Medicaid, your parent must essentially be impoverished. The maximum total income your parent receives cannot exceed the level set by the state, which is the official poverty level (the amount is different in each state, but it's usually less than about $15,000 per year). In addition, your parents cannot have any significant assets other than their house, household goods, and personal effects. The exact number is set by each state and is generally less than $60,000.

Medicaid Benefits

Medicaid pays all the required costs of nursing home care. However, the rate it pays is set by the state, not by the home. It covers only the required nursing care, room charges, and meals. No incidentals or options are covered, just as under Medicare. However, prescription drugs and dental work are covered. Furthermore, there are no co-payments required, nor are there any limits to the number of days Medicaid will pay benefits.

Spending Down Assets to Qualify for Medicaid

If your parents have assets greater than the maximum allowed under state regulations, it's possible to transfer these assets to someone else and thereby qualify for Medicaid. In fact, many people have done this and many more will do so. The benefit is obvious—thousands and thousands of dollars are at stake.

But there are several risks inherent in this practice that should be pointed out:

Note: Some nursing homes that don't usually accept Medicaid patients *will* accept them if they start out as full-pay residents but later become Medicaid-eligible. Make sure that you know the nursing home's policy if this is a possible situation for your parent.

- ◆ Regulations allow states to go back three years to determine whether your parent transferred assets to qualify for Medicaid. They can disqualify people for the three-year period, so early planning is a necessity.

- ◆ Funds transferred to another person belong to the transferee, not your parent. He or she loses control of the funds unless they're put into a trust.

- ◆ If the funds are put into a trust, the trust must be an irrevocable trust. Trusts also require using attorneys and filing income tax returns, and may involve gift taxes and estate taxes.

- ◆ Since funds transferred belong to the transferee, they're considered available to creditors in the event that there are judgments against the transferee.

- ◆ If the funds are transferred to you, you may have income tax, gift tax, and estate tax consequences.

- ◆ Finally, there's the moral concern that you're doing something to get around the very purpose of Medicaid. (Look at the irony: many of the same people who complain about paying taxes to subsidize welfare recipients because "they should be earning their own money" don't see that transferring assets to qualify for Medicaid is no more than white-collar welfare.)

Private Long-Term-Care Insurance

As we discussed in chapter 5, "I Got You Covered," long-term-care (LTC) insurance is a relatively new product offered by insurance companies, and the number of people purchasing these policies is growing rapidly. Currently, less than 5 percent of nursing home residents rely on LTC insurance to pay their nursing home expenses. But with about 40 percent of nursing home residents currently relying on their own funds (or the family's money) to pay the bills, the use of LTC insurance will likely grow in the next few years.

Most LTC policies don't concern themselves with what services are covered, like Medicare (which pays only for skilled nursing care). Rather, they simply pay whatever amount the policy calls for, since the policy is for both skilled and custodial care. The amount the insurance company pays is based on the premium charged, which in turn is based on:

Note: As the health insurance industry has changed, more and more people are covered under health maintenance organizations (HMOs) or managed-care programs. Most of these plans cover only medical expenses and skilled nursing care. They don't, as a rule, cover custodial care.

- ◆ the insured's age
- ◆ the insured's health at the time the policy is taken out
- ◆ the length of the waiting period
- ◆ the duration of benefits
- ◆ the kind of inflation factor built in
- ◆ the exclusions in the policy
- ◆ the maximum lifetime benefit
- ◆ the level of care offered (including whether Alzheimer's and other mental health conditions are covered)

In 1997, a lifetime benefit policy that paid about $100 per day for custodial care with a twenty-day deductible will cost a healthy sixty-five-year-old about $2,000 per year. For a healthy seventy-five-year-old, the premium for that same policy could run closer to $5,000 per year. The key for your parents will be to compare policies and insurance companies. They're not all the same and don't offer the same products or service. When considering an LTC insurance policy, be sure to look at all the factors outlined in chapter 5.

For information about which companies are offering products (and at what price), you can contact:

United Seniors Health Cooperative
1331 H Street NW, Suite 500
Washington, DC 20005
202-393-6222

Veterans' Benefits

Long-term care is available to veterans and their eligible dependents or survivors through facilities operated under the Department of Veterans Affairs. These facilities provide both skilled nursing care and custodial care for those veterans requiring services. For more information about these services, your parent should check with the local VA office.

Self-Pay

Currently, more than half the residents in nursing homes rely on their own funds, or their family's money, to pay their expenses. As we said above, this is likely to change for a number of reasons, among them:

- ◆ the expenses of nursing home care continue to skyrocket and fewer people will be able to afford it

- ◆ demographics: the number of senior citizens is growing

- ◆ people are living longer and therefore more are requiring both skilled and custodial care

- ◆ the insurance industry is offering more LTC products that people can rely on rather than using their own funds

Nevertheless, many people rely on their own money and many people will do so in the future. The key to making sure that your parents can afford long-term care when they need it is good estate planning. If your parents are planning to pay for their own long-term care (essentially, being "self-insured"), you and they should review chapters 4, "Blind Justice," and 6, "Show Me the Money." In particular, pay close attention to the section "Financial Planning 101" in chapter 6, which helps guide you through budgets, cash flow, and the use of assets. In addition, your parents should make sure that they speak with legal and financial advisors to ensure they take advantage of trusts and gifts. Finally, for those who will choose to remain self-insured, that is, who will use their own money to pay for their long-term care in a nursing home or in-home care, they should make absolutely certain that they take full advantage of the many free and low-cost services available to them as seniors, that they have adequate medical coverage, and that they keep close track of medical reimbursements.

For more information about paying for long-term care, you can call any of the following:

American Association of Retired Persons (AARP)
800-424-3410

American Association of Homes for the Aging
801-783-2242

Health Care Financing Administration
800-638-6833

National Association of Insurance Commissioners
816-842-3600

In the next chapter, "Facing the Inevitable," we'll talk about what you have to do after your parent dies, from making all the funeral arrangements through filing the final income tax return.

FACING THE INEVITABLE

In the natural order of life, children outlive their parents. At least that's what most of us hope will occur. And, naturally, we all hope that our parents live a long and fruitful life, that their last years are happy and productive, that they don't suffer too much as they approach death, and that they don't outlive their resources, which would likely diminish the quality of their lives.

The many things we've discussed throughout this book we hope will make it easier for you, as the survivors, to deal with seeing your parents get closer to that moment when they die. And, hopefully, everything you've done so far will have brought more quality to their aging years.

But what about after they die? How can you best ensure that their dying wishes are met? How can you make sure that everything that must be done is done, with as little impact as possible on you and the rest of the family, so that you can get on with your mourning and deal with your own grief?

In this chapter we'll discuss making the arrangements, dealing with a funeral service (or however your parents remains will be disposed of), the family dynamics you can expect (with some suggestions about how to limit infighting), the legal issues you'll have to face, and some financial considerations so that whatever estate is left goes to whomever your parents have designated.

Again, we emphasize that we are *not* offering legal or financial advice. Every situation is different—every family has its own dynamic. Therefore, we strongly suggest that you and your aging parent seek the advice of a trained professional so you can be certain that all the required forms are completed and that your parents' wishes are met.

We also strongly encourage you to look back at chapter 2, "Tough Talk," to make sure that your parents have completed a signed and legal will and that you know what your parents would like done with their remains. Having a will is just about the only way they can be sure that their wishes about their estate will be met. It's also one of the best ways to limit the amount of family infighting that could occur when certain possessions are divided up. If, for example, your parents told their niece that a piece of jewelry, a family heirloom, will go to her, but they didn't put it in their will, and you had expected that your daughter would get it, imagine the confusion and disappointment that will occur. Now multiply that confusion by the amount of stress all of you are experiencing as you first face life without your parent (especially if it's your last surviving parent). Is there any wonder that some of the worst fights in families center around relatively worthless pieces of family history?

A will can prevent much of the fighting—at least those fights that are about your parents' possessions.

A will can also have another important function, one that will affect you greatly right away. And this is that the will names the person who will handle the arrangements after your parent dies, the "executor" or "executrix." That person will be named by your parent in the will and will be given the responsibility of making sure that his or her wishes are met, to the extent that that's possible (and legal).

Decisions, Decisions

When a parent dies, there is an incredible number of decisions that must be made, often very quickly, before you've even had a chance to accept the fact that your parent is dead. Here are some of the first decisions that will have to be made, most of which are centered around a funeral or service and which must be made while you're grieving:

Important: What a will often does not do is talk about how the survivors are supposed to deal with the dead parent's remains. We suggest two things:

1. Have your parents clearly state in their will exactly what arrangements they have made (or would like made) about the disposal of their remains.

2. Make sure that your parents have told you and other key members of the family what arrangements they have made (or would like made) about the disposal of their remains.

◆ Who to notify that your parent has died

Note: As a general rule, you should probably call immediate family members personally. But don't feel that you must notify everyone yourself. It's common practice to ask people to make calls to others to make sure that they're notified.

◆ What to do with the remains of the body (embalming or cremation)

Note: Embalming is not required by law in every state. However, it may be necessary if death is due to certain diseases, if burial or cremation is not done within a pre-scribed period of time, if there is no refrigeration available, or if the body must be transported out of state or some distance. In addition, if the body will be viewed, the funeral director may require that it be embalmed.

◆ Whether an autopsy will be performed

Note: If a death is suspicious, the coroner or medical examiner may insist on conducting an autopsy. If that's the case, you have no choice but to comply. If the doctor recommends an autopsy for research or teaching purposes, you must give your permission. Autopsies can be quite disfiguring, so make sure that you're comfortable with your decision. For most older people, unless you must know the exact cause of death, an autopsy is unnecessary.

◆ Whether your parent's organs will be donated

Note: Most older people's organs are not accepted for donation, except by some eye banks and medical schools.

◆ What funeral home to use

Note: If you're trying to make the arrangements from out of town and don't know any of the "local" funeral homes, you can get a list from the National Funeral Directors Association by calling them at 414-541-2500. The association will merely provide a list, not a recommendation. To make sure that you're getting a reputable funeral director, ask a friend or relative who lives nearby to make a recommendation. You can also ask your parent's clergy for the name of the funeral home he or she recommends.

- How much to spend on the funeral

  Note: This is an extremely touchy subject. Read the section on funeral expenses later in this chapter.

- If a burial, what kind of casket

  Note: Don't be pressured into spending more than you can afford. See appendix I, "Funeral Directors Code of Ethics."

- What kind of vault and liner, if any

- In what clothes your parent will be dressed

- Whether to have the casket open or closed

- When to schedule "viewing" hours

- Whether to have a picture on display

- What kinds of flowers to have (and where to buy them and how much to spend)

- What kind of service to conduct (what prayers, readings, etc. will be included)

- Whether there will be music at the service (what songs or hymns, who will sing, and whether there will be any accompaniment)

- Who will officiate at a service

  Note: Usually this person is your or your parent's clergy. If there is no specific person, the funeral home director can make a recommendation.

  Important: If the person who will officiate did not know your parent, insist on talking to him or her beforehand so that the service can be personalized.

- Who will get to speak at the service (and for how long)

- Who is considered "immediate family" (this often gets touchy and leads to many hard feelings that linger years afterward)

  Suggestion: When in doubt, if a family member or close friend *wants* to be considered "immediate family," it's usually best to let that person be included, without making a fuss. There's little or no special privilege, which means little or no emotional or financial cost to the other immediate family members. On the other hand, the emotional cost of excluding the person could be significant later on.

◆ Whether to have a procession to the cemetery with a limousine

◆ Who gets to ride in the family limousine (see the discussion above, although in this instance space is likely to be a consideration)

◆ If a burial, which cemetery and which plot

Note: This is one of the items you should have learned from your conversation with your parent beforehand. If your parent already owns a plot, you'll simply need to notify the cemetery when the funeral will be held (the funeral home will probably do that for you). If your parent does not own a plot, you'll need to purchase one. Many families use one or two cemeteries that are nearby and, if there's space (and sufficient resources), you'll probably want to purchase a plot there. If not, get recommendations or visit a few.

◆ If a cremation, what to do with the ashes

Note: If you plan on spreading the ashes somewhere, make sure that it's legal to do so. Check with the local health authority to be sure.

◆ Whether there will be a graveside service (and, again, who will officiate and what kind of service)

◆ How soon to have the funeral

Note: Keep in mind that certain religions have specific "regulations" about when a funeral must be held (for example, Jewish law states that Jews usually must be buried within 24 hours). If your parent belonged to a religion with specific rules, you'll want to make sure that you're familiar with the rules.

Suggestion: If your parent is a member of a specific religion but does not necessarily adhere strictly to its laws while other close family members do, it's probably best to adhere to the law, to the extent that that's possible and practical. It won't matter much to your parent, but it could cause a problem with the other family members.

Because of distance and complicated arrangements that must be made very quickly, it's quite common that a very close family member will not able to get to where the funeral is being held until after the funeral is scheduled.

This could cause an incredible amount of pain and hurt for years, that could, perhaps, have been prevented. Use your best judgment, certainly. But if the funeral can be delayed so that the close family member can be there, we suggest doing so (unless a religious "law" would be broken and you or your parent would be greatly offended).

♦ Who gets to make the decisions about arrangements, cemetery, casket and liner, who officiates, etc.

♦ How many "official" death certificates will be ordered (you'll need official death certificates for most financial institutions; see the information about probate below)

♦ In what newspaper an obituary will be placed

Suggestion: Make certain that an obituary appears in the "old hometown" paper and any alumni or company magazine (your parents will probably have some old friends and colleagues who'd like to know, even if your parents haven't lived in that town or worked for the company in some time).

♦ What the obituary will say, who will write it (assuming your parent is not famous and, therefore, will have a professional journalist write it), and whether a photo will be included

Note: Most funeral homes will arrange for a standard obituary to be sent if you tell them which newspapers you want notified. It will be up to the newspaper whether the obituary is simply one of the listings or is given special attention. Smaller newspapers and alumni or company newsletters will likely want more information and, perhaps, interesting facts or anecdotes.

♦ Whether or not you prefer charitable contributions in lieu of flowers, and which organization(s) will be the preferred recipient(s)

♦ Whether there will be a gathering of family and friends after the funeral and/or graveside service, and if so, where

♦ Who will be invited, what will be served, and whether it will be catered, potluck, or hosted

♦ Whether there will be a grave marker (and what it will say, when it will be done, by what company, and whether there will be any kind of ceremony when the marker is erected)

Who's in Charge Here?

The determination of who's in charge could be a very obvious choice or it may be a touchy one. Each family situation will be different.

We suggest looking over that section of chapter 9, "For the Long Haul," that deals with who makes the key decision about placing your parent in a nursing home. The dynamics of making decisions about funeral arrangements are not too different from deciding about nursing homes: the same people are involved with the decisions, emotions are running high, you'll want to get some professional advice (although, clearly, not from the same people), and the same interactions will occur. The long-distance caregiver will still be as frustrated by an inability to be there for the smaller decisions, the primary caregiver (or executor) will be overwhelmed with the details and amount of work, everyone will have an opinion, there will be great pressure to make decisions quickly, and you'll feel as if you've constantly made the wrong decisions (you'll even feel responsible for the weather!). You're not alone. This is a tough time. Rely on your family and friends for guidance. And if you've chosen a reputable funeral home, you can rely on the funeral director for assistance and advice.

Here are five points to remember about making decisions regarding funeral arrangements:

1. A surviving spouse is the ultimate decision-maker, to the extent that he or she is able to carry out that function.

2. Try to be as accommodating as you can. With all the emotions everyone is feeling at this difficult time, it's easy to get locked into decisions and lose sight of the bigger picture. At the same time, if you feel strongly about something, don't hesitate to voice your opinion.

3. Try to accommodate what your parent would have wanted, but don't try to second guess yourself on everything— you're doing the best you can. If your parent had felt really strongly about something, he or she could have put that in writing or told you personally.

4. If you have the decision-making responsibility, don't be pressured by any "salesman" type to spend more on funeral arrangements than you're comfortable with. Professional funeral directors will not use high-pressure sales tactics. If they do, remind them of their Code of Ethics (see appendix I).

5. Remember to speak with the person officiating at the service beforehand, even if he or she knew your parent. If the person did not know your parent, you'll want to make sure that some personal information is included (it's not uncommon for a visiting clergy to refer to the deceased by the wrong name!).

Should Children Attend the Funeral?

In the olden days, children were exposed to death routinely. At a relatively young age they may have experienced the death of a sibling, friend, or parent. Or if they lived in a rural area they saw animals die or be slaughtered. Children in those days usually attended a funeral or service.

Suggestion: When deciding, consider not only the impact on the children themselves, but also on the others present (or those who might not be able to attend if their children were not permitted to do so).

In more modern times, children became more and more protected from death and, as a result, more families kept them away from funerals or services.

We may have come full circle since now, it seems, more and more children are attending funerals and wakes.

Whether you choose to have your young children attend your parent's funeral is a decision that you and your spouse must make yourselves. Keep in mind that you'll also have to decide whether to encourage or discourage other children in your family to attend your parent's funeral.

There are no "general rules" for these decisions. Most counselors suggest talking with the children, telling them as much as possible about what it will be like and what will go on, then letting them make their own decision about whether to attend.

Here are a few other suggestions:

- If you're concerned about whether a young child will be able to sit still for the entire service, plan on having the child attend only a part of it.

- Bring along a baby-sitter, or encourage others to bring a sitter, so that they or you don't have to leave early if the child gets restless and needs to leave.

- Bring along a favorite toy he or she can play with quietly.

- Bring some snacks to keep them occupied.

- Be extra careful about noise or disruption. It's already a very emotional time for people.

The Funeral Director Is Your Friend

Losing a loved one is tough, particularly when it's a parent. At a time when you're stricken with grief, all those decisions listed above must be made. Needless to say, you must rely on some people to help you through this difficult period.

One of those people is the funeral director. If you've chosen wisely, you should be able to rely upon him or her in several ways.

Ten Ways a Funeral Director Can Help You

The funeral director can:

1. arrange to have the body brought to the funeral home

2. get the proper authorities to sign and file a death certificate

3. give you guidance and information about how the remains should be disposed of, including helping you to decide what kind of funeral to have and where and when to have it

4. help you choose a casket or other burial container

5. help to organize the service if you choose to have one

6. arrange for transportation to and from the cemetery

7. take care of logistics on the day of the funeral

8. arrange for funeral and obituary notices to be sent to the newspapers and organizations you designate

9. file a claim form to the Social Security Administration

10. refer you or other grieving family members to professional counseling services

Paying for the Funeral

Funerals can be simple and low-cost or they can be extraordinarily lavish and you could have the Taj Mahal built or your parent's tomb guarded by thousands of terra-cotta warriors. It's up to you where in that continuum you want to be. Money is not something you especially want to deal with at this point, but, of course, you must.

Suggestion: Don't feel bad about shopping around for the best price or about negotiating. You can get prices from funeral homes over the phone or by mail or fax. Just be sure that all the costs are included so you can compare. Also, many people negotiate lower prices, so don't feel badly about doing so yourself. If you're not comfortable negotiating, ask another family member to help you out. You could save hundreds of dollars or more.

Many older people qualify for financial assistance to help defray the cost of a funeral. The Social Security Administration will pay a lump sum of $250 to the surviving spouse of a Social Security recipient. The spouse does not have to apply for this. Rather, a check will be sent once the Social Security Administration is notified of the death of the recipient (which is usually taken care of by the funeral director).

In addition, some union and employer pension funds, insurance policies, and fraternal or professional organizations in which your parent was a member will have funds available to help with funeral costs. You should be sure to notify these organizations to see if they offer financial assistance. They will usually require an official death certificate, which the funeral director can provide.

Table 12-1 shows the range of costs for various elements of a funeral, and Figure 12-1 is a sample itemized bill from a funeral home.

Prearranged Funerals

It's possible to prearrange a funeral (or the funeral of a spouse). Many older people do so for three reasons:

Table 12-1: Average Range of Funeral Costs

Item	Range
Professional services of funeral director	$800–$1,200
Casket (simple pine box to top of the line)[1]	$200–$4,000
Vaults and liners (if required by cemetery)	$400–$1,500
Cremation	$200–$300
Urns	$100–$1,000
Use of facilities for service	$200–$500
Embalming (not required in all states)	$300–$400
Other body preparation (dressing, makeup, etc.)[2]	$100–$200
Transporting the body to the funeral home	$100–$200
airline transport	variable
hearse	$100–$200

1. You can rent a fancy casket for viewing but have the burial in a less expensive casket.
2. Often included in other charges.
Source: National Funeral Directors Association.

1. to make certain that their wishes are carried out exactly

2. to make it easier on the survivors during a time of grief

3. so that they can prepay the costs and relieve any burden on the family

Prearranging a funeral can be appropriate for many people. However, some questions arise that you and your parents should consider, especially if your parents prepay:

1. What happens to the money if the funeral home goes bankrupt? (Chances are that your parents would be in a long line of creditors who would not get reimbursed the full amount paid.)

2. What happens to the money if your parents move to another town? Can they get a refund? Is there a penalty?

3. What happens to the money if your parents decide to cancel the prearrangement for any other reason?

Prearranging a funeral can be an excellent idea so that your parents' wishes are clearly spelled out and you won't have the difficult task of making decisions about what they would want. But because of the three considerations listed above, it's probably best not to *prepay* for a funeral unless it is clearly spelled out that any moneys paid are fully refundable and that this debt cannot be discharged through bankruptcy.

Figure 12-1: Itemized Funeral Home Bill

ACME Funeral Home, Inc.
1234 Spruce Street
Anytown, NJ 00375

Invoice

Professional and Personal Services Rendered	$1,050.00
Use of Facilities and Equipment	$295.00
Poplar Casket	$1,650.00
Creter Vault and Setup	$870.00
Transfer of Deceased to Funeral Home	$105.00
Funeral Coach (Hearse)	$185.00
Five (5) Transcripts of Death Certificate	$21.00
Memorial Folders	$55.00
Airline to Transport Deceased	$345.00
Mortuary Service	$395.00
TOTAL	$4,971.00

Due and payable within 15 days. Any balance outstanding
after this date will be subject to a late charge of 12% per year.

If your aging parent wishes to prearrange his or her funeral, you can assist by suggesting the use of the following questionnaire. Your parent can then submit and discuss the completed questionnaire with a funeral director he or she has personally chosen.

Questionnaire for Prearranging Your Funeral

Adapted from the National Funeral Directors Association booklet "Making Funeral Arrangements."

1. Full name (legal name as well as aliases and nicknames)

2. Maiden name

3. Social Security number

4. Date and place of birth

5. Name, address, and phone number of spouse

6. Date and place of marriage

7. Names, addresses, and phone numbers of all children

8. Names, addresses, and phone numbers of previous spouses

9. Date(s) of divorce

10. Names, addresses, and phone numbers of brothers and sisters

11. Names, addresses, and phone numbers of other friends and relatives who should be notified

12. Names, addresses, and phone numbers of present and previous employers

13. Religious affiliation

14. Name, address, and phone number of clergy you wish to officiate

15. Veteran status

    ♦ date of enlistment

    ♦ date of discharge

    ♦ location of discharge papers

    ♦ rank and service number

    ♦ organization or outfit

    ♦ commendations or medals awarded

16. Professional and fraternal organizations

17. Names, dates attended, and degrees awarded from all colleges and universities attended

18. Names of newspapers in which you wish to have an obituary printed

19. Organ donation instructions (including anyone who should be notified)

20. Funeral home you prefer

21. Kind of service you would like (including music, hymns, or special readings)

22. Visitation instructions

23. Names and addresses of organizations to which you would like donations sent in lieu of flowers

24. Names, addresses, and phone numbers of pall bearers

25. Name, address, and phone number of cemetery (including lot and grave number)

26. Kind of casket and vault or liner preferred

27. If you wish to be cremated, what you would like done with your ashes

28. The location of your will, including the name, address, and phone number of your executor

29. Name, address, and phone number of your attorney

30. Location of any insurance policies

31. Additional instructions or comments

The Will

The will is the legal document your parents have written that gives instructions about how their property should be passed on to their heirs after they die. It's also the document that names a person who will act as a personal representative, or, more formally, executor or executrix. Usually only a written will is legal, and one or two witnesses must sign that they were in your parent's presence when the will was signed and dated. If a person dies without a will, it is called dying "intestate." In such instances, the state will be responsible for making sure all creditors are paid from the estate and then deciding where the remaining balance will go. Usually, the balance will go to a surviving spouse. If there is none, it will usually be split equally among the surviving children.

For more information about wills, see chapter 4, "Blind Justice."

The Executor/Executrix

The executor (for males) or executrix (for females) is the person responsible for carrying out the distribution of a person's estate. The designation of a specific person as executor/executrix is usually done in the will. Often it's the spouse or son or daughter who is named to handle this task. But just as often it's the person's attorney or financial advisor who will be given the responsibility.

Administering a person's estate can be an overwhelming task, particularly with large estates. First off, you're grieving over your loss and therefore probably cannot think too straight. Yet you're the one responsible for making sure that the funeral is arranged and paid for, all debts and bills are paid, all assets are distributed among the heirs according to the terms of the will, and all the required paperwork is completed.

Suggestion: If it's truly an overwhelming task for you, consider hiring an attorney to serve as executor on your behalf. Choosing your parent's attorney is probably a better idea than choosing yours, but either will do. An attorney will charge either a flat fee (ranging from a few hundred dollars to over a thousand dollars, depending on the complexity and size of the estate), a variable fee (based on an hourly rate, which you should agree to beforehand with, if possible, a maximum fee), or a percentage of the estate (which can be 10 percent or more).

In addition, there are a number of books available in bookstores and libraries that will guide you through the probate process. One is *How to Administer an Estate* by Stephen G. Christianson (Citadel Press, 1997).

If your parent's estate is worth more than $600,000 (the amount under which no federal estate tax is assessed), it's probably wise to consult with an attorney and/or a tax advisor, even if you decide to handle the duties of executor.

If your parent dies "intestate," that is, without a will, the court may give you the responsibility of handling the estate. In that case, you might also consider consulting with an attorney, just to make sure that you're doing everything you're supposed to do.

The Funeral Bill and Life Insurance

The first thing you'll probably have to do as executor is make sure that the funeral is arranged and taken care of. Most funeral homes expect payment for their services within thirty to sixty days. Depending on the complexity and liquidity of your parent's estate, that could pose a cash-flow problem if the funeral is to be paid out of the estate.

Important: If your parent has a life insurance policy, you can direct the insurance company to pay the funeral home directly from the proceeds of the policy. Most funeral homes will wait to get their money from an insurance policy if you show them proof that the policy exists.

If the funeral home you've chosen will not wait for payment from the insurance company, you can either pay it directly from other funds (it's often recommended that the executor open a new estate checking account for these purposes) or from your own funds (and be sure to document this so that you can reimburse yourself). Hopefully, when you selected the funeral home, you arranged with the director to pay either from insurance proceeds or after some of the estate was liquidated.

To notify the insurance company, simply write a letter directing the company to pay the funeral home. Enclose a copy of the bill from the funeral home and a copy of the death certificate. (The letter should come from your parent's primary beneficiary. If the primary beneficiary is no longer living—a common occurrence since most people don't remember to change the beneficiaries—you'll also have to include a copy of the other parent's death certificate and a copy of the letter from the probate court naming you as executor.)

If your parent's estate will not go into probate (see the discussion of probate, below), you can simply tell the insurance company that. It will then pay the funeral home the appropriate amount and forward any balance to the beneficiary.

If you don't have a copy of the life insurance policy, you should call the insurance company directly. Often, no copy of the policy is required since the company will already have one on file. You may have to fill out additional papers, but if the payments were up-to-date and the policy was still in force, you shouldn't have any trouble getting the money.

Probate

Probate is the process by which your parent's estate is accounted for, all debts and taxes paid, and whatever is left goes to the rightful heirs. It's in officially registering the will and making sure that it's publicly recorded that you have the legal right to serve as executor of the estate.

To get your parent's will probated, go to the appropriate county office, usually in the hall of records in the central county building or court. The name of the office handling probate differs from state to state (surrogate's office, probate court, register of wills, etc.), but you should be able to find the appropriate office by calling the main county government office phone and asking which office handles probate. In most states you must wait a period of time (perhaps ten days) before you can get the will probated.

When you go to the office, bring an official copy of the death certificate and the will showing you as the designated executor (don't forget to bring personal identification). You should receive a certified letter stating that you are the official executor (you might want to get several copies of this letter since you may need to send one to various banks, brokerages, insurance companies, etc.; there's usually a small charge for additional copies).

When getting the will probated, you should also get an "Order to Limit Creditors," which will protect the estate from frivolous and bogus lawsuits that could drag on endlessly. This protective order limits creditors to six months from the date of publication for filing claims on the estate. The order will be published in the newspaper of the city or town in which the deceased lived.

The steps of probate are:

1. A will is presented to the probate court and a judge decides that it was legally prepared and, therefore, valid.

2. The executor/executrix or personal representative is officially confirmed by the court. If there is no will, the judge will appoint someone to serve as executor.

3. Creditors, heirs, and beneficiaries are informed that probate has started.

4. An inventory and appraisal of the estate is done.

5. Creditors and taxes are paid.

6. A final accounting of the remaining estate is done.

7. The estate is distributed to the rightful heirs. If there is no will, a judge will make the decision as to how the estate is divided among those claiming a portion.

Can You Avoid Probate?

The probate process can be cumbersome and costly. There are numerous fees that will have to be paid: court fees, fees to file legal papers, and fees to appraisers and to other professionals. And if an attorney probates the will, you'll also have to pay the attorney's fee, which can be substantial. The amount an attorney charges will vary based on the size of the estate and whether the attorney charges a flat fee or by the hour. For an estate valued at $100,000, the attorney's fee for probating the will generally range from about $2,000 to $3,000.

The question, then, is: Can you avoid probate? The short answer is "yes." There are a couple of ways: joint ownership and revocable living trusts.

Joint Tenancy

Joint tenancy concerns property that is owned jointly with a right of survivorship. By law, ownership passes to the co-owner(s) upon the death of one of the partners, outside the probate process. So if you've opened a joint account with your parent, the money in that account automatically is yours when your parent dies.

Like most things, joint ownership has positives and negatives. On the positive side, joint tenancy means that you get to avoid probate (thus saving some money and a great deal of hassle). In addition, you have immediate use of the funds (or immediate access to the safe deposit box), which can be quite important when you're trying to take care of your deceased parent's obligations. On the negative side, joint tenancy means co-ownership.

This means, of course, that any of the owners can take any or all of the funds, at any time and for any purpose—there are no limits. In addition, if there are any judgments against any of the joint owners of the property, that property is considered available to settle any of the joint owner's debts. The money will not be protected from lawsuits or judgments against you (or your spouse if you live in a community property state).

Revocable Living Trusts

A revocable living trust is very much like a will: it's a written document, legally prepared and witnessed; it allows your parents (or grantors) to pass on to heirs a portion of their estate after they die; and it appoints an executor, or trustee, to make sure that everything is taken care of and that the terms of the trust are carried out. One major difference is that any property placed in a revocable living trust does *not* go through probate after the grantor dies. Other advantages of a revocable living trust are: your parent can put an age limit on when the heir gets the property (which means that there's no worry about bequeathing property to a minor); if your parent becomes incapacitated, the trustee can handle the legal and financial affairs, thus making guardianship or conservatorship unnecessary; if your parent owns property in more than one state, the will does not have to go through probate in more than one state; and a trust is totally private, while a will is a public document, open to anyone once it's submitted for probate.

Note: Filing for probate is not always necessary, and not all property is subject to probate. If you and your deceased parent own all the property "jointly with right of survivorship," you don't need to probate the property. Property owned jointly passes by law to the surviving co-owner(s), outside the probate process. In addition, life insurance and pension benefits go directly to the beneficiaries or survivors without going through probate.

The primary disadvantages of a living trust are that it's more expensive to draft than a will, at least up front (a trust costs about twice as much as a will); that attorneys and companies that set up trusts often require a minimum balance; and that for many people it's totally unnecessary. So if your parent's estate is relatively small, you or the executor will be able to handle probate with no cost and a minimum of hassle, especially if your parent's state offers assistance to "do-it-yourself" probate or an expedited probate.

For more information about revocable living trusts and joint tenancy, you and your parents should consult an attorney or financial advisor.

What You Must Do As Executor of a Will

The funeral is certainly one of the first things you must take care of as executor of your parent's estate. Once that's over, now you have to start on all the other administrative responsibilities. Being executor is not a difficult task—it's just time-consuming and tedious.

Important: One thing to keep in mind is that absolutely nothing must be done immediately! Every creditor can wait, every legal task you must do can wait, and every heir can wait.

One of the hardest parts of being an executor is dealing with your own emotional stress: Your parent has just died and you're grieving over the loss. You have your own life to get back together (and are probably also dealing with your family's stress). You've put aside all your own financial, legal, and daily business. And you probably also had to take some time off from work and are now paying the price for that time away. Yet now you must deal with all the administrative trivia and personal finances of another person's life!

Here are the things to take care of as executor:

1. Deal with the funeral and arrange to have your parent's life insurance pay the bill. (If there's no policy or if the amount is not sufficient, either pay the bill from your own resources or arrange to pay a little later, after you've had a chance to get organized.)

2. Go through your parent's house or room and do a quick inventory of what's there. Pick out the clothes your parent will be buried in and give them to the funeral director.

3. Go through your parent's papers (in the desk or dresser drawer, safe, filing cabinet, etc.). Make a list of what you find and where you found it. You should specifically look for:

   ◆ the will

   ◆ life insurance policies

- ◆ safe deposit box key

- ◆ checkbook

- ◆ bank statements (make a list of all accounts since there are likely several)

- ◆ tax returns

- ◆ unpaid bills

- ◆ brokerage accounts

- ◆ stock or bond certificates

- ◆ medical insurance policies

- ◆ medical claims

- ◆ the deed to the house

- ◆ other financial records of assets and liabilities

You can put everything official in one place if you want. Don't forget to check your parent's purse or wallet, boxes in the attic and/or basement, and "secret hiding places" such as a fake book or can in the pantry (hopefully your parent told you about a secret place—otherwise you could be spending a lot of time shaking soup cans).

4. Read your parent's will and make sure that you're named as executor. (If not, contact the designated executor. If the executor is no longer alive and there's no provision for anyone else to assume the responsibility, you'll have to go through the probate process to get yourself named as executor.)

   If the will is not in the house, check with your parent's attorney or advisor to see if he or she has a copy. If your parent has a safe deposit box, there's likely a copy of the will there. If you have access to the box, you can go there and remove the contents. If you don't have access, you'll have to go through the probate process to gain access.

5. Clean out the safe deposit box and close the box account.

6. Call the life insurance companies and ask how to file a claim. Usually you'll need to send a copy of the will that names you executor and the death certificate. The company will then send a check to the primary beneficiary or to the funeral home if you've directed it there.

Note: If your parent has been ill for a while, it's possible that the premiums were not paid and therefore that the insurance company will claim that the policy is no longer in effect. You can appeal based on the fact that your parent was ill and ask for a waiver. Be persistent, and if one person says no, appeal to the next level.

7. Go to the county probate clerk's office in the county in which the your parent was a legal resident and begin to probate the will (don't forget to ask for the "Order to Limit Creditors").

8. Set up a checking account for the estate. You can pay all bills and put any assets you liquidate into this account. If you had already set up a joint account with your parent, you don't have to open a new one. Just make sure that your parent's Social Security number is the number on record so that any tax liability is your parent's, not yours.

9. If you need to close any bank accounts (and are not already an authorized signatory), you may have to contact the state tax authority to get permission (the state tax board may have to certify that your parent does not owe any past taxes).

10. Go through the pile of unpaid bills as time and funds permit. As you pay each bill, notify the creditor that your parent is now deceased and that all correspondence should go to your address.

11. File any unfiled medical claims. Any payments due should be made payable to "The Estate of . . ." so you'll have no trouble depositing the checks into the new account.

12. Pay the heirs what is due them. Consider transferring stocks, bonds, real estate, and other assets to the heirs rather than liquidating them so that you can avoid paying any capital gains taxes. The heir will only have to pay an inheritance tax if the inheritance was over $1 million. Also, when the heirs sell the stock and calculate the capital gains taxes they owe, they can then use the fair market value of the stock or bond at the time of transfer.

13. Have any valuables appraised (unless they've been designated to go to someone and are not to be included in the estate). Your local jeweler should be able to give you a fair appraisal. For valuables other than jewelry (for example,

collections, antiques, etc.) or if you don't have a local jeweler who can give you an appraisal, you can check with the Appraisers Association of America (212-889-5404), the American Society of Appraisers (800-ASA-VALU or 703-478-2228; Web site: http://www.appraisers.org), or the International Society of Appraisers (206-241-0359).

14. Keep track of all your expenses as you appraise and distribute assets. The law allows you to take a commission based on the value of the estate (just as an attorney would do if he or she acted as executor). Whether you take a commission is up to you. You're certainly permitted to do so, and at the very least you should make sure that, to the extent possible, the estate pays all expenses, not you.

15. By April 15 of the following year, file final income tax returns for the deceased. On the top of the first page, in big, bold letters, write "DECEASED." And on the signature line you should sign your own name.

16. If necessary, file estate or inheritance tax returns.

17. Once all bills are paid, all income due is received, and all tax returns are filed, close the estate checking account.

STATE AGENCIES ON AGING

Alabama
Commission on Aging
770 Washington Avenue,
Suite 470
Montgomery, AL 36130
334-242-5743

Alaska
Older Alaskans Commission
Department of Administration
Pouch C—Mail Station 0209
Juneau, AK 99811-0209
907-465-3250

Arizona
Aging and Adult
Administration
1789 West Jefferson—950A
Phoenix, AZ 85007
602-542-4446

Arkansas
Division of Aging and Adult
Services
Arkansas Department of
Human Services
7th and Main Streets
(P.O. Box 1417, Slot 1412)
Little Rock, AK 72201
501-682-2441

California
Department of Aging
1600 K Street
Sacramento, CA 95814
916-322-5290

Colorado
Aging and Adult Services
Department of Social Services
1575 Sherman Street,
10th Floor
Denver, CO 80203-1714
303-866-3851

Connecticut
Department on Aging
175 Main Street
Hartford, CT 06106
203-566-3238

Delaware
Division on Aging
Department of Health and
Social Services
1901 North Dupont Highway
New Castle, DE 19720
302-421-6791

District of Columbia
Office on Aging
1424 K Street NW, 2nd Floor
Washington, DC 20005
202-724-5626

Florida
Program Office of Aging and
Adult Services
Department of Health and
Rehabilitative Services
1317 Winewood Boulevard
Tallahassee, FL 32301
904-488-8922

Georgia
Office of Aging
878 Peachtree Street NE,
Room 632
Atlanta, GA 30309
404-894-5333

Hawaii
Executive Office on Aging
335 Merchant Street,
Room 241
Honolulu, HI 96813
808-548-2593

Idaho
Office on Aging
Room 108—Statehouse
Boise, ID 83720
208-334-3833

Illinois
Department on Aging
421 East Capitol Avenue
Springfield, IL 62701
217-785-2870

Indiana
Choice/Home Care Services
P.O. Box 7083
Indianapolis, IN 46207-7083
317-232-7020

Iowa
Department of Elder Affairs
Jewett Building
914 Grand Avenue, Suite 236
Des Moines, IA 50319
515-281-5187

Kansas
Department on Aging
Docking State Office Building,
122-S
915 SW Harrison
Topeka, KS 66612-1500
913-296-4986

Kentucky
Divison of Aging Services
Cabinet for Human Resources
CHR Building, 6th Floor
275 East Main Street
Frankfort, KY 40621
502-564-6930

Louisiana
Office of Elderly Affairs
4550 North Boulevard,
2nd Floor
(P.O. Box 80374)
Baton Rouge, LA 70806
504-925-1700

Maine
Bureau of Elder and Adult
Services
Department of Human
Services
State House, Station 11
Augusta, ME 04333
207-626-5335

Maryland
Office on Aging
State Office Building
301 West Preston Street,
Room 1004
Baltimore, MD 21202
301-225-1100

Massachusetts
Executive Office of
Elder Affairs
38 Chauncy Street
Boston, MA 02111
617-727-7750

Michigan
Office of Services to the Aging
P.O. Box 30026
Lansing, MI 48909
517-373-8230

Minnesota
Board on Aging
444 Lafayette Road
St. Paul, MN 55155-3843
612-296-2770

Mississippi
Council on Aging
Divison of Aging and
Adult Services
421 West Pasagoula Street
Jackson, MI 39203-3524
601-949-2070

Missouri
Division of Aging
Department of Social Services
615 Howerton Court
(P.O. Box 1337)
Jefferson City, MO 65102
314-751-3082

Montana
The Governor's Office
on Aging
State Capitol Building
Capitol Statino, Room 219
Helena, MT 59620
406-444-3111

Nebraska
Department on Aging
301 Centennial Mall–South
(P.O. Box 95044)
Lincoln, NE 68509
402-471-2306

Nevada
Division for Aging Services
Department of Human
Services
340 North 11th Street,
Suite 114
Las Vegas, NE 89101
702-486-3545

New Hampshire
Divison of Elderly and
Adult Services
6 Hazen Street
Concord, NH 03301-6501
603-271-4680

New Jersey
Division on Aging
Department of Community
Affairs
CN 807
South Broad and Front Streets
Trenton, NJ 08625-0807
609-292-3766

New Mexico
State Agency on Aging
La Villa Rivera Building
224 East Palace Avenue,
4th Floor
Santa Fe, NM 87501
505-827-7640

New York
Office of the Aging
New York State Plaza
Agency Building #2
Albany, NY 12223
518-474-4425

North Carolina
Division of Aging
693 Palmer Drive
Raleigh, NC 27603
919-733-3983

North Dakota
Aging Services
Department of Human
Services
State Capitol Building
Bismarck, ND 58505
701-224-2577

Ohio
Department of Aging
50 West Broad Street,
9th Floor
Columbus, OH 43266-0501
614-466-5500

Oklahoma
Aging Services Divison
Department of Human
Services
P.O. Box 25352
Oklahoma City, OK 73125
405-521-2327

Oregon
Senior and Disabled Services
Division
313 Public Service Building
Salem, OR 97310
503-378-4728

Pennsylvania
Department of Aging
231 State Street
Harrisburg, PA 17101-1195
717-783-1550

Puerto Rico
Gericulture Commission
Department of Social Services
Cal Box 50063
San Juan, PR 00902
809-721-0753

Rhode Island
Department of Edlerly Affairs
160 Pine Street
Providence, RI 02903-3708
401-277-2858

South Carolina
Commision on Aging
400 Arbor Lake Drive,
Suite B-500
Columbia, SC 29223
803-735-0210

South Dakota
Office of Adult Services
and Aging
Kneip Building
700 North Illinois Street
Pierre, SD 57501
605-773-3656

Tennessee
Commission on Aging
Suite 201
706 Church Street
Nashvile, TN 37243-0860
615-741-2056

Texas
Department on Aging
1949 I-35 South
(P.O. Box 12786, Capitol
Station)
Austin, TX 78741-3702
512-444-2727

Utah
Divison of Aging and Adult
Services
Department of Social Services
120 North 200 West
(P.O. Box 45500)
Salt Lake City, UT 84145-0500
801-538-3910

Vermont
Aging and Disabilities
103 South Main Street
Waterbury, VT 05676
802-241-2400

Virginia
Department for the Aging
700 Centre, 10th Floor
700 East Franklin Street
Richmond, VA 23219-2327
804-225-2271

Virgin Islands
Senior Citizens Affairs
Department of Human
Services
#19 Estate Diamond,
Fredericksted
St. Croix, VI 00840
809-772-4950 ext. 46

Washington
Aging and Adult Services
Administration
Department of Social and
Health Services
OB-44A
Olympia, WA 98504
206-586-3768

West Virginia
Commission on Aging
Holly Grove—State Capitol
Charleston, WV 25305
304-348-3317

Wisconsin
Bureau of Aging
Division of Community
Services
217 South Hamilton Street,
Suite 300
Madison, WI 53707
608-266-2536

Wyoming
Commission on Aging
Hathaway Building, Room 139
Cheyenne, WY 82002-0710
307-777-7986

AMERICAN HEALTH CARE ASSOCIATION STATE AFFILIATES

Alabama
Alabama Nursing Home
Association
4156 Carmichael Road
Montgomery, AL 36106
334-271-6214

Alaska
Alaska State Hospital and
Nursing Home Association
319 Seward Street
Juneau, AK 99801
907-586-1790

Arizona
Arizona Health Care
Association
1440 East Missouri Avenue,
Suite 215
Phoenix, AZ 85014
602-265-5331

Arkansas
Arkansas Health Care
Association
501 Woodlane Drive, Suite 300
Little Rock, AR 72201
501-374-4422

California
California Association of
Health Facilities
1251 Beacon Boulevard
West Sacramento, CA 95691
916-371-4700

Colorado
Colorado Health Care
Association
225 East 16th Avenue,
Suite 1100
Denver, CO 80203
303-861-8228

Connecticut
Connecticut Association of
Health Care Facilities
131 New London Turnpike,
Suite 318
Glastonbury, CT 06033
203-659-0391

Delaware
Delaware Health Care Facilities
Association
1013 Centre Road, Suite 101
Wilmington, DE 19805
302-633-7880

District of Columbia
D.C. Health Care Association
1233 20th Street NW, Suite 800
Washington, DC 20036
202-778-1220

Florida
Florida Health Care
Association
P.O. Box 1459
Tallahassee, FL 32302
904-224-3907

Georgia
Georgia Nursing Home
Association
3735 Memorial Drive
Decatur, GA 30032
404-284-8700

Hawaii
Healthcare Association
of Hawaii
932 Ward Avenue, Suite 430
Honolulu, HI 96814
808-521-8961

Idaho
Idaho Health Care Association
P.O. Box 2623
Boise, ID 83701
208-343-9735

Illinois
Illinois Health Care
Association
1029 South 4th Street
Springfield, IL 62703
217-528-6455

Indiana
Indiana Health Care
Association
1 North Capitol, Room 1115
Indianapolis, IN 46204
317-636-6406

Iowa
Iowa Health Care Association
950 12th Street
Des Moines, IA 50309
515-282-0666

Kansas
Kansas Health Care
Association
221 SW 33rd
Topeka, KS 66611
913-267-6003

Kentucky
Kentucky Association of
Health Care Facilities
9403 Mill Brook Road
Louisville, KY 40223
502-425-5000

Louisiana
Louisiana Nursing Home
Association
7921 Picardy Avenue
Baton Rouge, LA 70809
504-769-3705

Maine
Maine Health Care
Association
303 State Street
Augusta, ME 04330
207-623-1146

Maryland
Health Facilities Association
of Maryland
229 Hanover Street
Annapolis, MD 21401
301-269-1390

Massachusetts
Massachusetts Federation of
Nursing Homes
990 Washington Street,
Suite 207-S
Dedham, MA 02026
617-326-8967

Michigan
Health Care Association
of Michigan
P.O. Box 80050
Lansing, MI 48908
517-627-1561

Minnesota
Care Providers of Minnesota
2850 Metro Drive, Suite 200
Minneapolis, MN 55425
612-854-2844

Mississippi
Mississippi Health Care
Association
114 Marketridge Drive
Jackson, MI 39213
601-956-3472

Missouri
Missouri Health Care
Association
236 Metro Drive
Jefferson City, MO 65109
314-893-2060

Montana
Montana Health Care
Association
36 South Last Chance Gulch,
Suite A
Helena, MT 59601
406-443-2876

Nebraska
Nebraska Health Care
Association
421 South 9th Street, Suite 137
Lincoln, NE 68508
402-435-3551

Nevada
Nevada Health Care
Association
P.O. Box 3226
Carson City, NV 89702
702-885-1006

New Hampshire
New Hampshire Health Care
Association
125 Airport Road
Concord, NH 03301
603-225-0900

New Jersey
New Jersey Association of
Health Care Facilities
2131 Route 33
Trenton, NJ 08690
609-890-8700

New Mexico
New Mexico Health Care
Association
6400 Uptown Boulevard,
Suite 520W
Albuquerque, NM 87110
505-880-1088

New York
New York State Health
Facilities Association
33 Elk Street, Suite 300
Albany, NY 12207
518-462-4800

North Carolina
North Carolina Health Care
Facilities Association
5109 Bur Oak Circle
Raleigh, NC 27612
919-782-3827

North Dakota
North Dakota Long-Term Care
Association
120 West Thayer Avenue
Bismarck, ND 58501
701-222-0660

Ohio
Ohio Health Care Association
55 Green Meadows Drive
South
Westerville, OH 43081
614-436-4154

Oklahoma
Oklahoma Health Care
Association
5801 North Broadway,
Suite 500
Oklahoma City, OK 73118
405-848-8338

Oregon
Oregon Health Care
Association
15895 SW 72nd Avenue,
Suite 250
Portland, OR 97224
503-620-9300

Pennsylvania
Pennsylvania Health Care
Association
2401 Park Drive
Harrisburg, PA 17111
717-657-4902

Rhode Island
Rhode Island Health Care
Association
144 Bignall Street
Warwick, RI 02888
401-785-9530

South Carolina
South Carolina Health Care
Association
170 Laurelhurst Drive
Columbia, SC 29210
803-772-7511

South Dakota
South Dakota Health Care
Association
804 North Western Avenue
Sioux Falls, SD 57104
605-339-2071

Tennessee
Tennessee Health Care
Association
P.O. Box 100129
Nashville, TN 37224
615-834-6520

Texas
Texas Health Care Association
P.O. Box 4554
Austin, TX 78765
512-458-1257

Utah
Utah Health Care Association
4190 South Highland Drive,
Suite 113
Salt Lake City, UT 84124
801-272-4368

Vermont
Vermont Health Care
Association
2 Moonlight Terrace
Montpelier, VT 05602
802-229-5700

Virginia
Virginia Health Care
Association
2112 West Laburnum Avenue,
Suite 206
Richmond, VA 23227
804-353-9101

Washington
Washington Health Care
Association
2120 State Street NE, Suite 102
Olympia, WA 98506
206-352-3304

West Virginia
West Virginia Health Care
Association
8 Capitol Street, Suite 700
Charleston, WV 25301
304-346-4575

Wisconsin
Wisconsin Health Care
Association
14 South Carroll Street,
Suite 200
Madison, WI 53703
608-257-0125

Wyoming
Wyoming Health Care
Association
2020 Club House Road
Greeley, CO 80634
303-330-7222

State Home Care Association Phone Numbers

Alabama
Alabama Association of
Home Health Agencies
334-277-2130

Alaska
Alaska Home Care Association
907-463-3113

Arizona
Arizona Association for
Home Care
602-967-2624

Arkansas
Home Care Association
of Arkansas
501-376-2273

California
California Association for
Health Services at Home
916-443-8055

Colorado
Home Care Association
of Colorado
303-694-4728

Connecticut
Connecticut Association
for Home Care, Inc.
203-265-9931

Delaware
Delaware Association for
Home and Community Care
302-455-1500

District of Columbia
Capital Home Health
Association
202-686-8728

Florida
Associated Home Health
Industries of Florida, Inc.
904-222-8967

Georgia
Georgia Association of
Home Health Agencies
770-984-9704

Georgia Association of
Community Care Providers
770-948-4507

Hawaii
Hawaii Association for
Home Care
808-735-2970

Idaho
Idaho Association of
Home Health Agencies
208-334-0500

Illinois
Illinois Home Care Council
312-335-9922

Indiana
Indiana Association for
Home Care
317-844-6630

Iowa
Iowa Association for
Home Care
515-282-3965

Kansas
Kansas Home Care
Association
913-841-8611

Kentucky
Kentucky Home Care
Association
606-268-2574

Louisiana
Homecare Association
of Louisiana
504-924-4144

Maine
Visiting Nurse Service
of Southern Maine
207-284-4566

Maryland
Maryland Association
for Home Care
410-242-1973

Massachusetts
Massachusetts Council for
Home Care Aid Services
617-523-6400

Michigan
Michigan Home Health
Association
517-349-8089

Minnesota
Minnesota Home Care
Association
612-635-0607

Mississippi
Mississippi Association
for Home Care
601-355-8900

Missouri
Missouri Alliance for
Home Care
314-634-7772

Montana
Montana Association of
Home Health Agencies
406-247-3240

Nebraska
Nebraska Association of Home
and Community Health
Agencies
402-334-0456

Nevada
Home Health Care Association
of Nevada
702-388-8429

New Hampshire
Home Care Association of
New Hampshire
603-225-5597

New Jersey
Home Care Council of
New Jersey
201-857-3333

Home Health Services and
Staffing Association
908-303-8599

Home Health Assembly
of New Jersey
609-275-6100

New Mexico
New Mexico Association
for Home Care
505-889-4556

New York
Home Care Association
of New York State
518-426-8764

New York State Assocation
of Health Care Providers
518-463-1118

Healthcare Assocation of
New York State
518-431-7732

North Carolina
North Carolina Association
for Home Care
919-878-0500

North Dakota
North Dakota Association of
Home Health Services
701-224-1815

Ohio
Ohio Council for Home Care
614-885-0434

Oklahoma
Oklahoma Association for
Home Care
405-943-6242

Oregon
Oregon Association for
Home Care
503-253-9237

Pennsylvania
Pennsylvania Association of
Home Health Agencies
717-975-9448

Puerto Rico
Puerto Rico Home Health
Agencies and Hospices
Association
809-774-8181

Rhode Island
Rhode Island Partnership
for Home Care
401-788-2000

Rhode Island Visiting Nurses
Council
401-737-6050

South Carolina
South Carolina Home Care
Association
803-254-7355

South Dakota
South Dakota Home Health
Association
605-353-6271

Tennessee
Tennessee Association for
Home Care
615-885-3399

Texas
Texas Association for
Home Care
512-338-9293

Utah
Utah Association of Home
Health Agencies
801-272-5785

Vermont
Vermont Assembly of
Home Health Agencies
802-229-0579

Virginia
Virginia Association for
Home Care
804-285-8636

Washington
Home Care Association
of Washington
206-775-8120

West Virginia
West Virginia Council of
Home Health Agencies
304-292-5826

Wisconsin
Wisconsin Homecare
Association
608-833-8118

Wyoming
Home Health Care Alliance
of Wyoming
307-778-5616

Sample Power of Attorney

This Power of Attorney is made on this _____ day of _____, 19_____, by and between _____, residing at _____

_____

and _____
residing at _____

_____.

I, _____, hereby make, constitute, and appoint the Agents, with full power of substitution, as my true and lawful attorneys in my name, and said Power of Attorney shall take effect on the date hereof and remain in effect in the event that I become disabled (as that term is defined in state law), to do each and every act which I could personally do for the following uses and purposes:

1. To make, execute, acknowledge, and deliver any and all contracts, leases, assignments, applications, bonds, mortgages, deeds, and other instruments of whatsoever kind and nature;

2. To purchase, acquire, buy, sell, convey, mortgage, pledge, lease, or otherwise transfer, assign, and dispose of any and all property, real and personal, wheresoever situate, of whatsoever kind and nature, tangible or intangible, owned by me or in which I may have any interest or to which I may become entitled; and to manage, operate, and control all or any part of the same;

3. To demand, sue for, collect, recover, and receive any and all goods, claims, debts, moneys, interests, and demands whatsoever now due or that may hereafter become due to me; and to make, execute, and deliver receipts, releases, and other discharges therefor;

4. To defend, settle, adjust, compound, submit to arbitration and compromise all actions, claims, accounts, suits, and demands whatsoever which now or hereafter shall be pending between me and any other person, firm, association, or corporation, in such manner as my said attorney shall deem fit;

5. To make, draw, sign, endorse, negotiate, and deliver checks, drafts, and withdrawals drawn against my account in any bank, trust company, or other financial institution wheresoever the same may be situate, which I may have;

6. To make, draw, endorse, and otherwise negotiate any and all instruments, whether the same be negotiable or non-negotiable;

7. To endorse or in any other way further negotiate any checks, drafts, or other obligations of the United States drawn to my order or made payable to me;

8. To sell, assign, transfer, redeem, collect, and in any other manner dispose of any and all United States Treasury Bonds, certificates, or other evidence of indebtedness of the United States of America owned by me or registered in my name;

9. To obtain insurance of any kind, nature, or description whatsoever on my person and property, whether real or personal, and to make, execute, and file proof of all loss or losses sustained or claimable thereto; and to make, execute, and deliver receipts or discharges thereto;

10. To have free access at all times to any safe deposit box which I may have in any bank.

This Power of Attorney shall not be affected by the physical or mental disability of the principal.

The grants above specifically enumerated shall not be construed as limitations of the powers hereby conferred, it being intended that my said attorney shall have full power and authority, without limit to the powers specifically enumerated herein, to act in my name and in my place and stead, giving and granting unto my said attorney full power and authority to do and perform any and every act and thing requisite and necessary to be done in and about the premises as fully, to all intents and purposes, as I might or could do if personally present, with full power of substitution and revocation, hereby ratifying and confirming all that my said attorney or his substitutes shall lawfully do or cause to be done by virtue thereof.

In the event that my attorney herein named dies or otherwise becomes incapable of acting, I do hereby substitute for him/her and appoint _____,
now residing at _____
_____, in place and stead of the
said _____, and confer
upon him/her all the powers and authority herein conferred upon my attorney in full and complete a manner to all intents and purposes as though the name of such substituted attorney had been used herein instead of the name of said original attorney.

IN WITNESS WHEREOF, I have hereunto set my hand and seal this _____ day of _____, 19_____.

Signed, Sealed, and Delivered _____

in the presence of:

State of _____ County of _____

BE IT REMEMBERED, that on this _____ day of _____, 19___, before me the subscriber personally appeared _____, who I am satisfied is the person mentioned in the within instrument, and who thereupon acknowledged that he/she signed, sealed, and delivered the same as his/her voluntary act and deed, for the uses and purposes therein expressed.

Notary Public Endorsement _____

SAMPLE LIVING WILL

DIRECTIVE MADE this _____ day of _____, 19____, to my physicians, attorneys, clergymen, family, and others responsible for my health, welfare, or affairs.

BE IT KNOWN, that I, _____, of _____, State of _____, being of sound mind, willfully and voluntarily make known my desire that my life shall not be artificially prolonged under the circumstances set forth below and do hereby declare that, if at any time I should have an incurable injury, disease, or illness certified to be a terminal condition by two physicians and where the application of life-sustaining procedures would serve only to artificially prolong the moment of my death and where my physician determines that my death is imminent or needlessly prolonged whether or not life-sustaining procedures are utilized, I direct that such procedures be withheld or withdrawn and that I be permitted to die naturally with only the merciful administration of medication to eliminate or reduce pain to my mind and body or the performance of any medical procedure deemed necessary to provide me with comfort care.

In the absence of my ability to give directions regarding the use of such life-sustaining procedures, it is my intention that this directive shall be honored by my family and physician(s) as the final expression of my legal right to refuse medical or surgical treatment and I accept the consequences from such refusal.

If I have bequeathed organs, I ask that I be kept alive for a sufficient time to enable proper withdrawal and transplant of said organs.

Special Provisions:_____
_____
_____

IN WITNESS WHEREOF, I have hereunto set my hand and seal this _____ day of _____, 19_____.

_____

As a witness to this act I state the declarer has been personally known to me and I believe said declarer to be of sound mind.

Signed in the presence of:

_____

Witness   Address

_____

Witness   Address

State of _____County of _____ SS.

BE IT KNOWN, that the above named _____
_____, personally known to me as the same person described in and who executed the within Living Will, acknowledged to me that said instrument was freely and voluntarily executed for the purposes therein expressed, and that said Living Will was duly executed in my presence.

_____

Notary Public

My Commission Expires: _____

HOME CARE AIDE JOB APPLICATION

Personal Information

Name: _____

Social Security Number: _____

Address: _____

_____

Phone number: _____

Current landlord: _____

Landlord's address: _____

_____

Landlord's phone number: _____

How long have you lived at this address? _____

If less than two years, previous address: _____

_____

Previous landlord: _____

Previous landlord's address: _____

_____

Previous landlord's phone number: _____

Do you have a driver's license? _____

If so, driver's license number: _____

State issuing license: _____

Do you own a car? _____ If so, year and make: _____

_____

Do you have auto insurance? _____

With what company? _____

Education

College: _____

Address: _____

_____

Dates attended: _____

Degree: _____

High school: _____

Address: _____

_____

Dates attended: _____

Date graduated: _____

Other schooling: _____

Address: _____

_____

Dates attended: _____

Degree: _____

Other schooling: _____

Address: _____

_____

Dates attended: _____

Degree: _____

Work Experience

List your most recent employer first.

Employer: _____

Address: _____

_____

Job title: _____

Date hired: _____ Date left: _____

Supervisor's name: _____

Supervisor's phone number: _____

Describe your duties: _____

_____

_____

Explain why you left this position: _____

_____

_____

Employer: _____

Address: _____

_____

Job title: _____

Date hired: _____ Date left: _____

Supervisor's name: _____

Supervisor's phone number: _____

Describe your duties: _____

_____

_____

Explain why you left this position: _____

_____

_____

Employer: _____

Address: _____

_____

Job title: _____

Date hired: _____ Date left: _____

Supervisor's name: _____

Supervisor's phone number: _____

Describe your duties: _____
_____
_____

Explain why you left this position: _____
_____
_____

Working as a Caregiver

Describe your experience as a caregiver: _____
_____
_____

Describe why you want to be a caregiver: _____
_____
_____

What days and hours are you available? _____
_____

When can you begin work? _____

Miscellaneous

Is English your native language? _____

Which (if any) other languages do you speak? _____
_____

What other skills do you have that would be useful in a position
as a caregiver? _____
_____
_____

Have you ever been charged with any violations of law (including
traffic offenses)? _____

If yes, please describe: _____
_____
_____

Personal References

Name: _____
Phone number: _____

Name: _____
Phone number: _____

Name: _____
Phone number: _____

Name: _____
Phone number: _____

Declaration

I, _____, have applied for a position as a caregiver for an older person. I hereby testify that, to the best of my knowledge, all the information on this application is true.

Signature: _____

NATIONAL ASSOCIATION FOR HOME CARE: PATIENT BILL OF RIGHTS

Home care patients have the right to:

- be fully informed of all their rights and responsibilities by the home care agency.

- choose care providers.

- receive appropriate and professional care in accordance with physician orders.

- receive a timely response from the agency to their request for service.

- be admitted for service only if the agency has the ability to provide safe, professional care at the level of intensity needed.

- receive reasonable continuity of care.

- receive information necessary to give informed consent prior to the start of any treatment or procedure.

- be advised of any change in the plan of care, before the change is made.

- refuse treatment within the confines of the law and be informed of the consequences of their action.

- be informed of their rights under state law to formulate advanced directives.

- have health care providers comply with advance directives in accordance with state law requirements.

- be informed within reasonable time of anticipated termination of service or plans for transfer to another agency.

- be fully informed of agency policies and charges for services, including eligibility for third-party reimbursements.

- be referred elsewhere, if denied service solely on their inability to pay.

- voice grievances and suggest changes in service or staff without fear of restraint or discrimination.

- receive a fair hearing for any individual to whom any service has been denied, reduced, or terminated, or who is otherwise aggrieved by agency action. The fair hearing procedure shall be set forth by each agency as appropriate to the unique patient situation (i.e., funding source, level of care, diagnosis).

- be informed of what to do in the event of any emergency.

- be advised of the telephone number and hours of operation of the state's home health hot line, which receives questions and complaints about Medicare-certified and state-licensed home care agencies.

QUESTIONS TO ASK ABOUT LONG-TERM-CARE FACILITIES

Cleanliness

1. Is the facility clean and free of unpleasant odor?

Patient Rights

2. Is there a written description of patient rights and responsibilities?

3. Is the staff trained to protect patient dignity and privacy?

4. Are restraining devices used or has every effort been made to seek alternatives?

Care Planning

5. Are patients and families involved in developing their own care plan?

6. Are services provided for terminally ill patients and their families?

7. Is there a subacute care program?

Staff

8. How many staff are on duty for each shift?

9. What is the turnover rate for nurse's aides and other unskilled help?

10. Does the staff show interest in, and respect for, individual patients?

11. Does the staff respond quickly to patient calls for assistance?

12. Does the staff interact respectfully and in a friendly manner with other staff?

13. Is the administrator available to answer questions, hear complaints, or discuss problems?

Licensure and Certification

14. Do the facility and administrator have a current license from the state?

15. Is the facility certified to provide Medicare and/or Medicaid coverage?

16. Does the facility have a formal quality assurance program?

Location

17. Is the facility convenient for frequent visits of family and friends?

18. Is the facility near a cooperating hospital?

19. Can the patient continue to use a personal physician and, if so, is the facility convenient?

20. Will the facility assist in finding a new personal physician and specialists if necessary?

Costs

21. What is the basic charge and what services are covered?

22. Is a list of specific services not covered in the basic rate available?

23. Are there any financial requirements for residence (for example, must a patient buy the unit or make a large lump-sum payment before admission)?

24. How much money must be paid initially?

25. Are advance payments returned if the patient leaves the home?

26. Can the contract be modified?

27. What happens if funds are depleted?

Medical

28. Who performs the initial needs assessment?

29. What if the patient's needs change?

30. Is a physician available in an emergency?

31. Are medical records and plans of care kept?

32. Are patients and their families involved in plans for treatment?

33. Is confidentiality of medical records assured?

34. What other medical services are available (dentists, optometrists, podiatrists, etc.)?

35. Will the patient's personal physician be notified in an emergency?

36. Does the facility periodically report to the patient's personal physician?

37. If the facility provides a physician, how often are the visits?

38. Does the facility have an arrangement with a nearby hospital?

39. Is emergency transportation readily available?

40. Does the facility make accommodations for holding beds when patients are hospitalized?

41. Are there rooms set aside for physical examinations?

42. Is there at least one bed and bathroom available for patients with a contagious disease?

Pharmacy

43. Are routine and emergency drugs available?

44. Does a pharmacist review patient drug regimens?

45. Is a pharmacist available for staff and patients?

Therapy/Social Services

46. Is there a physical therapy program available under the direction of a qualified physical therapist?

47. Are services of an occupational therapist and speech pathologist available?

48. Is a social worker available to assist residents and their families?

Safety and Accident Prevention

49. Is the facility well lighted inside?

50. Is the facility free of hazards underfoot?

51. Are chairs sturdy and not easily tipped?

52. Are warning signs posted on freshly waxed floors?

53. Are there handrails in hallways and grab bars in bathrooms?

54. Does the facility meet federal and/or state fire codes?

55. Are exits clearly marked and unobstructed?

56. Are written emergency evacuation plans posted with floor plans throughout the facility?

57. Are fire drills conducted?

58. Are exit doors unlocked on the inside?

59. Are doors to stairways kept closed?

Bedrooms

60. Do bedrooms open onto the hall?

61. Does each patient's room have a window?

62. How many beds are in each room? Is there a limit?

63. Is there a privacy curtain for each bed?

64. Is there a nurse call button by each bed?

65. Is fresh drinking water beside each bed?

66. Is there at least one comfortable chair per patient?

67. Is there a clothes closet or separate set of drawers for each patient?

68. Is there sufficient space for personal items and clothes?

69. Is extra storage space available?

70. Is there room for a wheelchair to maneuver around the room?

71. How are roommates selected?

72. Are patients encouraged to decorate rooms with personal items such as pictures?

73. Can patients bring any of their own furniture?

74. Are there units available both furnished and unfurnished?

Toilet Facilities

75. Are toilets convenient to the bedrooms?

76. Are they easy for a wheelchair patient to use?

77. Is there a sink in each bathroom?

78. Are nurse call buttons near toilets?

79. Are hand grips on or near toilets?

80. Are there bathtubs and/or showers in each bathroom?

81. If so, do they have nonslip surfaces and hand grips?

82. If not, where is the bath or shower facility and is it clean and safe?

Grooming

83. Is assistance in bathing and grooming available?

84. Are barbers and beauticians available?

85. Are basic personal laundry services available?

Lobby and Common Space

86. Is the atmosphere welcoming?

87. Is the furniture attractive and comfortable?

88. Is there a bulletin board with the activities schedule posted?

89. Are certificates and licenses on display?

90. Is there a courtyard or patio for patients and visitors?

91. Is there adequate parking nearby for visitors?

92. Are the grounds well maintained?

93. Is the facility well secured?

94. Are the halls large enough for two wheelchairs to pass easily?

95. Do the halls have hand grip railings?

96. Are the halls well lighted?

Dining Room, Kitchen, and Food

97. Is the dining area attractive and inviting?

98. Are tables convenient for those in wheelchairs?

99. Is the food tasty and attractively served?

100. Is there adequate time to eat meals?

101. Do meals match the posted menu?

102. Are those needing help to eat receiving it?

103. Is food needing refrigeration not standing on counters?

104. Does the kitchen help observe sanitation rules?

105. Does a dietician plan menus for patients on special diets?

106. Are personal likes and dislikes taken into consideration?

107. Does the menu vary from meal to meal?

108. Are snacks available?

109. Is food delivered to patients unable or unwilling to eat in the dining room?

110. Are warm foods served warm?

111. Is the patient permitted to have wine or liquor with meals?

112. Are patients permitted to go out for meals with visitors?

Activities

113. Are patient preferences observed?

114. Are group and individual activities available?

115. Are patients encouraged to participate?

116. Are patients involved with the surrounding community?

117. Do volunteers work with patients?

118. Are outside trips planned and, if so, where, how often, and is transportation available to patients in wheelchairs?

119. Are separate rooms available for patient activities?

120. Is equipment available, such as games, easels, yarn, kiln, etc.?

121. Are patients using the equipment?

122. Is there adequate supervision?

123. Does the activities calendar have many and varied activities?

124. Are there arrangements made for patients to worship?

125. Are there varied kinds of religious services available?

FUNERAL DIRECTORS CODE OF ETHICS

As funeral directors, we herewith fully acknowledge our individual and collective obligations to the public, especially to those we serve, and our mutual responsibilities for the benefit of the funeral service profession.

To the public we pledge vigilant support of public health laws; proper legal regulations for the members of our profession; devotion to high moral and service standards; conduct befitting good citizens; honesty in all offerings of funeral service and in all business transactions.

To those we serve we pledge confidential business and professional relationships; cooperation with the customs of all religions and creeds; observance of all respect due the deceased; high standards of competence and dignity in the conduct of all service; truthful representation of all funeral service offerings.

To our profession we pledge support of high educational standards and licensing laws; encouragement of scientific research; adherence to sound business practices; adoption of improved techniques; observance of legal standards of competition; maintenance of favorable personnel relations.

We subscribe to the principles set forth in the Code of Ethics of the National Funeral Directors Association and pledge our best efforts to make them effective.

GENERAL RELEASE— BACKGROUND CHECKS

Authorization to Obtain and Disclose Information*

I, _____, hereby authorize _____ to contact my former employers and references and to conduct a complete background review, including criminal, motor vehicle, and medical history. I authorize the release of this information and discharge each employer, reference, police department, motor vehicle department, educational institution, and medical practice from any and all liability of any kind or nature whatsoever relative to my background review. I further specifically request that all agencies, representatives, and references fully cooperate with this investigation.

If employed, I further authorize periodic checks of all the above-referenced sources as may be deemed necessary by my employer.

A photocopy shall be as effective as the original.

_____

Job Applicant's Full Name

_____

Signature   Date

_____

Date of Birth

_____

Social Security Number

_____

Driver's License Number and State

*Reprinted from *Hiring Home Caregivers* by D. Helen Susik (Impact Publishing, 1995).

Medicare supplement insurance (Medigap) can be sold in any of the ten standard plans, A through J, shown below.

Note: Basic Benefits (which are a part of all plans) include:

1. Hospitalization: Part A coinsurance plus coverage for 365 additional days after Medicare benefits end.

2. Medical Expenses: Part B coinsurance (generally 20% of Medicare-approved expenses).

3. Blood: The first three pints of blood each year.

Coverage	Plan A	Plan B	Plan C	Plan D	Plan E	Plan F	Plan G	Plan H	Plan I	Plan J
Basic Benefits	X	X	X	X	X	X	X	X	X	X
Skilled Nursing Coinsurance			X	X	X	X	X	X	X	X
Part A Deductible		X	X	X	X	X	X	X	X	X
Part B Deductible			X	X		X				X
Part B Excess (100%)						X	X		X	X
Foreign Travel Emergency	X	X	X	X	X	X	X	X	X	X
At-Home Recovery				X			X		X	X
Basic Drugs ($1,250)								X	X	X
Preventive Care					X					X
Monthly Cost	$36.75	$61.00	$70.25	$66.00	$69.75	$88.25	$81.75	$88.25	$104.25	$137.00

RESOURCES AND REFERRALS

Books/Magazines/Newsletters

Caring and Coping When Your Loved One Is Seriously Ill (Beacon Press, 1995) Earl Grollman

A Consumer's Guide to Aging (The Johns Hopkins University Press, 1992) David H. Solomon, Elyse Salend, Anna N. Rahman, Marie E. B. Liston, and David B. Reuben

The Healthy Caregiver A Quarterly Resource Magazine for Adults Caring for Their Aging Parents 12 West Willow Grove Avenue, Suite 190 Philadelphia, PA 19118-9712 ($15 per year)

The Magazine for Adult Children of Aging Parents 75 Seabreeze Drive Richmond, CA 04804 ($21.95 per year)

My Parent My Turn (Broadman & Holman, 1995) Harris McIlwain, M.D., and Debra Bruce

Mom & Dad Can't Live Alone Anymore: A Family Decision (Lion Publishing, 1994) Eldon Weisheit

Wiser Now Alzheimer's Disease Caregiver Tips 800-999-0795 ($27.95 per year for 12 issues)

E-zines (Electronic Newsletters and Electronic Magazines)

Active Senior Electronic Newsmagazine write to jlgiffor@prairienet.org

Connections (Alzheimer's Disease Education and Referral Center) http://www.cais.com/adear/connect.html

Mainstream Online (Web-based newsletter for people with disabilities) http://www.mainstream-mag.com

Senior Group Newsletter write to olsonjam@cnsvax.uwec.edu

Web Sites

Administration on Aging
http://www.aoa.dhhs.gov

Alzheimer's Association
http://www.alz.org

Alzheimer's Disease Education
and Referral Center (ADEAR)
at the National Institute on
Aging
http://www.alzheimers.org/
adear

American Physical Therapy
Association, Section on
Geriatrics
http://www.geriatricspt.org

Arthritis Foundation
http://www.arthritis.org

Breast Cancer Information
Center
http://nysernet.org/breast/
default.html

Centers for Disease Control
and Prevention
http://www.cdc.gov

Choice in Dying
http://www.echonyc.com

Diabetes, Digestive and
Kidney Diseases (at the
National Institutes of Health)
http://www.niddk.nih.gov

Diabetesnet
http://www.diabetesnet.com

Elderhostel
http://www.elderhostel.org

FindLaw (a shopping guide to
the law)
http://www.findlaw.com

Griefnet
http://rivendell.org

Health Care Financing
Administration
http://www.ssa.gov/hcfa

Incontinence
http://IncontiNet.com

National Aging Information
Center
http://www.ageinfo.org

National Library Service for
the Blind and Physically
Disabled
http://lcweb.loc.gov/
nls.nls.html

National Senior Citizens Law
Center (for legal issues that
"affect the security and welfare of older persons of limited
income")
http://www.nsclc.org

Pension Research Council
http://prc.wharton.upenn.edu/
prc/prc.html

Sagesite
http://www.utmb.edu/aging

SeniorCom (chat room for
seniors, resource for commer-
cial shopping and services)
http://www.senior.com

SeniorLaw Home Page (information about elder law, Medicare, Medicaid, estate planning, trusts, and rights)
http://www.seniorlaw.com

SeniorLink (resource of eldercare professionals and programs)
http://www.seniorlink.com

SeniorNet (bookclubs and learning centers)
http://www.seniornet.org

Seniors-Site
http://seniors-site.com

Information and Referral Resources

Agency for Health Care Policy
Research Publications
Clearinghouse
P.O. Box 8547
Silver Spring, MD 20907

Alzheimer's Disease and
Related Disorders Association
919 North Michigan Avenue,
Suite 1000
Chicago, IL 60611
800-272-3900

National Institute of Mental
Health
5600 Fishers Lane, Room 76C2
Rockville, MD 20857
301-443-4513

TriAd (Three for the
Management of Alzheimer's
Disease)
888-874-2343

Services/Associations

Administration on Aging
U.S. Department of Health
and Human Services
330 Independence Avenue SW
Washington, DC 20201
202-401-4541
http://aoa.dhhs.gov

American Association for
International Aging
1900 L Street NW, Suite 510
Washington, DC 20036
202-833-8893

American Association
of Homes and Services
for the Aging
901 E Street NW, Suite 500
Washington, DC 20004
202-783-2242

American Association of
Retired Persons (AARP)
601 E Street NW
Washington, DC 20049
800-424-3410
http://www.aarp.org

American College of Health Care Administrators
325 South Patrick Street
Alexandria, VA 22314
703-739-7932

American Geriatrics Society
770 Lexington Avenue, Suite 300
New York, NY 10021
212-308-1414

American Health Care Association
1201 L Street NW
Washington, DC 20005
202-842-4444

American Optometric Association
243 North Lindbergh Boulevard
St. Louis, MO 63141

American Society on Aging
833 Market Street, Suite 511
San Francisco, CA 94103
415-974-9600

Asociacion Nacional Pro Personas Mayores
3325 Wilshire Boulevard, Suite 800
Los Angeles, CA 90010
213-487-1922

Assisted Living Facilities Association of America
9411 Lee Highway, Suite J
Fairfax, VA 22031
703-691-8100

Catholic Golden Age
430 Penn Avenue
Scranton, PA 18505
717-342-3294

Children of Aging Parents
1609 Woodbourne Road
Levittown, PA 19057
800-227-7294
215-945-6900

Commission on Legal Problems of the Elderly
American Bar Association
1800 M Street NW
Washington, DC 20036
202-331-2297

Concern for Dying
250 West 57th Street
New York, NY 10107
212-246-6962

Corporation for National Service
1201 New York Avenue NW
Washington, DC 20525
202-606-5000

Eldercare Locator
800-677-1116

Families USA Foundation
1334 G Street NW, Suite 300
Washington, DC 20005
202-628-3030

Federal Council on the Aging
330 Independence Avenue SW, Room 4661
Washington, DC 20201
202-619-2451

Foundation Aiding the Elderly
P.O. Box 254849
Sacramento, CA 96865
916-481-8550

Generations United
℅ CWLA
440 1st Street NW, Suite 310
Washington, DC 20001
202-638-2952

Gray Panthers Project
2025 Pennsylvania Avenue
NW, Suite 821
Washington, DC 20006
202-466-3132

International Executive
Service Corps
P.O. Box 10005
Stamford, CT 06904
800-243-4372

International Federation
on Aging
380 St. Antoine Street West,
Suite 3200
Montréal, PQ H2Y 3X7,
CANADA
514-987-9101

Legal Counsel for the Elderly
601 E Street NW
Washington, DC 20049
202-434-2120

National Academy of Elder
Law Attorneys
1604 North Country Club
Road
Tucson, AZ 85716
520-881-4005
325-7925 fax
http://www.primenet.com/
~rbf/naela.html

National Alliance of Senior
Citizens
1700 18th Street NW,
Suite 401
Washington, DC 20009
202-986-0117

National Asian Pacific Center
on Aging
Melbourne Tower, Suite 914
1511 3re Avenue
Seattle, WA 98101
206-624-1221

National Association for
Home Care
519 C Street NE
Washington, DC 20002
202-547-7424
http://www.nahc.org

National Association of Area
Agencies on Aging
1112 16th Street NW, Suite 100
Washington, DC 20036
202-296-8130

National Association of
Private Geriatric Care
Managers
655 North Alvernon Way,
Suite 108
Tucson, AZ 85711
602-881-8008

National Association of
Social Workers
7981 Eastern Avenue
Silver Spring, MD 20910

National Association of State
Units on Aging
1225 I Street NW, Suite 725
Washington, DC 20005
202-898-2578

National Caucus and Center
on Black Aged
1424 K Street NW, Suite 500
Washington, DC 20005
202-637-8400

National Citizens' Coalition
for Nursing Home Reform
1424 16th Street NW,
Suite 202
Washington, DC 20036
202-332-2275

National Committee to
Preserve Social Security
and Medicare
2000 K Street NW, Suite 800
Washington, DC 20006
202-822-9459

National Council of
Senior Citizens
Nursing Home Information
Services
1331 F Street NW
Washington, DC 20004
202-347-8800

National Council on the Aging
409 3rd Street SW, Suite 200
Washington, DC 20024
202-479-1200

National Executive
Service Corps
257 Park Avenue South,
2nd Floor
New York, NY 10010
212-529-6660

National Family Caregivers
Association
9621 East Bexhill Drive
Kensington, MD
800-896-3650
301-942-6430

National Funeral Directors
Association
11121 West Oklahoma Avenue
Milwaukee, WI 53227

National Hispanic Council
on Aging
2713 Ontario Road NW
Washington, DC 20009
202-745-2521

National Hospice
Organization
1901 North Moore Street,
Suite 901
Arlington, VA 22209
703-243-5900

National Indian Council
on Aging
6400 Uptown Boulevard NE,
Suite 510W
Albuquerque, NM 87110
505-888-3302

National Institute on
Adult Day Care
409 3rd Street SW, 2nd Floor
Washington, DC 20024
202-479-6680

National Institute on Aging
National Institutes of Health
Building B1
Center Drive, MSC 2292
Bethesda, MD 20892
301-496-1752

National Senior Citizens
Law Center
1815 H Street NW, Suite 700
Washington, DC 20006
202-887-5280

Nursing Home Advisory and
Research Council
P.O. Box 18820
Cleveland Heights, OH 44118
216-321-4499

Older Women's League
666 11th Street NW, Suite 700
Washington, DC 20001
202-783-6686

Service Corps of Retired
Executives (SCORE)
409 3rd Street SW
Washington, DC 20024
202-205-6762
http://www.senior.com/
score.html

Social Security Administration
6401 Security Boulevard
Baltimore, MD 21235
800-772-1213
http://www.ssa.gov

Society for the Right to Die
250 West 57th Street
New York, NY 10107
212-246-6962

U.S. Department of
Veterans Affairs
810 Vermont Avenue NW
Washington, DC 20420
202-273-5700
http://www.va.gov

Women Work
The National Network for
Women's Employment
1625 K Street NW, Suite 300
Washington, DC 20006
202-467-6346

EMERGENCY RESPONSE SYSTEMS

Health Care Technology
Corporation
295 Treadwell Street
Hamden, CT 06514
800-841-3800

HelpLine
Henry Ford Health System
24445 Northwestern Highway,
#110
Southfield, MI 48075
313-972-1640

Home Technology Systems
200 Main Street, Suite 200
PO Box 598
Dubuque, IA 52001

Independent Living, Inc.
770 Frontage Road
Suite 118
Northfield, IL 60093
312-441-6963

JD Monitoring, Inc.
5411 Amberwood Lane
Rockville, MD 20853
800-782-7582

Knight Protective Industries
7315 Lankershim Boulevard
North Hollywood, CA 91605
800-356-4448

LifeGuard Systems Co.
Abington, PA 19001
800-752-9900
215-657-7222

Lifeline Systems, Inc.
Dept. RP
1 Arsenal Marketplace
Watertown, MA 02172
800-451-0525
800-451-04514 (in
Massachusetts)

Lifeline Program
St. Agnes Medical Center
1900 South Broad Street
Philadelphia, PA 19145
215-339-41459

Life Safety Systems, Inc.
2100 M Street NW
Washington, DC 20037
202-296-1873

Lifewatch 24
PO Box 34050
West Bethesda, MD 20817
301-469-9564

Link to Life through Jewish
Family Services
2250 Palm Beach Lakes
Boulevard, S-104
West Palm Beach, FL 33409
800-227-3772
407-684-1991

MediAlert
475 Fifth Avenue
Suite 1812
New York, NY 10017
212-213-4510

Newart Electronics
Science, Inc.
1009 Twelve Oaks Center
Box 129
Wayzata, MN 55391
612-473-4484

Courtesy of Children of Aging Parents

SAMPLE EMPLOYMENT CONTRACT

This agreement is between _____ (insert your name), located at _____ _____ (hereafter referred to as Employer) and _____ (insert employee's name), located at _____ (hereafter referred to as Employee).

The purpose of this contract is to identify the terms of the employment contract under which the Employee is hired to care for

_____

(insert name of your parent).

1. Hours and Days of Employment

Employee's regular schedule shall be as follows:

Sunday   _____ to _____ and _____ to _____.

Monday   _____ to _____ and _____ to _____.

Tuesday   _____ to _____ and _____ to _____.

Wednesday   _____ to _____ and _____ to _____.

Thursday   _____ to _____ and _____ to _____.

Friday   _____ to _____ and _____ to _____.

Saturday   _____ to _____ and _____ to _____.

Total hours worked per week shall be: _____. Any hours worked over that amount shall be considered overtime.

2. Compensation

Employee shall earn $_____ per hour worked (or per week, per month, per year). For hours worked over regularly scheduled hours, employee shall earn $_____ per hour.

Employee shall be paid by check every other Friday (or at whatever schedule you agree). All appropriate federal, state, and local taxes, including workers compensation, shall be deducted from the wages. By January 31 of each year, Employer will provide a W-2 statement to the Employee on which the total wages paid, taxes withheld, and any other appropriate information, are itemized.

Raises shall be made on an annual basis. The amount of any raise shall be based on the performance of the Employee, and shall be made at the discretion of the Employer.

3. Expenses

Employer shall reimburse the Employee for all expenses incurred on behalf of the person being cared for. If the Employee uses his or her own car to transport the person being cared for, Employee shall be reimbursed at the rate of $.35 per mile. To be reimbursed, a written report must be filed for any expenses incurred. Report must be signed and dated, and, if reimbursement for mileage is claimed, actual mileage must be detailed. Employee agrees to abide by all laws of the state, and, if the person being cared for is in the car, will make certain seat belts are used. No reimbursement will be made to Employee for expenses incurred in normal commuting to and from the place of employment.

Employee agrees to maintain adequate automobile insurance and to furnish a copy of the insurance policy to the Employer. If automobile is provided by the Employer, Employer is responsible for maintaining adequate insurance and providing a copy of the policy to the Employee.

4. Leave and Vacation

Employee shall not (or shall) accrue paid time off (at the rate of one day per month worked), but shall be permitted up to two weeks unpaid leave to be taken as arranged with consent of the Employer. No leave or vacation can be taken until after Employee has worked at least six months (one year).

Employee shall not accrue nor be paid for any sick days.

5. Meals

Employer shall not (shall) pay for the Employee's meals while on the job.

6. Rules of Employment

- ◆ No physical, mental, or verbal abuse shall be permitted.
- ◆ No alcohol or drug use shall be permitted while Employee is on the job.
- ◆ No personal telephone calls may be made while on the job.
- ◆ No personal visitors may be received while Employee is on the job except in case of emergency.
- ◆ No exchanges of gifts or money between the Employee and the person being cared for shall be permitted.

Violation of any of the above rules is grounds for immediate dismissal.

In addition, Employee may be terminated after _____ absences, or _____ tardies, unless approved by the Employer.

Employee agrees that Employer has the right to terminate Employee at any time, and for any reason or without a reason, and prior notification is not necessary. No additional compensation will be due Employee (unless paid leave has been agreed to under number four above). Employee has the same right to terminate the employment agreement.

We agree to the terms of this employment contract:

_____

Employee   Date

_____

Employer   Date

INDEX

A

Activities of Daily Living (ADLs), 160
acute care, 68
addiction to prescription drugs, 46
agencies
 1-800-DOCTORS, 50
 Administration on Aging, 267–268
 Agency for Health Care Policy Research Publication, 268
 Alzheimer's Disease and Related Disorders Association, 268
 Alzheimer's Disease Education and Referral Center (ADEAR), 266–267
 American Association for International Aging, 268
 American Association of Homes for the Aging, 206, 268
 American Association of Retired Persons (AARP), 27, 206, 268
 American Health Care Association, 235–239, 269
 American Optometric Association, 269
 American Society of Appraisers, 55, 229
 American Society on Aging, 269
 Appraisers Association of American, 55, 229
 Asociacion Nacional Pro Personas Mayores, 269
 Assisted Living Facilities Association of America, 269
 Centers for Disease Control and Prevention, 267
 Children of Aging Parents (CAPS), 17, 269
 Choice in Dying, 59
 Corporation for National Service, 269
 Eldercare Locator, 269
 Families USA Foundation, 269
 Federal Council on the Aging, 269
 Foundation Aiding the Elderly, 270
 Generations United, 270
 Gray Panthers Project, 270
 Health Care Financing Administration, 205
 International Executive Service Corps, 270
 International Federation on Aging, 270
 Legal Counsel for the Elderly, 270
 National Academy of Elder Law Attorneys (NAELA), 66, 270
 National Alliance of Senior Citizens, 270
 National Asian Pacific Center on Aging, 270
 National Association for Home Care, 254–255, 270
 National Association of Area Agencies on Aging, 270
 National Association of Private Geriatric Care Managers, 270
 National Association of Social Workers, 270
 National Association of State Units on Aging, 270
 National Caucus and Center on Black Aged, 271
 National Citizens' Coalition for Nursing Home Reform, 271
 National Committee to Preserve Social Security/Medicare, 271
 National Family Caregivers Association, 271
 National Funeral Directors Association, 209, 271
 National Hispanic Council on Aging, 271
 National Hospice Organization, 271
 National Indian Council on Aging, 271
 National Institute of Mental Health, 268
 National Institute on Adult Day Care, 271
 National Right to Life Committee, 59
 National Senior Citizens Law Center, 267, 271
 Nursing Home Advisory and Research Council, 272
 Older Women's League, 272
 Service Corps of Retired Executives (SCORE), 272
 Society for the Right to Die, 272
 TriAd, 268
 U.S. Department of Veterans Affairs, 205, 272
 United Seniors Health Cooperative, 205
 Women Work, 272
Alabama
 Association of Home Health Agencies, 240
 Commission on Aging, 230
 Nursing Home Association, 235
alcoholism, 32
Alzheimer's disease, 35–36
Arizona
 Aging and Adult Administration, 230
 Association for Home Care, 240
 Health Care Association, 235
Arkansas
 Division of Aging and Adult Services, 230
 Health Care Association, 235
 Home Care Associations, 240
assisted-living facilities, 161–163
attorneys, elder law, 65–67

B

background checks, 264
bank accounts, 18, 21, 63
behavior, changes, 119–120, 126
bills, paying, 116, 122
birth certificates, 19, 22
body temperatures, 32, 36
burial plots, 20–22

C

California
  Association for Health
    Services at Home, 240
  Association of Health
    Facilities, 235
  Department of Aging, 230
  Health Care Technology
    Corporation, 274
  Knight Protective
    Industries, 273
caregivers
  geriatic care managers,
    155–157
  home, 141–142
    applications, 249–253
    contracts, 155,
      275–276
    cost, 145, 154
    employment
      applications,
      249–253
    hiring, 142–144,
      147–153
    patient bill of rights,
      254–255
    reponsibilities,
      145–147
    self-directed, 145
    state agencies,
      240–243
  long-distance, 17, 129–133
  primary, 13
cars, 19–20
checking accounts, 116
clergy, 21
code of ethics for funeral
  directors, 263
codicils, see wills
Colorado
  Aging and Adult Services,
    230
  Health Care Association,
    235
  Home Care Association,
    240
community property, 115
con artists, 97
confusion, 35
Connecticut
  Association for Home
    Care, Inc., 240
  Association of Health
    Care Facilities, 235
  Department on Aging,
    230
  Health Care Technology
    Corporation, 273
conservatorships, 61
continuing-care community
  centers, 162–163
credit cards, 18, 22, 115

D

death certificates, 23
  see also funerals
dehydration, 30, 37
Delaware
  Association for Home and
    Community Care, 240
  Division on Aging, 230
  Health Care Facilities
    Association, 235
delirium, 35
dementia, 35–36
denial, 15
dental and gum disease,
  37–38
dependents, claiming on tax
  returns, 112
depression, 30–34
  Seasonal Affective
    Disorder, 31
diabetes, nutrition, 27
diet, see nutrition
disabilities, 20, 26
divorce decrees, 23
DNR (Do Not Resuscitate)
  order, 60
doctors, 25, 48–52
durable power of attorney,
  58

E

elder law attorneys, 65–67
emergencies
  contacts, 22, 137
  medical alert tags,
    135–136
  on-call services, 136
  panic buttons, 136–137
  response systems,
    273–274
  transportation, 138
employment
  contracts, 275–276
  home care applications,
    249–253
exercise, 25–26
eyesight, 39–40

F

Federal Insurance
  Compensation Act (FICA),
  98
finances, 14, 18, 97–98,
  102–103
  accounts, 21, 63
  affinity cards, 116
  bills, 116, 123
  budgeting, 104–105
  checking accounts, 116,
    123
  credit cards, 18, 22, 116

  debts, 21
  discounts, 116
  expenses, 106
  fraud, 97
  income, 103
  investments, 106–108
  joint ownership, 114–115
  liabilities, 21, 102
  living expenses, 102
  mortgages, 21
  partnerships, 22
  pension plans, 21
  safe deposit boxes, 21, 63,
    117
  seminars, 96–97
  stocks and bonds, 63
  taxes, 21, 64
  valuables, 21
Florida
  Associated Home Health
    Industries of Florida, Inc.,
    240
  Health Care Association,
    235
  Link to Life through Jewish
    Family Services, 273
  Program Office of Aging
    and Adult Services, 230
friends, 22, 137
full-care facilities, 163–165
funerals, 21–22, 209–211,
  213–219, 222, 263

G

generic prescription drugs,
  48
Georgia
  Association of Community
    Care Providers, 240
  Association of Home
    Health Agencies, 240
  Nursing Home
    Association, 236
  Office of Aging, 231
geriatric care managers,
  155–157
glaucoma, 39
grandchildren, 122
green cards, 19
guardianships, 61

H

health care, 19, 179
  deteriorating, 124
  insurance, 18, 20, 47–48,
    61, 69, 140–141, 258,
    265
  monitoring, 120, 126
  proxy, 60
hearing aids, 43–45
hearing loss, 40–43
holidays, 121

home caregivers
  contracts, 155
  cost, 145, 154
  employment applications,
    249–253
  geriatic care managers,
    155–157
  hiring, 142–144, 147–153
  patient bill of rights,
    254–255
  reponsibilities, 145–147
  state agencies, 240–243
homes, 18, 21
  deed/title, 19
  equity conversions (HEC),
    110
  insurance, 20
  refinancing, 109
  selling, 109
hyperthermia (heat stress),
  36–37
hypothermia, 36

I

Idaho
  Association of Home
    Health Agencies, 240
  Health Care Association,
    236
  Office on Aging, 231
identification cards,
  Medicare/Medicaid, 18
Illinois
  Department on Aging,
    231
  Health Care Association,
    236
  Home Care Council, 241
  Immigration and
    Naturalization Service
    card (green card), 19
  Independent Living, Inc.,
    273
independence, 160
Indiana
  Association for Home
    Care, 241
  Choice/Home Care
    Services, 231
  Health Care Associations,
    236
insurance, 14, 20
  employer and group, 69
  HMOs, 69, 71
  long-term-care, 20, 83–85
    adult day care, 79
    assisted-living facilities,
      78
    costs, 80–81, 257
    custodial care, 79
    deductibles, 92
    guaranteed
      renewability, 89

home health care, 78
    intermediate care, 79
    private, 204–205
    respite care, 79
    skilled care, 79
    underwriting, 90
  managed-care, 68
  Medicaid, 68-69, 75, 82,
    265
  Medicare, 68–69, 265
    acute care, 82
    Part A plan, 73–74
    Part B plan, 69–73
  Medigap, 69, 75–77
  nonforfeiture benefit, 91
  premiums, 88, 123
  renter's, 20
  risk management, 84
  veteran's benefits, 68–69,
    83–84
  waiver of premium, 91
Iowa
  Association for Home
    Care, 241
  Department of Elder
    Affairs, 231
  Health Care Association,
    236
  Home Technology
    Systems, 273

J–K

joint ownership, 62, 114, 224

Kansas
  Department on Aging, 231
  Health Care Association,
    236
  Home Care Association,
    241
Kentucky
  Association of Health
    Care Facilities, 236
  Division of Aging Services,
    231
  Home Care Association,
    241

L

landlords, 18
liabilities, 21
licensure/certification,
  long-term-care facilities, 257
life insurance, 20
  funeral payment, 222
  loans, 111
  viatical settlements,
    113–114
lifestyle changes, 33
living wills, 20, 59, 247–248
loans, 110–111
long-distance caregivers, 17,
  129–133

long-term-care, 14
  activities, 262
  bedrooms, 259
  care planning, 256
  cleaniness, 256
  costs, 80–81, 167, 257
  facilities, 167–170
    assisted-living,
      161–163
    full-care, 163–165
  finding, 256
  grooming, 260
  health care, 258
  insurance, 20, 61, 84–85
    adult day care, 79
    assisted-living facilities,
      78
    custodial care, 79
    deductibles, 92
    home health care, 78
    intermediate care, 79
    nonforfeiture benefit,
      91
    private, 204–205
    respite care, 79
    skilled care, 79
    underwriting, 90
    waiver of premium, 91
  licensure/certification, 257
  location, 166, 257
  nutrition, 261
  patient rights, 256
  pharmacies, 258
  premiums, 88
  safety and accident
    prevention, 259
  staff, 256
  therapy/social service,
    259
  toilet facilities, 260
Louisiana
  Home Association, 241
  Nursing Home
    Association, 236
  Office of Elderly Affairs,
    231

M

Maine
  Bureau of Elder and Adult
    Services, 231
  Health Care Association,
    236
  Visiting Nurse Service of
    Southern Maine, 241
malnutrition, see nutrition
managed-care insurance, 69
marriage certificates, 19, 23
Maryland
  Association for Home
    Care, 241
  Health Facilities
    Association, 236

JD Monitoring, Inc., 273
Lifewatch 24, 273
Office on Aging, 231
Massachusetts
Council for Home Care
Aid Services, 241
Executive Office of Elder
Affairs, 232
Federation of Nursing
Homes, 236
Lifeline Systems, Inc., 273
meals-on-wheels, 29
Medicaid, 68–69, 75, 82–83,
269
nursing homes, 201–203
medical alert tags, 135–136
medical savings accounts
(MSA), 70
medical supplies, 140–141
Medicare, 68–69, 269
coverage, 265
identification cards, 18, 20
nursing homes, 200–201
Part A plan, 73–74
Part B plan, 69–72
see also health care,
insurance
Medigap, 20, 69, 75–77
Michigan
Health Care Association,
237
HelpLine, 273
Home Health Association,
241
Office of Services to the
Aging, 232
military discharge, 19
Minnesota
Board on Aging, 232
Care Providers, 237
Home Care Association,
241
Newart Electronics
Science, Inc., 274
Mississippi Association for
Council on Aging, 232
Health Care Association,
237
Home Care, 241
Missouri
Alliance for Home Care,
241
Division of Aging, 232
Health Care Association,
237
mixing prescription drugs, 32
Montana
Association of Home
Health Agencies, 241
Governor's Office on
Aging, 232
Health Care Association,
237
mortgages, see homes

N

Nebraska
Association of Home and
Community Health
Agencies, 241
Department on Aging,
232
Health Care Association,
237
neighbors, 22, 137
Nevada
Division for Aging
Services, 232
Health Care Association,
237
Home Health Care
Association, 241
New Hampshire
Division of Elderly and
Adult Services, 232
Health Care Association,
237
Home Care Association,
241
New Jersey
Association of Health
Care Facilities, 237
Division on Aging, 232
Home Care Council, 241
Home Health Assembly,
242
Home Health Services
and Staffing Association,
242
New Mexico
Association for Home
Care, 242
Health Care Association,
237
State Agency on Aging,
232
New York
Healthcare Association,
242
Home Care Association,
242
MediAlert, 274
Office of the Aging, 233
State Association of
Health Care Providers,
242
State Health Facilities
Association, 237
North Carolina
Association for Home
Care, 242
Division of Aging, 233
Health Care Facilities
Association, 237
North Dakota
Aging Services, 233
Association of Home
Health Services, 242

Long-Term Care
Association, 238
notary publics, 54
nursing homes
activities, 179
attitudes about, 174–176
costs, 196–198
gifts, 191–193
health care, 179
Medicaid, 201–203
Medicare, 200–201
nutrition, 179
quality, 177
roommates, 182–183
staff, 178, 180
transition, 176, 181, 184
veterans' benefits, 205
visiting, 185–190
nutrition, 27–28
dehydration, 30
dental and gum disease,
37–38
diabetes, 27
long-term-care facilities,
261
meals-on-wheels, 29
vitamins, 30
nursing homes, 179
monitoring, 120, 122

O

Ohio
Council for Home Care,
242
Department of Aging,
233
Health Care Association,
238
Oklahoma
Aging Services Division,
233
Association for Home
Care, 242
Health Care Association
on-call services, 136
Oregon
Association for Home
Care, 242
Health Care Association,
238
Senior and Disabled
Services, 233

P

panic buttons, 136–137
parents, 14
aging, 10–12
changes in behavior,
119–120, 126
claiming as dependents,
112
health, 120
independence, 160

parents, *(cont.)*
  personal information, 18
  visiting, 120–122,
    126–129
partnerships, 22
patient rights, 256
Pennsylvania
  Association of Home
    Health Agencies, 242
  Department of Aging, 233
  Health Care Association,
    238
  LifeGuard Systems Co.,
    273
  Lifeline Program, 273
pension plans, 21
physical illness, 32, 125
  see also health care
power of attorney, 22, 57,
  244–246
  asset access, 62
  durable, 58
prescription drugs, 19, 45
  addiction, 46
  buying, 47–48
  depression from, 32
  generic, 48
  health insurance, 47
  mixing, 32
  side effects, 46–47
primary caregivers, 13, 17
probate, 56, 223–225

R

recreation, 179
relatives, 137
religious concerns, 21
renter's insurance, 20
resident-care facilities, 162
retirement
  accounts, loans, 110–111
  communities, 14
revocable living trusts, 225
Rhode Island
  Department of Elderly
    Affairs, 233
  Health Care Association,
    238
  Partnership for Home
    Care, 242
  Visiting Nurses Council,
    242
risk management insurance,
  84
roommates, 182–183

S

safe deposit boxes, 18, 21,
  63, 117
Seasonal Affective Disorder,
  31

self-directed home care,
  145
senior discounts, 116
sensorineural hearing loss,
  41–42
side effects from prescription
  drugs, 46–47
Social Security benefits, 18,
  98–101, 272
South Carolina
  Commission on Aging,
    233
  Health Care Association,
    238
  Home Care Association,
    242
South Dakota
  Health Care Association,
    238
  Home Health Association,
    242
  Office of Adult Services
    and Aging, 233
state agencies, 230–234,
  240–243
stocks and bonds, 63
suicide, 32
support groups, 17, 36

T

taxes, 21, 64
  claiming parents as
    dependents, 112
  filing after death, 229
  gifts, 112
tenacy by the entirety/
  in common, 114
Tennessee
  Association for Home
    Care, 242
  Commission on Aging,
    233
  Health Care Association,
    238
Texas
  Association for Home
    Care, 242
  Department on Aging,
    234
  Health Care Association,
    238
transportation, 138–140

U–V

Utah
  Association of Home
    Health Agencies, 243
  Division of Aging and
    Adult Services, 234
  Health Care Association,
    238

valuables, 21, 55
Vermont
  Aging and Disabilities, 234
  Assembly of Home Health
    Agencies, 243
  Health Care Association,
    238
veteran's benefits, 68–69,
  83–84, 205, 272
viatical settlements, 113–114
Virgin Islands Senior Citizens
  Affairs, 234
Virginia
  Association for Home
    Care, 243
  Department for the Aging,
    234
  Health Care Association,
    239
vision, see eyesight
visiting parents, 120–122,
  126–129, 134, 185–191

W

Washington state
  Aging and Adult Services
    Administration, 234
  Health Care Association,
    239
  Home Care Association,
    243
Washington, D.C.
  Capital Home Health
    Association, 240
  Health Care Association,
    235
  Life Safety Systems, Inc.,
    273
  Office on Aging, 230
Web sites, 267–268
West Virginia
  Commission on Aging,
    234
  Council of Home Health
    Agencies, 243
  Health Care Association,
    239
wills, 20, 55–56, 220–221,
  223–228, 247–248
Wisconsin
  Bureau of Aging, 234
  Health Care Association,
    239
  Homecare Association,
    243
Wyoming
  Alliance of Wyoming, 243
  Commission on Aging,
    234
  Health Care Association,
    239